COMPLETE

Math

47 to 50

23 to 20

ROUND UP

ROUND DOWN

Carson-Dellosa Publishing LLC
Greensboro, North Carolina

Carson-Dellosa Publishing LLC
P.O. Box 35665
Greensboro, NC 27425 USA

ISBN 978-1-60996-179-4

1 2 3 4 5 6 7 8 WCR 15 14 13 12 11

030118454

Table of Contents

Addition Facts

Directions: Add.

1.
$$\begin{array}{r} 3 \\ +1 \\ \hline \end{array} \quad \begin{array}{r} 8 \\ +2 \\ \hline \end{array} \quad \begin{array}{r} 1 \\ +6 \\ \hline \end{array} \quad \begin{array}{r} 4 \\ +7 \\ \hline \end{array} \quad \begin{array}{r} 6 \\ +3 \\ \hline \end{array} \quad \begin{array}{r} 2 \\ +8 \\ \hline \end{array} \quad \begin{array}{r} 4 \\ +5 \\ \hline \end{array} \quad \begin{array}{r} 7 \\ +9 \\ \hline \end{array}$$

2.
$$\begin{array}{r} 6 \\ +4 \\ \hline \end{array} \quad \begin{array}{r} 1 \\ +8 \\ \hline \end{array} \quad \begin{array}{r} 3 \\ +9 \\ \hline \end{array} \quad \begin{array}{r} 2 \\ +1 \\ \hline \end{array} \quad \begin{array}{r} 5 \\ +0 \\ \hline \end{array} \quad \begin{array}{r} 0 \\ +2 \\ \hline \end{array} \quad \begin{array}{r} 9 \\ +1 \\ \hline \end{array} \quad \begin{array}{r} 3 \\ +2 \\ \hline \end{array}$$

3.
$$\begin{array}{r} 2 \\ +7 \\ \hline \end{array} \quad \begin{array}{r} 6 \\ +9 \\ \hline \end{array} \quad \begin{array}{r} 4 \\ +8 \\ \hline \end{array} \quad \begin{array}{r} 9 \\ +3 \\ \hline \end{array} \quad \begin{array}{r} 2 \\ +2 \\ \hline \end{array} \quad \begin{array}{r} 8 \\ +0 \\ \hline \end{array} \quad \begin{array}{r} 0 \\ +4 \\ \hline \end{array} \quad \begin{array}{r} 7 \\ +1 \\ \hline \end{array}$$

4.
$$\begin{array}{r} 5 \\ +2 \\ \hline \end{array} \quad \begin{array}{r} 8 \\ +3 \\ \hline \end{array} \quad \begin{array}{r} 1 \\ +5 \\ \hline \end{array} \quad \begin{array}{r} 7 \\ +8 \\ \hline \end{array} \quad \begin{array}{r} 6 \\ +2 \\ \hline \end{array} \quad \begin{array}{r} 4 \\ +6 \\ \hline \end{array} \quad \begin{array}{r} 5 \\ +4 \\ \hline \end{array} \quad \begin{array}{r} 9 \\ +4 \\ \hline \end{array}$$

5.
$$\begin{array}{r} 2 \\ +3 \\ \hline \end{array} \quad \begin{array}{r} 9 \\ +0 \\ \hline \end{array} \quad \begin{array}{r} 4 \\ +3 \\ \hline \end{array} \quad \begin{array}{r} 2 \\ +9 \\ \hline \end{array} \quad \begin{array}{r} 1 \\ +1 \\ \hline \end{array} \quad \begin{array}{r} 8 \\ +8 \\ \hline \end{array} \quad \begin{array}{r} 3 \\ +5 \\ \hline \end{array} \quad \begin{array}{r} 5 \\ +7 \\ \hline \end{array}$$

6.
$$\begin{array}{r} 8 \\ +9 \\ \hline \end{array} \quad \begin{array}{r} 3 \\ +3 \\ \hline \end{array} \quad \begin{array}{r} 9 \\ +5 \\ \hline \end{array} \quad \begin{array}{r} 6 \\ +6 \\ \hline \end{array} \quad \begin{array}{r} 3 \\ +8 \\ \hline \end{array} \quad \begin{array}{r} 0 \\ +6 \\ \hline \end{array} \quad \begin{array}{r} 7 \\ +3 \\ \hline \end{array} \quad \begin{array}{r} 2 \\ +6 \\ \hline \end{array}$$

7.
$$\begin{array}{r} 7 \\ +7 \\ \hline \end{array} \quad \begin{array}{r} 4 \\ +1 \\ \hline \end{array} \quad \begin{array}{r} 3 \\ +6 \\ \hline \end{array} \quad \begin{array}{r} 8 \\ +7 \\ \hline \end{array} \quad \begin{array}{r} 0 \\ +0 \\ \hline \end{array} \quad \begin{array}{r} 9 \\ +8 \\ \hline \end{array} \quad \begin{array}{r} 9 \\ +2 \\ \hline \end{array} \quad \begin{array}{r} 7 \\ +5 \\ \hline \end{array}$$

8.
$$\begin{array}{r} 2 \\ +4 \\ \hline \end{array} \quad \begin{array}{r} 0 \\ +3 \\ \hline \end{array} \quad \begin{array}{r} 5 \\ +8 \\ \hline \end{array} \quad \begin{array}{r} 2 \\ +5 \\ \hline \end{array} \quad \begin{array}{r} 1 \\ +9 \\ \hline \end{array} \quad \begin{array}{r} 1 \\ +0 \\ \hline \end{array} \quad \begin{array}{r} 5 \\ +9 \\ \hline \end{array} \quad \begin{array}{r} 8 \\ +4 \\ \hline \end{array}$$

Addition Facts

Directions: Add.

1.
$$\begin{array}{r} 8 \\ +2 \\ \hline \end{array}\qquad \begin{array}{r} 7 \\ +0 \\ \hline \end{array}\qquad \begin{array}{r} 0 \\ +1 \\ \hline \end{array}\qquad \begin{array}{r} 1 \\ +1 \\ \hline \end{array}\qquad \begin{array}{r} 6 \\ +4 \\ \hline \end{array}\qquad \begin{array}{r} 5 \\ +2 \\ \hline \end{array}\qquad \begin{array}{r} 4 \\ +9 \\ \hline \end{array}\qquad \begin{array}{r} 2 \\ +7 \\ \hline \end{array}$$

2.
$$\begin{array}{r} 1 \\ +0 \\ \hline \end{array}\qquad \begin{array}{r} 6 \\ +3 \\ \hline \end{array}\qquad \begin{array}{r} 3 \\ +0 \\ \hline \end{array}\qquad \begin{array}{r} 2 \\ +3 \\ \hline \end{array}\qquad \begin{array}{r} 7 \\ +1 \\ \hline \end{array}\qquad \begin{array}{r} 8 \\ +1 \\ \hline \end{array}\qquad \begin{array}{r} 6 \\ +5 \\ \hline \end{array}\qquad \begin{array}{r} 1 \\ +9 \\ \hline \end{array}$$

3.
$$\begin{array}{r} 0 \\ +5 \\ \hline \end{array}\qquad \begin{array}{r} 1 \\ +2 \\ \hline \end{array}\qquad \begin{array}{r} 6 \\ +6 \\ \hline \end{array}\qquad \begin{array}{r} 3 \\ +5 \\ \hline \end{array}\qquad \begin{array}{r} 9 \\ +5 \\ \hline \end{array}\qquad \begin{array}{r} 5 \\ +7 \\ \hline \end{array}\qquad \begin{array}{r} 7 \\ +6 \\ \hline \end{array}\qquad \begin{array}{r} 3 \\ +8 \\ \hline \end{array}$$

4.
$$\begin{array}{r} 4 \\ +2 \\ \hline \end{array}\qquad \begin{array}{r} 6 \\ +8 \\ \hline \end{array}\qquad \begin{array}{r} 8 \\ +5 \\ \hline \end{array}\qquad \begin{array}{r} 2 \\ +6 \\ \hline \end{array}\qquad \begin{array}{r} 5 \\ +8 \\ \hline \end{array}\qquad \begin{array}{r} 9 \\ +8 \\ \hline \end{array}\qquad \begin{array}{r} 0 \\ +0 \\ \hline \end{array}\qquad \begin{array}{r} 4 \\ +4 \\ \hline \end{array}$$

5.
$$\begin{array}{r} 7 \\ +2 \\ \hline \end{array}\qquad \begin{array}{r} 9 \\ +7 \\ \hline \end{array}\qquad \begin{array}{r} 0 \\ +8 \\ \hline \end{array}\qquad \begin{array}{r} 4 \\ +7 \\ \hline \end{array}\qquad \begin{array}{r} 7 \\ +9 \\ \hline \end{array}\qquad \begin{array}{r} 5 \\ +9 \\ \hline \end{array}\qquad \begin{array}{r} 3 \\ +3 \\ \hline \end{array}\qquad \begin{array}{r} 5 \\ +4 \\ \hline \end{array}$$

6.
$$\begin{array}{r} 1 \\ +3 \\ \hline \end{array}\qquad \begin{array}{r} 9 \\ +0 \\ \hline \end{array}\qquad \begin{array}{r} 2 \\ +2 \\ \hline \end{array}\qquad \begin{array}{r} 5 \\ +1 \\ \hline \end{array}\qquad \begin{array}{r} 7 \\ +7 \\ \hline \end{array}\qquad \begin{array}{r} 6 \\ +0 \\ \hline \end{array}\qquad \begin{array}{r} 8 \\ +6 \\ \hline \end{array}\qquad \begin{array}{r} 9 \\ +4 \\ \hline \end{array}$$

7.
$$\begin{array}{r} 4 \\ +8 \\ \hline \end{array}\qquad \begin{array}{r} 9 \\ +3 \\ \hline \end{array}\qquad \begin{array}{r} 1 \\ +4 \\ \hline \end{array}\qquad \begin{array}{r} 2 \\ +9 \\ \hline \end{array}\qquad \begin{array}{r} 9 \\ +2 \\ \hline \end{array}\qquad \begin{array}{r} 8 \\ +3 \\ \hline \end{array}\qquad \begin{array}{r} 7 \\ +3 \\ \hline \end{array}\qquad \begin{array}{r} 0 \\ +9 \\ \hline \end{array}$$

8.
$$\begin{array}{r} 2 \\ +0 \\ \hline \end{array}\qquad \begin{array}{r} 2 \\ +8 \\ \hline \end{array}\qquad \begin{array}{r} 8 \\ +4 \\ \hline \end{array}\qquad \begin{array}{r} 4 \\ +0 \\ \hline \end{array}\qquad \begin{array}{r} 8 \\ +7 \\ \hline \end{array}\qquad \begin{array}{r} 9 \\ +1 \\ \hline \end{array}\qquad \begin{array}{r} 4 \\ +3 \\ \hline \end{array}\qquad \begin{array}{r} 5 \\ +5 \\ \hline \end{array}$$

Addition

2 ⟶ Find the 2 - row.
+6 ⟶ Find the 6 - column.
8 ⟵ The sum is named
where the 2-row and
6-column meet.

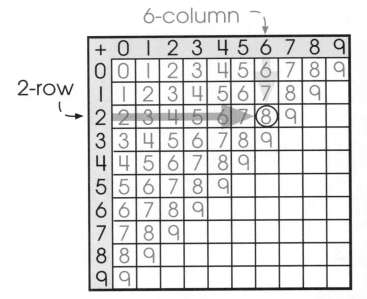

6-column

2-row

Directions: Add.

1.	2 +4	3 +1	1 +2	7 +0	0 +4	1 +4	5 +2	3 +3
2.	2 +0	6 +3	4 +4	3 +0	5 +3	1 +6	0 +5	8 +1
3.	2 +6	1 +0	1 +5	2 +2	3 +2	2 +1	5 +4	1 +7
4.	9 +0	5 +1	0 +3	4 +1	4 +5	1 +8	8 +0	4 +3
5.	0 +0	2 +3	7 +1	0 +9	4 +2	0 +2	0 +7	1 +1

Addition

5 ⟶ Find the 5 - row.
+7 ⟶ Find the 7 - column.
    ⟵ The sum is named where
        the 5-row and 7-column meet.

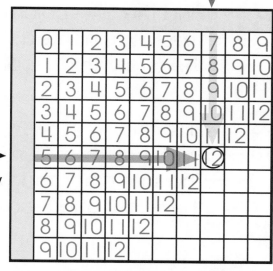

7-column

5-row

Directions: Add.

1. 6   7   2   8   9   6   2
      +5   +3   +7   +4   +2   +3   +6

2. 8   3   3   5   6   5   1
      +2   +9   +5   +2   +4   +5   +9

3. 5   9   6   3   4   9   3
      +3   +3   +6   +7   +7   +1   +8

4. 5   8   5   2   2   7   7
      +7   +1   +6   +8   +5   +5   +1

5. 3   4   4   2   8   4   7
      +4   +5   +6   +9   +3   +8   +4

Addition

6 ⟶ Find the 6 - row.
+7 ⟶ Find the 7 - column.
⟵ The sum is named where
the 6-row and 7-column meet.

9 ⟶ Find the 9 - row.
+8 ⟶ Find the 8 - column.
⟵ The sum is named where
the 9-row and 8-column meet.

8-column
7-column

0	1	2	3	4	5	6	7	8	9
1	2	3	4	5	6	7	8	9	10
2	3	4	5	6	7	8	9	10	11
3	4	5	6	7	8	9	10	11	12
4	5	6	7	8	9	10	11	12	13
5	6	7	8	9	10	11	12	13	14
6	7	8	9	10	11	12	13	14	15
7	8	9	10	11	12	13	14	15	16
8	9	10	11	12	13	14	15	16	17
9	10	11	12	13	14	15	16	17	18

6-row

9-row

Directions: Add.

1.
$$7 + 5$$ $$8 + 7$$ $$7 + 4$$ $$9 + 7$$ $$4 + 9$$ $$8 + 8$$ $$9 + 5$$

2.
$$5 + 9$$ $$6 + 4$$ $$6 + 8$$ $$5 + 8$$ $$8 + 4$$ $$7 + 8$$ $$6 + 6$$

3.
$$6 + 9$$ $$5 + 5$$ $$6 + 7$$ $$9 + 2$$ $$8 + 6$$ $$4 + 6$$ $$2 + 9$$

4.
$$5 + 7$$ $$8 + 9$$ $$9 + 6$$ $$5 + 6$$ $$9 + 4$$ $$9 + 9$$ $$4 + 8$$

5.
$$7 + 9$$ $$8 + 2$$ $$9 + 8$$ $$8 + 5$$ $$9 + 1$$ $$4 + 7$$ $$7 + 7$$

Addition

Directions: Add.

Example:

Add the ones.	Add the tens.
26	26
+21	+21
7	47

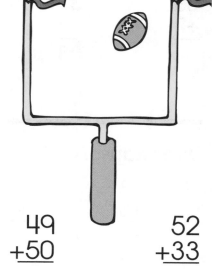

18	24	38	49	52
+11	+35	+21	+50	+33

75	83	67	44	28
+12	+16	+32	+25	+41

68 + 20 = ____   54 + 25 = ____   71 + 17 = ____

The Lions scored 42 points. The Clippers scored 21 points.
How many points were scored in all?   _____

Addition

	Add the ones.	Add the tens.		Add the ones.	Add the tens.
36 +2	36 +2 — 8	36 +2 — 38	6 +41	6 +41 — 7	6 +41 — 47

Directions: Add.

1.
3	23	2	42	5	25
+5	+5	+3	+3	+1	+1

2.
3	3	4	4	2	2
+4	+64	+5	+55	+5	+85

3.
2	12	22	32	42	52
+4	+4	+4	+4	+4	+4

4.
5	6	24	92	57	2
+63	+31	+3	+2	+1	+41

5.
41	21	3	2	21	4
+3	+2	+63	+84	+6	+14

6.
8	62	25	6	2	5
+51	+4	+3	+33	+51	+43

7.
36	42	2	60	5	34
+2	+5	+51	+8	+21	+2

Addition

Add the ones.   Add the tens.

```
  36          36          36
+43         +43         +43
            ___         ___
             9           79
```

```
  26
+61
___
 87
```
↑ ↖ Add the ones.
└─── Add the tens.

Directions: Add.

1.
```
  23        63        45        61        42        60
+45       +21       +22       +30       +35       +25
```

2.
```
  48        52        32        63        21        45
+41       +14       +54       +20       +38       +52
```

3.
```
  34        41        36        51        83        42
+22       +25       +22       +40       +12       +30
```

4.
```
  23        30        27        44        62        35
+24       +58       +12       +23       +14       +53
```

5.
```
  24        52        42        51        16        43
+31       +32       +27       +33       +20       +23
```

6.
```
  34        64        18        54        41        14
+25       +23       +41       +24       +27       +32
```

Magic Squares

The ancient Chinese believed that these number squares really were magic. To many people, the mystery of having each row, column, and diagonal be the same sum seemed like magic.

Example:
Magic Square for 12

7	0	5
2	4	6
3	8	1

Directions: Make a Magic Square for 15. Find the missing numbers for this magic square. The sum of each row, column, and diagonal must equal 15.

	1	6
3	5	
		2

Make a Magic Square for 21. Find the missing numbers for this magic square. The sum of each row, column, and diagonal must equal 21.

10	3	
	7	
		4

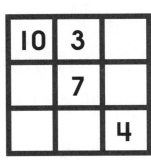

Make Your Own Magic Square. Start with one of the magic squares above. Change the numbers to make a different magic sum. Let someone else solve your magic square.

Dial - A - Word

Directions: Use the phone pad to calculate the "value" of the words.

Example: PHONE = 74663
 PHONE = 7 + 4 + 6 + 6 + 3 = 26

(your name) = _____ = _____

CALCULATOR = _____ = _____

DICTIONARY = _____ = _____

PET TRICKS = _____ = _____

BASEBALL GAME = _____ = _____

COMPUTERS = _____ = _____

TENNIS SHOES = _____ = _____

ADDITION = _____ = _____

MENTAL MATH = _____ = _____

Problem Solving

Directions: Solve each problem.

Work Space:

1. Andy played 2 games today. He played 9 games yesterday. How many games did he play in all?

Andy played _____ games today.

Andy played _____ games yesterday.

He played _____ games in all.

2. Jenna rode her bicycle 8 kilometres yesterday. She rode 4 kilometres today. How many kilometres did she ride in all?

Jenna rode _____ kilometres yesterday.

Jenna rode _____ kilometres today.

Jenna rode _____ kilometres in all.

3. Paul hit the ball 7 times. He missed 4 times. How many times did he swing at the ball?

Paul hit the ball _____ times.

Paul missed the ball _____ times.

Paul swung at the ball _____ times.

1.

2.

3.

Problem Solving

Directions: Solve each problem.

Work Space:

1. Luciana worked 9 hours Monday. She worked 7 hours Tuesday. How many hours did she work in all on those two days?

She worked _____ hours Monday.
She worked _____ hours Tuesday.
She worked _____ hours in all on those two days.

1.

2. Alex has 6 windows to wash. Nadia has 9 windows to wash. How many windows do they have to wash in all?

Alex has _____ windows to wash.
Nadia has _____ windows to wash.
Together they have _____ windows to wash.

2.

3. Seven cars are in the first row. Six cars are in the second row. How many cars are in the first two rows?

_____ cars are in the first two rows.

3.

4. There are 9 men and 8 women at work. How many people are at work?

There are _____ people at work.

4.

Problem Solving

Directions: Solve each problem.

Work Space:

1. John has 32 red marbles and 5 green marbles. How many red and green marbles does he have?

   John has _____ red and green marbles.

2. Su-Lee had 5 paper cups. She bought 24 more. How many paper cups did she have then?

   She then had _____ paper cups.

3. On the way to work, Michael counted 41 cars and 7 trucks. How many cars and trucks did he count?

   Michael counted _____ cars and trucks.

4. Mark worked all the problems on a test. He had 24 right answers and 4 wrong ones. How many problems were on the test?

   There were _____ problems on the test.

5. Shea works with 12 women and 6 men. How many people does she work with?

   Shea works with _____ people.

1.

2.

3.

4.

5.

Six Hundred Silkworms

Sally had hundreds of silkworm eggs in the spring. She couldn't wait for them to hatch. She loved watching them grow, spin cocoons, and hatch into moths.

But once they all hatched, she had 600 silkworms to take care of. Soon she was running out of room to keep them all. She had silkworms in her bedroom. She had silkworms in the family room. She even tried to put silkworms in the kitchen. That's when her mother couldn't take it anymore! "Sally," she said, "600 silkworms are just too many! You have to start giving some of them away."

So Sally took the silkworms to school to give away. The first day, she gave away 20 silkworms. The second day, she gave away 40 more. The third day, she gave away 60 silkworms. How many silkworms did Sally give away by the seventh day?

Directions: Fill in the table. Look for a pattern. It can help you solve the mystery.

Day	Silkworms Given Away	Total Number Given Away
1	20	20
2	40	60
3	60	120
4	80	
5		
6		
7		

Write Your Own Mystery: Think of something else a person might have to give away. Write some clues. Let someone else solve your mystery.

Using Number Concepts

Directions: Cut out the set of cards on the next page.

Use them to form number sentences that answer the questions below.

2 7 5 4 8

1. Use two cards to list each way that you can make the sum of 10.

_____

_____

2. Use two cards to list each way that you can make the sum of 13.

_____

_____

3. Use two cards to list each way that you can make the sum of 16.

_____

_____

4. Use two cards to list each way that you can make the sum of 12.

_____

_____

5. Use two cards to list each way that you can make the sum of 15.

_____

_____

6. Use two cards to list each way that you can make the sum of 17.

_____

_____

7. How did you know you found all the ways?

_____

_____

Extension: Repeat this exercise using three cards to make each sum.

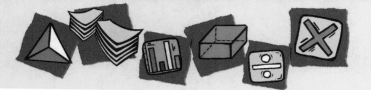

Using Number Concepts

0	1	2	3
4	5	6	
7	8	9	10
	11	12	13
14	15	16	17
+	+	=	

This page was left intentionally
blank for cutting activity on
previous page.

Subtraction Facts

Directions: Subtract.

1.	11 − 3	8 − 4	5 − 5	12 − 3	2 − 1	10 − 9	4 − 3	11 − 9

2.   10 −5   3 −3   6 −3   11 −4   7 −6   10 −6   9 −2   12 −4

3.   16 −7   9 −0   5 −4   13 −7   10 −2   15 −9   8 −8   14 −5

4.   13 −8   4 −2   7 −7   12 −9   2 −0   17 −9   6 −1   11 −7

5.   18 −9   9 −8   6 −4   11 −5   3 −1   15 −7   9 −9   10 −8

6.   12 −6   8 −7   3 −2   13 −9   10 −4   14 −6   7 −5   12 −7

7.   15 −8   8 −3   9 −5   12 −8   8 −6   16 −9   5 −3   12 −7

8.   14 −7   7 −1   6 −5   11 −6   4 −1   10 −7   1 −1   10 −3

Subtraction Facts

Directions: Subtract.

1.
$$\begin{array}{r} 4 \\ -2 \\ \hline \end{array}\qquad \begin{array}{r} 13 \\ -7 \\ \hline \end{array}\qquad \begin{array}{r} 3 \\ -2 \\ \hline \end{array}\qquad \begin{array}{r} 10 \\ -1 \\ \hline \end{array}\qquad \begin{array}{r} 6 \\ -5 \\ \hline \end{array}\qquad \begin{array}{r} 8 \\ -1 \\ \hline \end{array}\qquad \begin{array}{r} 14 \\ -5 \\ \hline \end{array}\qquad \begin{array}{r} 10 \\ -7 \\ \hline \end{array}$$

2.
$$\begin{array}{r} 8 \\ -2 \\ \hline \end{array}\qquad \begin{array}{r} 12 \\ -5 \\ \hline \end{array}\qquad \begin{array}{r} 6 \\ -3 \\ \hline \end{array}\qquad \begin{array}{r} 10 \\ -8 \\ \hline \end{array}\qquad \begin{array}{r} 2 \\ -1 \\ \hline \end{array}\qquad \begin{array}{r} 11 \\ -9 \\ \hline \end{array}\qquad \begin{array}{r} 14 \\ -8 \\ \hline \end{array}\qquad \begin{array}{r} 11 \\ -2 \\ \hline \end{array}$$

3.
$$\begin{array}{r} 4 \\ -0 \\ \hline \end{array}\qquad \begin{array}{r} 11 \\ -3 \\ \hline \end{array}\qquad \begin{array}{r} 9 \\ -1 \\ \hline \end{array}\qquad \begin{array}{r} 15 \\ -6 \\ \hline \end{array}\qquad \begin{array}{r} 5 \\ -0 \\ \hline \end{array}\qquad \begin{array}{r} 7 \\ -1 \\ \hline \end{array}\qquad \begin{array}{r} 13 \\ -8 \\ \hline \end{array}\qquad \begin{array}{r} 10 \\ -9 \\ \hline \end{array}$$

4.
$$\begin{array}{r} 6 \\ -4 \\ \hline \end{array}\qquad \begin{array}{r} 13 \\ -9 \\ \hline \end{array}\qquad \begin{array}{r} 1 \\ -0 \\ \hline \end{array}\qquad \begin{array}{r} 9 \\ -2 \\ \hline \end{array}\qquad \begin{array}{r} 7 \\ -3 \\ \hline \end{array}\qquad \begin{array}{r} 12 \\ -4 \\ \hline \end{array}\qquad \begin{array}{r} 15 \\ -7 \\ \hline \end{array}\qquad \begin{array}{r} 5 \\ -4 \\ \hline \end{array}$$

5.
$$\begin{array}{r} 0 \\ -0 \\ \hline \end{array}\qquad \begin{array}{r} 12 \\ -3 \\ \hline \end{array}\qquad \begin{array}{r} 8 \\ -4 \\ \hline \end{array}\qquad \begin{array}{r} 14 \\ -6 \\ \hline \end{array}\qquad \begin{array}{r} 8 \\ -5 \\ \hline \end{array}\qquad \begin{array}{r} 10 \\ -4 \\ \hline \end{array}\qquad \begin{array}{r} 16 \\ -9 \\ \hline \end{array}\qquad \begin{array}{r} 11 \\ -6 \\ \hline \end{array}$$

6.
$$\begin{array}{r} 9 \\ -9 \\ \hline \end{array}\qquad \begin{array}{r} 10 \\ -2 \\ \hline \end{array}\qquad \begin{array}{r} 3 \\ -2 \\ \hline \end{array}\qquad \begin{array}{r} 15 \\ -9 \\ \hline \end{array}\qquad \begin{array}{r} 5 \\ -1 \\ \hline \end{array}\qquad \begin{array}{r} 12 \\ -9 \\ \hline \end{array}\qquad \begin{array}{r} 14 \\ -9 \\ \hline \end{array}\qquad \begin{array}{r} 10 \\ -3 \\ \hline \end{array}$$

7.
$$\begin{array}{r} 7 \\ -5 \\ \hline \end{array}\qquad \begin{array}{r} 12 \\ -7 \\ \hline \end{array}\qquad \begin{array}{r} 7 \\ -0 \\ \hline \end{array}\qquad \begin{array}{r} 14 \\ -7 \\ \hline \end{array}\qquad \begin{array}{r} 7 \\ -2 \\ \hline \end{array}\qquad \begin{array}{r} 11 \\ -4 \\ \hline \end{array}\qquad \begin{array}{r} 16 \\ -7 \\ \hline \end{array}\qquad \begin{array}{r} 11 \\ -5 \\ \hline \end{array}$$

8.
$$\begin{array}{r} 4 \\ -4 \\ \hline \end{array}\qquad \begin{array}{r} 13 \\ -6 \\ \hline \end{array}\qquad \begin{array}{r} 5 \\ -2 \\ \hline \end{array}\qquad \begin{array}{r} 16 \\ -8 \\ \hline \end{array}\qquad \begin{array}{r} 9 \\ -4 \\ \hline \end{array}\qquad \begin{array}{r} 10 \\ -5 \\ \hline \end{array}\qquad \begin{array}{r} 13 \\ -4 \\ \hline \end{array}\qquad \begin{array}{r} 6 \\ -0 \\ \hline \end{array}$$

Subtraction

8 →Find 8 in
- 6 →the ⬚ 6 ⬚ - column.
 2 ←The difference is named in the
⬚ at the end of this row.

6-column →

−	0	1	2	3	4	5	6	7	8	9
0	0	1	2	3	4	5	6	7	8	9
1	1	2	3	4	5	6	7	8	9	
②	2	3	4	5	6	7	8	9		
3	3	4	5	6	7	8	9			
4	4	5	6	7	8	9				
5	5	6	7	8	9					
6	6	7	8	9						
7	7	8	9							
8	8	9								
9	9									

Directions: Subtract.

1.
$$\begin{array}{r}5\\-4\\\hline\end{array}\qquad\begin{array}{r}3\\-2\\\hline\end{array}\qquad\begin{array}{r}7\\-7\\\hline\end{array}\qquad\begin{array}{r}1\\-0\\\hline\end{array}\qquad\begin{array}{r}8\\-2\\\hline\end{array}\qquad\begin{array}{r}9\\-7\\\hline\end{array}\qquad\begin{array}{r}4\\-3\\\hline\end{array}$$

2.
$$\begin{array}{r}7\\-2\\\hline\end{array}\qquad\begin{array}{r}2\\-2\\\hline\end{array}\qquad\begin{array}{r}7\\-6\\\hline\end{array}\qquad\begin{array}{r}8\\-7\\\hline\end{array}\qquad\begin{array}{r}9\\-3\\\hline\end{array}\qquad\begin{array}{r}9\\-8\\\hline\end{array}\qquad\begin{array}{r}4\\-1\\\hline\end{array}$$

3.
$$\begin{array}{r}0\\-0\\\hline\end{array}\qquad\begin{array}{r}7\\-1\\\hline\end{array}\qquad\begin{array}{r}3\\-0\\\hline\end{array}\qquad\begin{array}{r}6\\-6\\\hline\end{array}\qquad\begin{array}{r}4\\-2\\\hline\end{array}\qquad\begin{array}{r}6\\-2\\\hline\end{array}\qquad\begin{array}{r}9\\-5\\\hline\end{array}$$

4.
$$\begin{array}{r}9\\-9\\\hline\end{array}\qquad\begin{array}{r}8\\-4\\\hline\end{array}\qquad\begin{array}{r}9\\-1\\\hline\end{array}\qquad\begin{array}{r}7\\-5\\\hline\end{array}\qquad\begin{array}{r}7\\-4\\\hline\end{array}\qquad\begin{array}{r}6\\-5\\\hline\end{array}\qquad\begin{array}{r}2\\-0\\\hline\end{array}$$

5.
$$\begin{array}{r}5\\-5\\\hline\end{array}\qquad\begin{array}{r}2\\-1\\\hline\end{array}\qquad\begin{array}{r}5\\-0\\\hline\end{array}\qquad\begin{array}{r}8\\-3\\\hline\end{array}\qquad\begin{array}{r}9\\-0\\\hline\end{array}\qquad\begin{array}{r}6\\-3\\\hline\end{array}\qquad\begin{array}{r}7\\-0\\\hline\end{array}$$

Subtraction

11 →Find 11 in
- 4 →the 4 - column.
← The difference is named in the
at the end of this row.

4-column

-	0	1	2	3	4	5	6	7	8	9
0	0	1	2	3	4	5	6	7	8	9
1	1	2	3	4	5	6	7	8	9	10
2	2	3	4	5	6	7	8	9	10	11
3	3	4	5	6	7	8	9	10	11	12
4	4	5	6	7	8	9	10	11	12	
5	5	6	7	8	9	10	11	12		
6	6	7	8	9	10	11	12			
7	7	8	9	10	11	12				
8	8	9	10	11	12					
9	9	10	11	12						

Directions: Subtract.

1.
$$\begin{array}{r} 11 \\ -\ 7 \\ \hline \end{array} \quad \begin{array}{r} 10 \\ -\ 4 \\ \hline \end{array} \quad \begin{array}{r} 10 \\ -\ 8 \\ \hline \end{array} \quad \begin{array}{r} 12 \\ -\ 9 \\ \hline \end{array} \quad \begin{array}{r} 8 \\ -\ 5 \\ \hline \end{array} \quad \begin{array}{r} 11 \\ -\ 2 \\ \hline \end{array} \quad \begin{array}{r} 7 \\ -\ 3 \\ \hline \end{array}$$

2.
$$\begin{array}{r} 10 \\ -\ 1 \\ \hline \end{array} \quad \begin{array}{r} 11 \\ -\ 8 \\ \hline \end{array} \quad \begin{array}{r} 7 \\ -\ 4 \\ \hline \end{array} \quad \begin{array}{r} 11 \\ -\ 6 \\ \hline \end{array} \quad \begin{array}{r} 12 \\ -\ 3 \\ \hline \end{array} \quad \begin{array}{r} 9 \\ -\ 6 \\ \hline \end{array} \quad \begin{array}{r} 10 \\ -\ 3 \\ \hline \end{array}$$

3.
$$\begin{array}{r} 12 \\ -\ 7 \\ \hline \end{array} \quad \begin{array}{r} 10 \\ -\ 7 \\ \hline \end{array} \quad \begin{array}{r} 9 \\ -\ 3 \\ \hline \end{array} \quad \begin{array}{r} 11 \\ -\ 9 \\ \hline \end{array} \quad \begin{array}{r} 12 \\ -\ 4 \\ \hline \end{array} \quad \begin{array}{r} 10 \\ -\ 5 \\ \hline \end{array} \quad \begin{array}{r} 12 \\ -\ 5 \\ \hline \end{array}$$

4.
$$\begin{array}{r} 8 \\ -\ 6 \\ \hline \end{array} \quad \begin{array}{r} 12 \\ -\ 8 \\ \hline \end{array} \quad \begin{array}{r} 9 \\ -\ 5 \\ \hline \end{array} \quad \begin{array}{r} 10 \\ -\ 6 \\ \hline \end{array} \quad \begin{array}{r} 11 \\ -\ 5 \\ \hline \end{array} \quad \begin{array}{r} 8 \\ -\ 8 \\ \hline \end{array} \quad \begin{array}{r} 8 \\ -\ 3 \\ \hline \end{array}$$

5.
$$\begin{array}{r} 12 \\ -\ 6 \\ \hline \end{array} \quad \begin{array}{r} 10 \\ -\ 9 \\ \hline \end{array} \quad \begin{array}{r} 9 \\ -\ 8 \\ \hline \end{array} \quad \begin{array}{r} 7 \\ -\ 6 \\ \hline \end{array} \quad \begin{array}{r} 11 \\ -\ 4 \\ \hline \end{array} \quad \begin{array}{r} 9 \\ -\ 7 \\ \hline \end{array} \quad \begin{array}{r} 11 \\ -\ 3 \\ \hline \end{array}$$

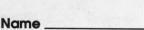

Subtraction

13 ⟶ Find 13 in
- 8 ⟶ the 8 - column.
⟵ The difference is named in the
       ▭ at the end of this row.

15 ⟶ Find 15 in
- 6 ⟶ the 6 - column.
⟵ The difference is named in the
       ▭ at the end of this row.

6-column ⟶   8-column

--	0	1	2	3	4	5	6	7	8	9
0	0	1	2	3	4	5	6	7	8	9
1	1	2	3	4	5	6	7	8	9	10
2	2	3	4	5	6	7	8	9	10	11
3	3	4	5	6	7	8	9	10	11	12
4	4	5	6	7	8	9	10	11	12	13
5	5	6	7	8	9	10	11	12	13	14
6	6	7	8	9	10	11	12	13	14	15
7	7	8	9	10	11	12	13	14	15	16
8	8	9	10	11	12	13	14	15	16	17
9	9	10	11	12	13	14	15	16	17	18

Directions: Subtract.

1.
$$\begin{array}{r} 13 \\ -5 \\ \hline \end{array}$$
$$\begin{array}{r} 14 \\ -8 \\ \hline \end{array}$$
$$\begin{array}{r} 16 \\ -7 \\ \hline \end{array}$$
$$\begin{array}{r} 10 \\ -9 \\ \hline \end{array}$$
$$\begin{array}{r} 12 \\ -5 \\ \hline \end{array}$$
$$\begin{array}{r} 14 \\ -6 \\ \hline \end{array}$$
$$\begin{array}{r} 15 \\ -7 \\ \hline \end{array}$$

2.
$$\begin{array}{r} 17 \\ -8 \\ \hline \end{array}$$
$$\begin{array}{r} 13 \\ -7 \\ \hline \end{array}$$
$$\begin{array}{r} 12 \\ -4 \\ \hline \end{array}$$
$$\begin{array}{r} 14 \\ -5 \\ \hline \end{array}$$
$$\begin{array}{r} 15 \\ -8 \\ \hline \end{array}$$
$$\begin{array}{r} 13 \\ -6 \\ \hline \end{array}$$
$$\begin{array}{r} 10 \\ -3 \\ \hline \end{array}$$

3.
$$\begin{array}{r} 11 \\ -7 \\ \hline \end{array}$$
$$\begin{array}{r} 18 \\ -9 \\ \hline \end{array}$$
$$\begin{array}{r} 15 \\ -6 \\ \hline \end{array}$$
$$\begin{array}{r} 11 \\ -8 \\ \hline \end{array}$$
$$\begin{array}{r} 14 \\ -7 \\ \hline \end{array}$$
$$\begin{array}{r} 13 \\ -9 \\ \hline \end{array}$$
$$\begin{array}{r} 17 \\ -9 \\ \hline \end{array}$$

4.
$$\begin{array}{r} 16 \\ -8 \\ \hline \end{array}$$
$$\begin{array}{r} 10 \\ -5 \\ \hline \end{array}$$
$$\begin{array}{r} 12 \\ -7 \\ \hline \end{array}$$
$$\begin{array}{r} 13 \\ -4 \\ \hline \end{array}$$
$$\begin{array}{r} 12 \\ -6 \\ \hline \end{array}$$
$$\begin{array}{r} 14 \\ -9 \\ \hline \end{array}$$
$$\begin{array}{r} 11 \\ -6 \\ \hline \end{array}$$

5.
$$\begin{array}{r} 13 \\ -8 \\ \hline \end{array}$$
$$\begin{array}{r} 12 \\ -9 \\ \hline \end{array}$$
$$\begin{array}{r} 10 \\ -1 \\ \hline \end{array}$$
$$\begin{array}{r} 15 \\ -9 \\ \hline \end{array}$$
$$\begin{array}{r} 11 \\ -3 \\ \hline \end{array}$$
$$\begin{array}{r} 10 \\ -7 \\ \hline \end{array}$$
$$\begin{array}{r} 16 \\ -9 \\ \hline \end{array}$$

Subtraction

Subtraction means "taking away" or subtracting one number from another to find the difference. For example, 10 - 3 = 7.

Directions: Subtract.

Example:

Subtract the ones.

```
  39
- 24
   5
```

Subtract the tens.

```
  39
- 24
 |5
```

```
  48
- 35
```

```
  95
- 22
```

```
  87
- 16
```

```
  55
- 43
```

```
  37
- 14
```

```
  69
- 57
```

```
  44
- 23
```

```
  99
- 78
```

66 - 44 = ____   57 - 33 = ____

The yellow car traveled 87 kilometres per hour. The orange car traveled 66 kilometres per hour. How much faster was the yellow car traveling? _____

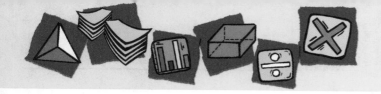

Subtraction

	Subtract the ones.	Subtract the tens.		Subtract the ones.	Subtract the tens.
47 - 2	47 - 2 5	47 - 2 45	64 - 23	64 - 23 1	64 - 23 41

Directions: Subtract.

1.   9 − 3   49 − 3   5 − 2   35 − 2   7 − 1   87 − 1

2.   8 − 2   78 − 2   4 − 3   64 − 3   9 − 9   89 − 9

3.   45 − 3   36 − 4   78 − 5   42 − 2   38 − 8   65 − 4

4.   49 − 26   37 − 16   58 − 23   49 − 31   78 − 45   73 − 20

5.   58 − 27   69 − 31   42 − 21   49 − 19   84 − 23   78 − 64

6.   78 − 21   67 − 31   40 − 20   56 − 36   45 − 23   92 − 21

Subtraction

To check
37 - 24 = 13,
add 24
to _____ .

$$\begin{array}{r} 37 \\ - 24 \\ \hline 13 \\ + 24 \\ \hline 37 \end{array}$$

To check
59 - 29 = 30,
add _____
to 30 .

$$\begin{array}{r} 59 \\ - 29 \\ \hline 30 \\ + 29 \\ \hline 59 \end{array}$$

These should be the same.

Directions: Subtract. Check each answer.

1.
$$\begin{array}{r} 59 \\ - 34 \end{array}$$
$$\begin{array}{r} 27 \\ - 14 \end{array}$$
$$\begin{array}{r} 85 \\ - 23 \end{array}$$
$$\begin{array}{r} 78 \\ - 23 \end{array}$$
$$\begin{array}{r} 47 \\ - 24 \end{array}$$
$$\begin{array}{r} 59 \\ - 26 \end{array}$$

2.
$$\begin{array}{r} 85 \\ - 25 \end{array}$$
$$\begin{array}{r} 48 \\ - 32 \end{array}$$
$$\begin{array}{r} 56 \\ - 24 \end{array}$$
$$\begin{array}{r} 96 \\ - 35 \end{array}$$
$$\begin{array}{r} 40 \\ - 30 \end{array}$$
$$\begin{array}{r} 92 \\ - 81 \end{array}$$

3.
$$\begin{array}{r} 74 \\ - 23 \end{array}$$
$$\begin{array}{r} 58 \\ - 26 \end{array}$$
$$\begin{array}{r} 75 \\ - 24 \end{array}$$
$$\begin{array}{r} 38 \\ - 23 \end{array}$$
$$\begin{array}{r} 45 \\ - 35 \end{array}$$
$$\begin{array}{r} 88 \\ - 35 \end{array}$$

4.
$$\begin{array}{r} 67 \\ - 24 \end{array}$$
$$\begin{array}{r} 87 \\ - 24 \end{array}$$
$$\begin{array}{r} 59 \\ - 36 \end{array}$$
$$\begin{array}{r} 58 \\ - 24 \end{array}$$
$$\begin{array}{r} 79 \\ - 54 \end{array}$$
$$\begin{array}{r} 84 \\ - 23 \end{array}$$

Mountaintop Getaway

Directions: Solve the problems. Find a path to the cabin by shading in all answers that have a **3** in them.

	98 -52	46 -12	68 -17
	79 -53	65 -23	63 -31	86 -32
	59 -45	75 -64	67 -24	87 -54	55 -43
87 -65	44 -32	57 -24	88 -25	75 -61	48 -26
69 -25	95 -24	48 -13	58 -16	35 -13	39 -17

SECRET
PATHS

Name _____

Problem Solving

Directions: Solve each problem.   **Work Space:**

1. There were 12 nails in a box. David used 3
   of them. How many nails are still in the box?

   _____ nails were in a box.
   _____ nails were used.
   _____ nails are still in the box.

   1.

2. There are 11 checkers on a board. Eight
   of them are black. The rest are red. How
   many red checkers are on the board?

   _____ checkers are on a board.
   _____ checkers are black and the
   rest are red.
   _____ red checkers are on the board.

   2.

3. Marty is 10 years old. Her brother Larry is 7.
   Marty is how many years older than Larry?

   Marty's age is _____ years.
   Larry's age is _____ years.
   Marty is _____ years older than Larry.

   3.

4. Twelve people are in a room. Five of
   them are men. How many are women?

   _____ women are in the room.

   4.

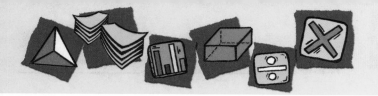

Problem Solving

Directions: Solve each problem.   **Work Space:**

1. Matt wants to collect 13 cars. He now has 5 cars. How many more cars does he need?

   Matt wants _____ cars.
   He now has _____ cars.
   He needs _____ cars.

2. Susan bought 18 valentines. She mailed 9 of them. How many valentines does she have left?

   Susan bought _____ valentines.
   She mailed _____ of them.
   She has _____ valentines left.

3. Courtney had 16 stamps. She used some, and had 7 left. How many stamps did she use?

   Courtney used _____ stamps.

4. Bret is 14 years old. Amy is 7. Bret is how much older than Amy?

   Bret is _____ years older than Amy.

5. Fifteen bolts and nuts were on the table. Seven were bolts. How many were nuts?

   There were _____ nuts.

1.

2.

3.

4.

5.

Problem Solving

Directions: Solve each problem.

Work Space:

1. Beth worked 27 problems. She got 6 wrong answers. How many answers did she get right?

   Beth got _____ answers right.

   1.

2. There were 96 parts in a box. Four parts were broken. How many parts were not broken?

   _____ parts were not broken.

   2.

3. At noon the temperature was 28 degrees Celsius. At nine o'clock in the evening, it was 14 degrees Celsius. How many degrees did the temperature drop?

   The temperature dropped _____ degrees.

   3.

4. Clark had 75 cents. Then he spent 25 cents for some paper. How many cents did he have left?

   Clark had _____ cents left.

   4.

5. There are 72 houses in Kyle's neighbourhood. Kyle delivers papers to all but 21 of them. How many houses does he deliver papers to?

   He delivers papers to _____ houses.

   5.

Problem Solving

Directions: Solve each problem.

Work Space:

1. Mr. Ming wants to build a fence 58 metres long. He has 27 metres of fence completed. How much of the fence is left to build?

   _____ metres of fence is left to build.

   1.

2. Mrs. Boyle is taking an 89-kilometre trip. She has traveled 64 kilometre. How much farther must she travel?

   Mrs. Boyle must travel _____ more kilometres.

   2.

3. Sean had 95 cents. Then he spent 45 cents. How many cents did he have left?

   Sean had _____ cents left.

   3.

4. Kevin scored 62 points and Bianca scored 78 points. How many more points did Bianca score than Kevin?

   Bianca scored _____ more points.

   4.

5. Darien lives 38 blocks from the ball park. Kelly lives 25 blocks from the park. How much farther from the ball park does Darien live than Kelly?

   Darien lives _____ blocks farther than Kelly.

   5.

Addition and Subtraction

To check
5 + 6 = 11,
subtract 6
from 11.

$$\begin{array}{r} 5 \\ + 6 \\ \hline 11 \\ - 6 \\ \hline 5 \end{array}$$

These should be the same.

To check
13 - 4 = 9,
add 4
to _____ .

$$\begin{array}{r} 13 \\ - 4 \\ \hline 9 \\ + 4 \\ \hline 13 \end{array}$$

These should be the same.

Directions: Add. Check each answer.

1.
$$\begin{array}{r} 9 \\ + 2 \\ \hline \end{array}$$
$$\begin{array}{r} 8 \\ + 4 \\ \hline \end{array}$$
$$\begin{array}{r} 7 \\ + 3 \\ \hline \end{array}$$
$$\begin{array}{r} 3 \\ + 8 \\ \hline \end{array}$$
$$\begin{array}{r} 1 \\ + 9 \\ \hline \end{array}$$
$$\begin{array}{r} 6 \\ + 6 \\ \hline \end{array}$$

2.
$$\begin{array}{r} 9 \\ + 3 \\ \hline \end{array}$$
$$\begin{array}{r} 5 \\ + 6 \\ \hline \end{array}$$
$$\begin{array}{r} 4 \\ + 8 \\ \hline \end{array}$$
$$\begin{array}{r} 5 \\ + 5 \\ \hline \end{array}$$
$$\begin{array}{r} 7 \\ + 4 \\ \hline \end{array}$$
$$\begin{array}{r} 9 \\ + 1 \\ \hline \end{array}$$

Directions: Subtract. Check each answer.

3.
$$\begin{array}{r} 10 \\ - 8 \\ \hline \end{array}$$
$$\begin{array}{r} 12 \\ - 7 \\ \hline \end{array}$$
$$\begin{array}{r} 11 \\ - 3 \\ \hline \end{array}$$
$$\begin{array}{r} 10 \\ - 4 \\ \hline \end{array}$$
$$\begin{array}{r} 11 \\ - 7 \\ \hline \end{array}$$
$$\begin{array}{r} 10 \\ - 7 \\ \hline \end{array}$$

4.
$$\begin{array}{r} 11 \\ - 9 \\ \hline \end{array}$$
$$\begin{array}{r} 12 \\ - 8 \\ \hline \end{array}$$
$$\begin{array}{r} 11 \\ - 8 \\ \hline \end{array}$$
$$\begin{array}{r} 12 \\ - 5 \\ \hline \end{array}$$
$$\begin{array}{r} 10 \\ - 6 \\ \hline \end{array}$$
$$\begin{array}{r} 10 \\ - 3 \\ \hline \end{array}$$

Addition and Subtraction

To check
6 + 8 = 14,
subtract 8
from 14.

$$\begin{array}{r} 6 \\ + 8 \\ \hline 14 \\ - 8 \\ \hline 6 \end{array}$$

These should
be the same.

To check
13 − 6 = 7,
add _____
to 7.

$$\begin{array}{r} 13 \\ - 6 \\ \hline 7 \\ + 6 \\ \hline 13 \end{array}$$

These should
be the same.

Directions: Add. Check each answer.

1.
$$\begin{array}{r} 5 \\ +9 \\ \hline \end{array}$$
$$\begin{array}{r} 9 \\ +7 \\ \hline \end{array}$$
$$\begin{array}{r} 6 \\ +6 \\ \hline \end{array}$$
$$\begin{array}{r} 7 \\ +4 \\ \hline \end{array}$$
$$\begin{array}{r} 9 \\ +8 \\ \hline \end{array}$$
$$\begin{array}{r} 3 \\ +7 \\ \hline \end{array}$$

2.
$$\begin{array}{r} 6 \\ +7 \\ \hline \end{array}$$
$$\begin{array}{r} 9 \\ +3 \\ \hline \end{array}$$
$$\begin{array}{r} 6 \\ +9 \\ \hline \end{array}$$
$$\begin{array}{r} 4 \\ +9 \\ \hline \end{array}$$
$$\begin{array}{r} 6 \\ +4 \\ \hline \end{array}$$
$$\begin{array}{r} 8 \\ +6 \\ \hline \end{array}$$

Directions: Subtract. Check each answer.

3.
$$\begin{array}{r} 14 \\ - 8 \\ \hline \end{array}$$
$$\begin{array}{r} 18 \\ - 9 \\ \hline \end{array}$$
$$\begin{array}{r} 13 \\ - 5 \\ \hline \end{array}$$
$$\begin{array}{r} 15 \\ - 6 \\ \hline \end{array}$$
$$\begin{array}{r} 16 \\ - 8 \\ \hline \end{array}$$
$$\begin{array}{r} 12 \\ - 7 \\ \hline \end{array}$$

4.
$$\begin{array}{r} 13 \\ - 6 \\ \hline \end{array}$$
$$\begin{array}{r} 12 \\ - 4 \\ \hline \end{array}$$
$$\begin{array}{r} 13 \\ - 4 \\ \hline \end{array}$$
$$\begin{array}{r} 16 \\ - 9 \\ \hline \end{array}$$
$$\begin{array}{r} 15 \\ - 7 \\ \hline \end{array}$$
$$\begin{array}{r} 13 \\ - 8 \\ \hline \end{array}$$

Addition and Subtraction

Directions: Add.

1.
```
   3      43       1       51       2       82
 + 6     + 6     + 4      + 4     + 5      + 5
```

2.
```
  57      26      44       23      42       21
 + 2     + 1     + 3      + 4     + 3      + 5
```

3.
```
   4       5       4        3       5        7
 + 31    + 43    + 62     + 43    + 12     + 20
```

4.
```
  54      26      45       67      42       22
 + 31    + 12    + 33     + 21    + 33     + 13
```

Directions: Subtract.

5.
```
   7      37       5       45       8       38
 - 4     - 4     - 2      - 2     - 6      - 6
```

6.
```
  38      27      54       29      68       26
 - 4     - 6     - 3      - 7     - 2      - 3
```

7.
```
  54      69      37       88      93       87
 - 23    - 24    - 21     - 24    - 21     - 37
```

8.
```
  28      54      87       54      50       37
 - 13    - 34    - 26     - 21    - 40     - 10
```

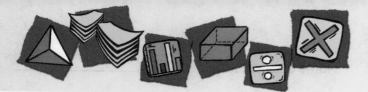

Addition and Subtraction

To check
43 + 14 = 57,
subtract 14
from _____.

```
   43
 + 14
 ─────
   57    These should
 - 14    be the same.
 ─────
   43
```

To check
57 - 14 = 43,
add _____
to 43 .

```
   57
 - 14
 ─────
   43    These should
 + 14    be the same.
 ─────
   57
```

Directions: Add. Check each answer.

1.
```
  27        42        26        14        23        65
+ 31      + 51      + 30      + 52      + 72      + 22
```

2.
```
  44        31        64        32        42        46
+ 24      + 27      + 14      + 20      + 36      + 23
```

Directions: Subtract. Check each answer.

3.
```
  78        48        27        58        67        38
- 23      - 13      - 16      - 26      - 24      - 16
```

4.
```
  75        46        39        45        67        38
- 61      - 26      - 10      - 23      - 41      - 15
```

Stay on Track

Directions: Add or subtract. Write each answer in the puzzle.

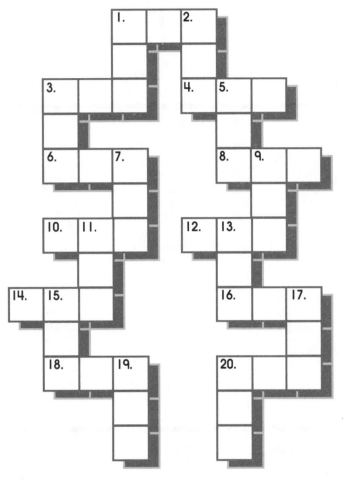

Across

1. 413
    +312

3. 102
    +415

4. 223
    +103

6. 131
    +253

8. 324
    +321

10. 207
    +222

12. 105
    +214

14. 315
    +400

16. 121
    +503

18. 451
    +421

20. 312
    +281

Down

1. 859
    -112

2. 985
    -402

3. 887
    -344

5. 789
    -583

7. 699
    -240

9. 589
    -100

11. 767
    -512

13. 497
    -321

15. 259
    -151

17. 974
    -511

19. 689
    -450

20. 797
    -236

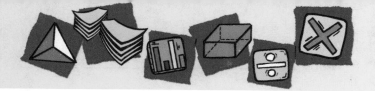

Problem Solving

Directions: Answer each question.

Work Space:

1. Ben had some marbles. He gave 2 of them away and had 9 left. How many marbles did he start with?

   Are you to add or subtract?_____
   How many marbles did he start with?_____

2. A full box has 10 pieces of chalk. This box has only 8 pieces. How many pieces are missing?

   Are you to add or subtract?_____
   How many pieces are missing?_____

3. Noah is 11 years old today. How old was he 4 years ago?

   Are you to add or subtract?_____
   How old was Noah 4 years ago?_____

4. Nine boys were playing ball. Then 3 more boys began to play. How many boys were playing ball then?

   Are you to add or subtract?_____
   How many boys were playing ball?_____

5. Tricia invited 12 people to her party. Seven came. How many people that were invited did not come?

   Are you to add or subtract?_____
   How many people did not come?_____

1.

2.

3.

4.

5.

Problem Solving

Directions: Answer each question.

Work Space:

1. Penny worked 9 addition problems. She worked 7 subtraction problems. How many problems did she work?

   Are you to add or subtract?_____
   How many problems did she work?_____

2. Six people were in the room. Then 8 more people came in. How many people were in the room then?

   Are you to add or subtract?_____
   How many people were in the room then?_____

3. There were 18 chairs in a room. Nine of them were being used. How many were not being used?

   Are you to add or subtract?_____
   How many chairs were not being used?_____

4. Mr. Noe and Miss Leikel had 17 students absent. Mr. Noe had 9 absent. How many did Miss Leikel have absent?

   Are you to add or subtract?_____
   How many students were absent from Miss Leikel's class?_____

1.

2.

3.

4.

Problem Solving

Directions: Solve each problem.

Work Space:

1. There are 12 boys and 13 girls in Jean's class. How many students are in her class?

   There are _____ students in her class.

2. Emily scored 32 baskets. She missed 23 times. How many times did she try to score?

   Emily tried to score _____ times.

3. One store ordered 52 bicycles. Another store ordered 45 bicycles. How many bicycles did both stores order?

   Both stores ordered _____ bicycles.

4. One bear cub weighs 64 kilograms. Another bear cub is 22 kilograms heavier. How much does the heavier cub weigh?

   The heavier bear cub weighs ____ kilograms.

5. 43 women and 35 men came to the meeting. How many people came to the meeting?

   _____ people came to the meeting.

6. 68 seats were filled, and 21 were empty. How many seats were there?

   There were _____ seats.

1.

2.

3.

4.

5.

6.

Problem Solving

Directions: Solve each problem.

Work Space:

1. Mrs. Dial weighs 55 kilograms. Her son weighs 32 kilograms. How much more than her son does Mrs. Dial weigh?

   She weighs _____ kilograms more.

2. Mitzi planted 55 flower seeds. Only 23 of them grew. How many did not grow?

   _____ seeds did not grow.

3. A city has 48 mail trucks. Twelve are not being used today. How many mail trucks are being used?

   _____ mail trucks are being used.

4. A mail carrier delivered 38 letters and picked up 15. How many more letters were delivered than were picked up?

   The carrier delivered _____ more letters.

5. A city has 89 mail carriers. One day 77 carriers were at work. How many carriers were not at work?

   _____ carriers were not at work.

1.

2.

3.

4.

5.

Outstanding Elephant Math

Directions: Connect the dots in order from least to greatest.

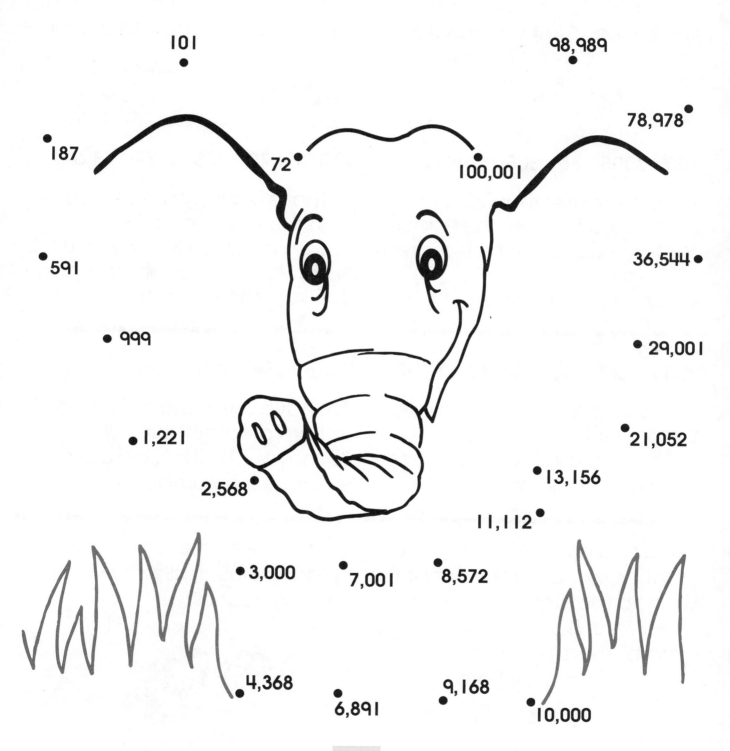

101

98,989

78,978

187

72

100,001

591

36,544

999

29,001

1,221

21,052

2,568

13,156

11,112

3,000

7,001

8,572

4,368

6,891

9,168

10,000

Place Value Riddles

Directions: Using the clues below, choose the number each riddle describes. As you read, draw an **X** on each number that does not fit the clue. After you have read all the clues for each riddle, there should be only one number left.

   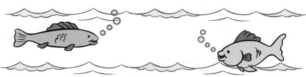

305   3005   35   3050   3500   **769   6,379   973   3,796   3,691**

1. I am greater than 300.
2. I have a 5 in the ones place.
3. I have a zero in the hundreds place.
4. Circle the number.

1. I have a number greater than 6 in the tens place.
2. I am between 3,000 and 4,000.
3. I have a 6 in the hundreds place.
4. Circle the number.

---

423   4023   324   3,412   2,143   **4058   584   845   5048   8540**

1. I have a 2 in the tens place.
2. I am less than 1,000.
3. I have a 4 in the ones place.
4. Circle the number.

1. I have a 4 in the tens place.
2. I am greater than 5,000.
3. I have a 0 in the hundreds place.
4. Circle the number.

Now, fold a blank sheet of paper in half three times to create eight boxes. Create eight of these place value riddles. You may want to use words like these when writing your clues:
ones, tens, hundreds, thousands place,
greater than, less than,
have a ___ somewhere

4 - 3 - 2 - 1 - Blast Off!

Directions: Colour these spaces **red**:

- three thousand five
- 1,000 less than 3,128
- six thousand eight hundred eighty-nine
- 100 more than 618,665
- 10 less than 2,981
- fifty-nine thousand two

Directions: Colour these spaces **blue**:

- 10 less than 4,786
- eight thousand six hundred two
- 1,000 less than 638,961
- two thousand four hundred fifty-one
- 100 more than 81,136
- 10,000 less than 48,472

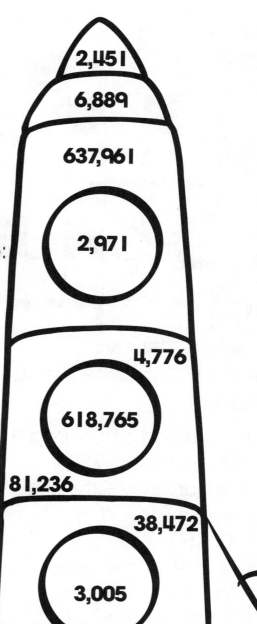

Place Value Puzzles

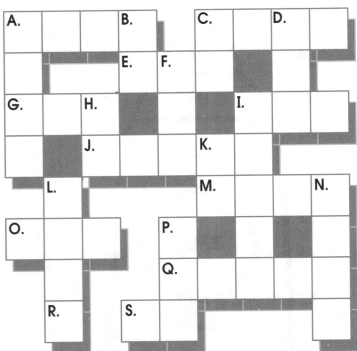

Directions: Complete the puzzle.

ACROSS

A. 3 thousand 5 hundred 9
C. 100 less than 8,754
E. one hundred sixty-two
G. seven hundred eighty-two
I. 100, 150, 200, ___
J. 1, 2, 3, 4, 5 mixed up
L. two
M. 100 less than 9,704
O. three zeros
P. eight
Q. 10,000 more than 56,480
R. one
S. 1 ten, 1 one

DOWN

A. 10 more than 3,769
B. ninety-one
C. 28 backwards
D. 5 hundreds, 8 tens, 5 ones
F. 100 less than 773
H. 5, 10, 15, 20, ___
I. ten less than 24,684
K. 2 tens, 9 ones
L. two thousand one
N. 1000, 2000, 3000, _____
P. eight hundreds, 6 tens, 1 one

Write That Number

Directions: Write the numeral form for each number.

Example: three hundred forty-two = 342

1. six hundred fifty thousand, two hundred twenty-five _____

2. nine hundred ninety-nine thousand, nine hundred ninety-nine _____

3. one hundred six thousand, four hundred thirty-seven _____

4. three hundred fifty-six thousand, two hundred two _____

5. Write the number that is two more than 356,909. _____

6. Write the number that is five less than 448,394. _____

7. Write the number that is ten more than 285,634. _____

8. Write the number that is ten less than 395,025. _____

Directions: Write the following numbers in word form.

9. 3,208 _____

10. 13,656 _____

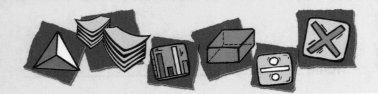

Big Numbers Game

Preparation: Cut out the spinners, number cards, and gameboard pattern on the next page. Glue the spinners and gameboard onto cardboard and let them dry. Cut them out. Attach a large paper clip or safety pin to the spinner base with a brad or paper fastener. The paper clip (or safety pin) should spin freely.

Give each player one set of ten cards. Also, each player will need a marker and a copy of the gameboard.

Rules: This game involves 2–6 players. The first player is the one who has the most letters in his/her last name. Play goes in a clockwise direction.

Directions: Player One spins the place value spinner first. Then, he or she spins the numerical spinner. Player One then puts the number marker on the place indicated by the spinner. (For example, if Player One spins hundreds on the place value spinner and 8 on the numerical spinner, he or she should put an 8 number marker in the hundreds place on the gameboard.) If the number shown on either spinner is already filled on the board, Player One loses his or her turn. The first player who fills all the spaces on his or her board and is able to read the number aloud is the winner.

HUNDRED MILLIONS	TEN MILLIONS	MILLIONS	HUNDRED THOUSANDS	TEN THOUSANDS	THOUSANDS	HUNDREDS	TENS	ONES
						8		

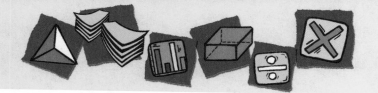

Game Parts for Big Numbers Game

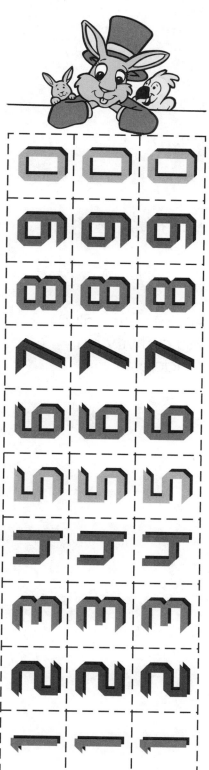

ONES	
TENS	
HUNDREDS	
THOUSANDS	
TEN THOUSANDS	
HUNDRED THOUSANDS	
MILLIONS	
TEN MILLIONS	
HUNDRED MILLIONS	

Numeral Spinner

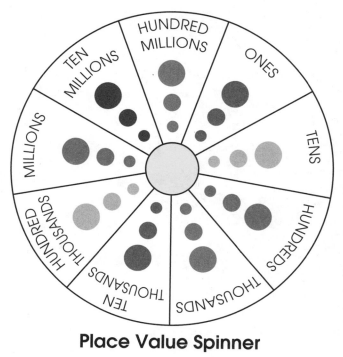

Place Value Spinner

This page was left intentionally
blank for cutting activity on
previous page.

Place Value

The place value of a digit, or numeral, is shown by where it is in the number. For example, in the number 1,234, **1** has the place value of thousands, **2** is hundreds, **3** is tens, and **4** is ones.

Hundred Thousands	Ten Thousands	Thousands	Hundreds	Tens	Ones
9	4	3	8	5	2

Directions: Match the numbers in Column A with the words in Column B.

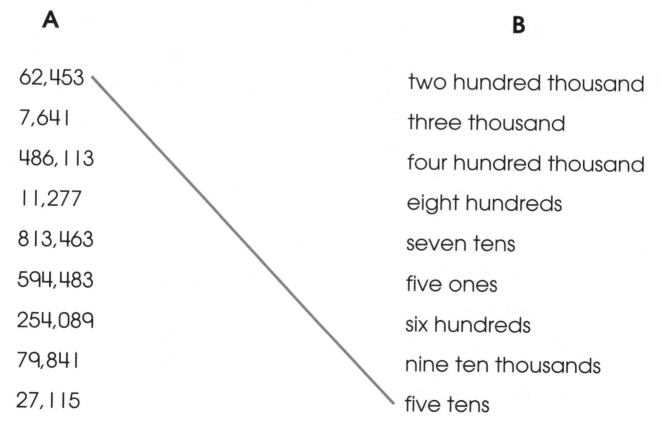

A	B
62,453	two hundred thousand
7,641	three thousand
486,113	four hundred thousand
11,277	eight hundreds
813,463	seven tens
594,483	five ones
254,089	six hundreds
79,841	nine ten thousands
27,115	five tens

Place Value

$$1\ ,\ 2\ 3\ 4\ ,\ 5\ 6\ 7$$

millions | hundred thousands | ten thousands | thousands | hundreds | tens | ones

Directions: Write each numeral in its correct place.

1. The number 8,672,019 has:

_____ thousands   _____ ten   _____ hundred thousands

_____ millions   _____ ones   _____ ten thousands

_____ hundreds

2. What number has:

6 ones   3 millions   9 tens

7 hundreds   4 ten thousands   8 thousands

5 hundred thousands

The number is _____ .

3. The number 6,792,510 has:

_____ ten thousands   _____ millions   _____ hundreds

_____ ones   _____ thousands   _____ ten

_____ hundred thousands

4. What number has:

5 millions   3 tens   6 thousands

1 hundred   8 ten thousands   4 ones

0 hundred thousands

The number is _____ .

Rounding: The Nearest Ten

Directions: If the ones number is **5** or greater, "round up" to the nearest **10**. If the ones number is **4** or less, the tens number stays the same and the ones number becomes a zero.

Examples:

15 round up to 20   **23** round down to 20   **47** round up to 50

7 _____

12 _____

33 _____

27 _____

73 _____

25 _____

39 _____

58 _____

81 _____

94 _____

44 _____

88 _____

66 _____

70 _____

Rounding: The Nearest Hundred

Directions: If the tens number is **5** or greater, "round up" to the nearest hundred. If the tens number is **4** or less, the hundreds number remains the same.

Remember... Look at the number directly to the right of the place you are rounding to.

Examples:

230 round down to 200   **470** round up to 500

150 round up to 200   **732** round down to 700

456 _____   120 _____

340 _____   923 _____

867 _____   550 _____

686 _____   231 _____

770 _____   492 _____

Estimate by Rounding Numbers

Directions: Estimate by rounding numbers to different place values. Use these rules.

Example: Round 283 to the nearest hundred.

- Find the digit in the place to be rounded.   ②83
- Now, look at the digit to its right.   ②83
- If the digit to the right is less than **5**, the digit being rounded remains the same.
- If the digit to the right is **5** or more, the digit being rounded is increased by **1**.   ②83
- Digits to the right of the place to be rounded become **0**s. Digits to the left remain the same.   Rounds to 300

Examples: Round 4,385 . . .

to the nearest thousand	to the nearest hundred	to the nearest ten
4,385	4,385	4,385
3 is less than **5**.	**8** is more than **5**.	**5 = 5**.
The **4** stays the same.	The **3** is rounded up to **4**.	The **8** is rounded up to **9**.
4,000	4,400	4,390

Directions: Complete the table.

NUMBERS TO BE ROUNDED	ROUND TO THE NEAREST THOUSAND	NEAREST HUNDRED	NEAREST TEN
2,725			
10,942			
6,816			
2,309			
7,237			
959			

Round, Round, Round You Go

Directions: Round numbers according to each set of directions.

Round each number to the nearest ten.

45 _____   72 _____   61 _____   255 _____

27 _____   184 _____   43 _____   97 _____

Round each number to the nearest hundred.

562 _____   1,246 _____   761 _____   4,593 _____

347 _____   859 _____   238 _____   76 _____

Round each number to the nearest thousand.

6,543 _____   83,246 _____   3,741 _____   66,357 _____

7,219 _____   9,814 _____   2,166 _____   8,344 _____

Round each number to the nearest ten thousand.

32,467 _____   871,362 _____   334,212 _____

57,891 _____   45,621 _____   79,356 _____

Round each number to the nearest hundred thousand.

116,349 _____   946,477 _____   732,166 _____

762,887 _____   365,851 _____   225,631 _____

Round each number to the nearest million.

2,765,437 _____   7,762,997 _____

1,469,876 _____   5,564,783 _____

14,537,123 _____   4,117,655 _____

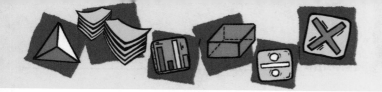

Big City

Directions: What city is home to the CN Tower? Follow the directions below to find out.

1. If 31,842 rounded to the nearest thousand is 31,000, put an **A** above number 2.

2. If 62 rounded to the nearest ten is 60, put an **O** above number 2 .

3. If 4,234 rounded to the nearest hundred is 4,200, put an **O** above number 7.

4. If 3,291 rounded to the nearest thousand is 3,000, put an **R** above number 3.

5. If 5,599 rounded to the nearest thousand is 6,000, put an **O** above number 4.

6. If 1,549 rounded to the nearest hundred is 1,500, put an **T** above number 6.

7. If 885 rounded to the nearest hundred is 800, put a **W** above number 2.

8. If 74 rounded to the nearest ten is 80, put an **R** above number 6.

9. If 248 rounded to the nearest hundred is 300, put an **R** above number 4.

10. If 615 rounded to the nearest ten is 620, put a **T** above number 1.

11. If 6,817 rounded to the nearest thousand is 7,000, put a **N** above number 5.

___   ___   ___   ___   ___   ___   ___
 1   2   3   4   5   6   7

Front-End Estimation

Front-end estimation is useful when you don't need to know the exact amount, but a close answer will do.

When we use front-end estimation, we use only the first number, and then add the numbers together to get the estimate.

Example:

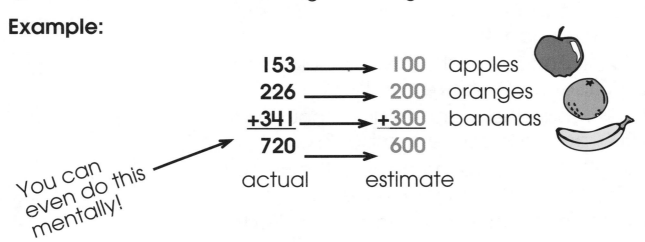

```
153  ———→   100   apples
226  ———→   200   oranges
+341 ———→  +300   bananas
720  ———→   600
```

actual   estimate

You can even do this mentally!

Directions: Estimate the sum of these numbers.

```
456  ———→           910  ———→           686  ———→
121  ———→           280  ———→           307  ———→
+438 ———→          +320  ———→          +711  ———→
```

Addition

Name _____

Add the ones.
Rename 13 as 10 + 3.   Add the tens.

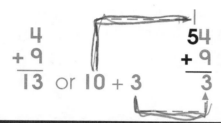

```
  54          4              54          |
+  9        + 9            +  9         54
            ‾‾‾‾                ‾‾       +  9
            13  or 10 + 3       3        ‾‾‾
                                         63
```

Directions: Add.

1.
```
  27        35        87        38        42        46
+  5       + 8       + 4       + 9       + 8       + 5
```

2.
```
  45        27         7        20        24         8
+  9       + 7       +38       +65       + 9       +38
```

3.
```
  27        45         8         9         6        42
+  3       + 6       +36       +29       +58       + 9
```

4.
```
  76         3         4        27         5         9
+  7       +47       +26       + 4       +18       +19
```

5.
```
   6        41        52        65         7         6
 +15       + 9       + 8       + 9       +38       +16
```

6.
```
   9        36        59         7         4         9
 +28       + 7       + 2       +36       +47       +38
```

Complete Math Grade 3   **59**   Addition: Regrouping

Addition

Add the ones.
Rename 15 as 10 + 5.

Add the tens.

$$\begin{array}{r} 4\,8 \\ +\ 2\,7 \\ \hline \end{array}$$

$$\begin{array}{r} 8 \\ +\ 7 \\ \hline 15 \end{array} \text{ or } 10 + 5$$

$$\begin{array}{r} 4\,8 \\ +\ 2\,7 \\ \hline 5 \end{array}$$

$$\begin{array}{r} 4\,8 \\ +\ 2\,7 \\ \hline 7\,5 \end{array}$$

Directions: Add.

1.
$$\begin{array}{r} 37 \\ +\ 25 \\ \hline \end{array}$$
$$\begin{array}{r} 48 \\ +37 \\ \hline \end{array}$$
$$\begin{array}{r} 26 \\ +54 \\ \hline \end{array}$$
$$\begin{array}{r} 35 \\ +\ 29 \\ \hline \end{array}$$
$$\begin{array}{r} 54 \\ +\ 18 \\ \hline \end{array}$$
$$\begin{array}{r} 62 \\ +\ 29 \\ \hline \end{array}$$

2.
$$\begin{array}{r} 29 \\ +\ 28 \\ \hline \end{array}$$
$$\begin{array}{r} 38 \\ +\ 37 \\ \hline \end{array}$$
$$\begin{array}{r} 47 \\ +25 \\ \hline \end{array}$$
$$\begin{array}{r} 63 \\ +27 \\ \hline \end{array}$$
$$\begin{array}{r} 79 \\ +\ 19 \\ \hline \end{array}$$
$$\begin{array}{r} 64 \\ +17 \\ \hline \end{array}$$

3.
$$\begin{array}{r} 58 \\ +\ 26 \\ \hline \end{array}$$
$$\begin{array}{r} 45 \\ +\ 18 \\ \hline \end{array}$$
$$\begin{array}{r} 27 \\ +57 \\ \hline \end{array}$$
$$\begin{array}{r} 44 \\ +29 \\ \hline \end{array}$$
$$\begin{array}{r} 36 \\ +36 \\ \hline \end{array}$$
$$\begin{array}{r} 77 \\ +\ 17 \\ \hline \end{array}$$

4.
$$\begin{array}{r} 49 \\ +\ 48 \\ \hline \end{array}$$
$$\begin{array}{r} 26 \\ +37 \\ \hline \end{array}$$
$$\begin{array}{r} 73 \\ +19 \\ \hline \end{array}$$
$$\begin{array}{r} 18 \\ +\ 28 \\ \hline \end{array}$$
$$\begin{array}{r} 15 \\ +47 \\ \hline \end{array}$$
$$\begin{array}{r} 29 \\ +27 \\ \hline \end{array}$$

5.
$$\begin{array}{r} 18 \\ +55 \\ \hline \end{array}$$
$$\begin{array}{r} 28 \\ +\ 24 \\ \hline \end{array}$$
$$\begin{array}{r} 38 \\ +\ 37 \\ \hline \end{array}$$
$$\begin{array}{r} 48 \\ +\ 43 \\ \hline \end{array}$$
$$\begin{array}{r} 58 \\ +16 \\ \hline \end{array}$$
$$\begin{array}{r} 68 \\ +28 \\ \hline \end{array}$$

6.
$$\begin{array}{r} 26 \\ +66 \\ \hline \end{array}$$
$$\begin{array}{r} 19 \\ +\ 54 \\ \hline \end{array}$$
$$\begin{array}{r} 57 \\ +\ 29 \\ \hline \end{array}$$
$$\begin{array}{r} 45 \\ +36 \\ \hline \end{array}$$
$$\begin{array}{r} 52 \\ +18 \\ \hline \end{array}$$
$$\begin{array}{r} 33 \\ +29 \\ \hline \end{array}$$

Addition: Regrouping

Addition means "putting together" or adding two or more numbers to find the sum. For example, 3 + 5 = 8. To regroup is to use ten ones to form one ten, ten tens to form one 100, and so on.

Directions: Add using regrouping.

Example:

Add the ones.

$$\begin{array}{r} 88 \\ + 21 \\ \hline 9 \end{array}$$

Add the tens with regrouping.

$$\begin{array}{r} 88 \\ + 21 \\ \hline 109 \end{array}$$

$$\begin{array}{r} 37 \\ + 72 \\ \hline \end{array}$$
$$\begin{array}{r} 56 \\ + 67 \\ \hline \end{array}$$
$$\begin{array}{r} 51 \\ + 88 \\ \hline \end{array}$$
$$\begin{array}{r} 37 \\ + 55 \\ \hline \end{array}$$
$$\begin{array}{r} 70 \\ + 68 \\ \hline \end{array}$$

$$\begin{array}{r} 93 \\ + 54 \\ \hline \end{array}$$
$$\begin{array}{r} 47 \\ + 82 \\ \hline \end{array}$$
$$\begin{array}{r} 81 \\ + 77 \\ \hline \end{array}$$
$$\begin{array}{r} 23 \\ + 92 \\ \hline \end{array}$$
$$\begin{array}{r} 36 \\ + 71 \\ \hline \end{array}$$

92 + 13 = _____   73 + 83 = _____   54 + 61 = _____

The Blues scored 63 points. The Reds scored 44 points.
How many points were scored in all?

_____

Addition: Regrouping

Directions: Study the example. Add using regrouping.

Examples:

Add the ones. Regroup.	Add the tens. Regroup.	Add the hundreds.

$$
\begin{array}{r} {\scriptstyle 1} \\ 156 \\ +\ 267 \\ \hline 3 \end{array}
\qquad
\begin{array}{r} 6 \\ +\ 7 \\ \hline 13 \end{array}
$$

$$
\begin{array}{r} {\scriptstyle 1} \\ 5 \\ +\ 6 \\ \hline 12 \end{array}
\qquad
\begin{array}{r} {\scriptstyle 11} \\ 156 \\ +\ 267 \\ \hline 23 \end{array}
$$

$$
\begin{array}{r} {\scriptstyle 1} \\ 156 \\ +\ 267 \\ \hline 423 \end{array}
$$

$$
\begin{array}{r} 29 \\ 46 \\ +\ 12 \\ \hline \end{array}
\qquad
\begin{array}{r} 81 \\ 78 \\ +\ 33 \\ \hline \end{array}
\qquad
\begin{array}{r} 52 \\ 67 \\ +\ 23 \\ \hline \end{array}
\qquad
\begin{array}{r} 49 \\ 37 \\ +\ 19 \\ \hline \end{array}
\qquad
\begin{array}{r} 162 \\ +\ 349 \\ \hline \end{array}
$$

$$
\begin{array}{r} 273 \\ +\ 198 \\ \hline \end{array}
\qquad
\begin{array}{r} 655 \\ +\ 297 \\ \hline \end{array}
\qquad
\begin{array}{r} 783 \\ +\ 148 \\ \hline \end{array}
\qquad
\begin{array}{r} 385 \\ +\ 169 \\ \hline \end{array}
\qquad
\begin{array}{r} 428 \\ +\ 122 \\ \hline \end{array}
$$

Sally went bowling. She had scores of 115, 129, and 103. What was her total score for three games?

_____

Addition: Regrouping

Directions: Add using regrouping. Then use the code to discover the name of a jungle animal.

$$\begin{array}{r} 348 \\ +752 \\ \hline 1,100 \end{array}$$

$$\begin{array}{r} 642 \\ +277 \\ \hline \end{array}$$

$$\begin{array}{r} 386 \\ +787 \\ \hline \end{array}$$

$$\begin{array}{r} 184 \\ +875 \\ \hline \end{array}$$

$$\begin{array}{r} 578 \\ +874 \\ \hline \end{array}$$

$$\begin{array}{r} 653 \\ +768 \\ \hline \end{array}$$

$$\begin{array}{r} 653 \\ +359 \\ \hline \end{array}$$

$$\begin{array}{r} 946 \\ +239 \\ \hline \end{array}$$

$$\begin{array}{r} 393 \\ +257 \\ \hline \end{array}$$

$$\begin{array}{r} 199 \\ +843 \\ \hline \end{array}$$

$$\begin{array}{r} 721 \\ +679 \\ \hline \end{array}$$

___ ___ ___ ___ ___ ___ ___ ___ ___

1012	1173	1059	1421	919	650	1452	1042	1100	1400	1185
R	L	L	I	A	F	G	F	T	E	A

Addition: Regrouping

Directions: Study the example. Add using regrouping.

Example:

Steps:

5,356
+3,976
9,332

1. Add the ones.
2. Regroup the tens. Add the tens.
3. Regroup the hundreds. Add the hundreds.
4. Add the thousands.

6,849 +3,276	1,846 +8,384	9,221 +6,769
2,758 +3,663	5,299 +8,764	7,932 +6,879

A plane flew 1,838 kilometres on the first day. It flew 2,347 kilometres on the second day. How many kilometres did it fly in all? _____

Addition: Mental Math

Directions: Try to do these addition problems in your head without using paper and pencil.

7 +4	6 +3	8 +1	10 +2	2 +9	6 +6
10 +20	40 +20	80 +100	60 +30	50 +70	100 +40
350 +150	300 +500	400 +800	450 +10	680 +100	900 +70
1,000 +200	4,000 400 +30	300 200 +80	8,000 500 +60	9,800 +150	7,000 300 +30

Mushrooming Addition

Name _____

Directions: Follow the arrows to **add**.

Example: 52 + 28 = 80
28 + 91 = 119
119 + 80 =   ?

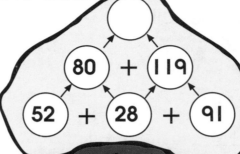

80 + 119

52 + 28 + 91

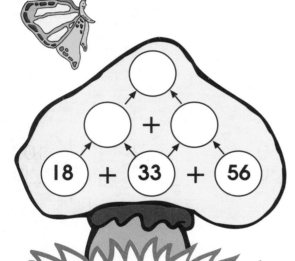

18 + 33 + 56

37 + 9 + 42 + 28

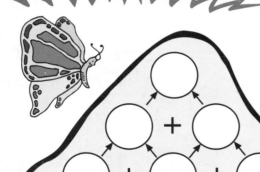

36 + 61 + 13 + 7

16 + 5 + 21

Addition: Regrouping   **66**   Complete Math Grade 3

Fishy Addition

Directions: Add.

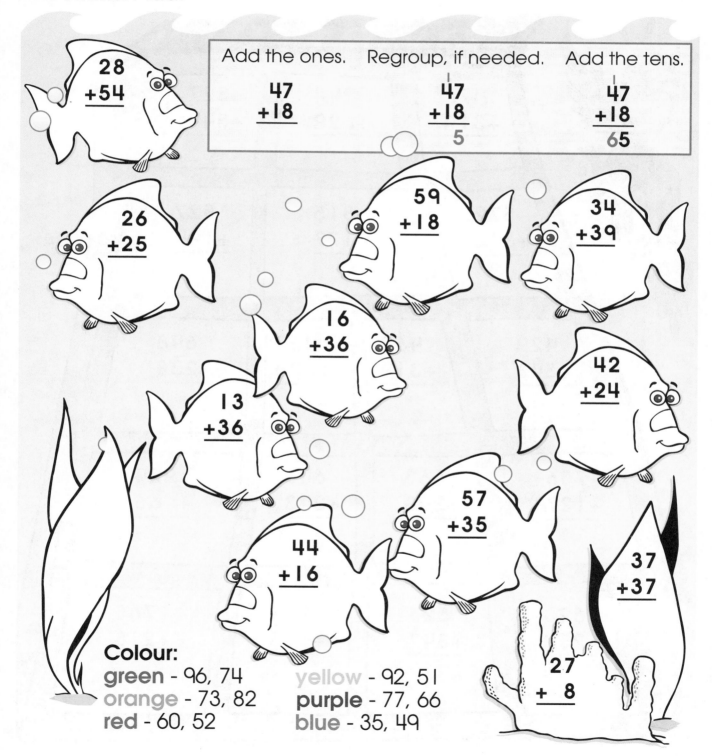

Add the ones.	Regroup, if needed.	Add the tens.
47 +18	47 +18 5	47 +18 65

28
+54

26
+25

59
+18

34
+39

16
+36

13
+36

42
+24

44
+16

57
+35

37
+37

27
+ 8

Colour:
green - 96, 74   yellow - 92, 51
orange - 73, 82   purple - 77, 66
red - 60, 52   blue - 35, 49

Make the Windows Shine!

Directions: Add.

476 +319	248 +629	327 +544	
572 +318	815 +177	527 +144	
429 +343	462 +319	462 +529	648 +238
756 +127	563 +208	646 +248	924 + 66
628 +259	526 +347	927 + 46	765 +218

Addition Ace

Directions: Add. Colour the ribbon according to the code below.

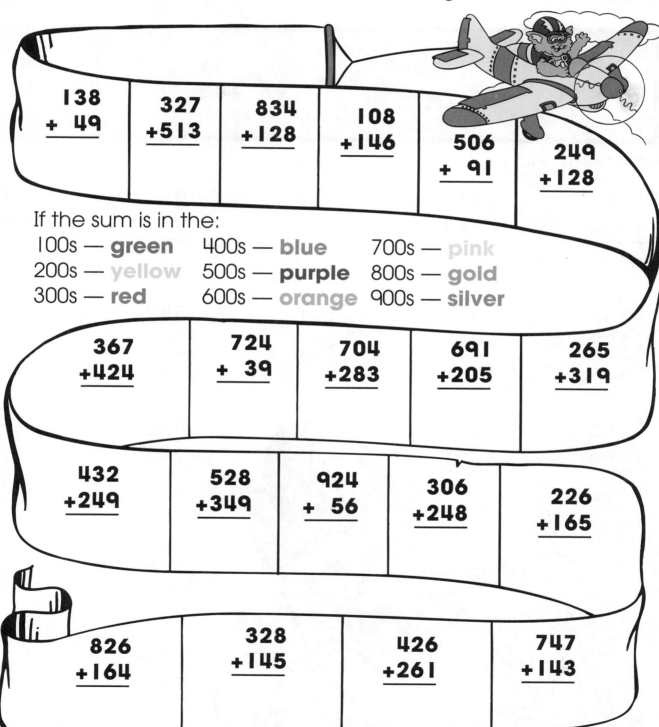

138 + 49	327 +513	834 +128	108 +146	506 + 91	249 +128

If the sum is in the:

100s — **green**	400s — **blue**	700s — pink
200s — yellow	500s — **purple**	800s — gold
300s — **red**	600s — orange	900s — silver

367 +424	724 + 39	704 +283	691 +205	265 +319

432 +249	528 +349	924 + 56	306 +248	226 +165

826 +164	328 +145	426 +261	747 +143

Name _____

Space Shuttle Addition

Add the ones.	Regroup.	Add the tens and regroup.	Add the hundreds.
362 +439	¹ 362 +439 1	¹¹ 362 +439 01	¹¹ 362 +439 801

Directions: Add.

```
 371      629      146      264      438
+439     +184     +587     +483     +290
```

```
 347      362      528      382      327
+328     +459     +391     +249     +649
```

```
 283      409               465      566
+346     +292              +193     +283
```

```
                            283      423
                           +519     +392
```

```
                            625      498
                           +246     +123
```

Underwater Addition

Directions: Add.

```
 446        476        509        251
+489       +527       +375       +368
```

```
            708        438        334
           +507       +419       +278
```

```
 464        589        288        811        609
+456       +322       +377       +386       +475
```

```
            531        810
           +249       +428
```

```
 831        445        211        230        319
+438       +476       +396       +284       +287
```

```
            714        767        911
           +185       +246       +427
```

Let's Climb to the Top!

Directions: Add.

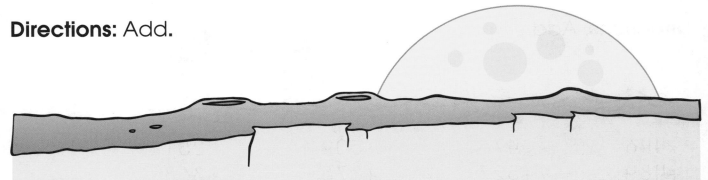

328 +449	246 +492	462 +781	621 +489	429 +636
	409 +736	921 + 87	562 +614	824 +597
	982 +220	207 +913		826 + 95
	547 +782	284 +493		506 +214
200 +489	684 +519	425 +594	536 +184	623 +192

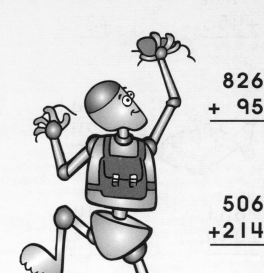

Picnic Problems

Directions: Help the ant find a path to the picnic. Solve the problems. Shade the box if an answer has a **9** in it.

836 + 90	536 + 248	952 + 8	362 + 47	486 + 293	368 + 529
789 526 + 214	2,846 + 6,478	932 + 365	374 + 299	835 + 552	956 874 + 65
4,768 + 2,894	38 456 + 3,894	4,507 + 2,743	404 + 289	1,843 + 6,752	4,367 + 3,574
639 + 77	587 342 + 679	5,379 1,865 + 2,348	450 + 145	594 + 278	459 + 367
29 875 + 2,341	387 29 + 5,614	462 379 + 248			

Grand Prix Addition

Directions: Solve each problem. Beginning at 7,000, run through this racetrack to find the path the race car took. When you reach 7,023, you're ready to exit and gas up for the next race.

3,536 +3,482	1,792 +5,225	3,838 +3,178	3,767 +3,248	1,874 +5,140	4,809 +2,204
3,561 +3,458	4,162 +2,858	3,771 +4,213	4,123 +2,887	5,879 +1,132	1,725 +5,287
3,544 +3,478	1,273 +5,748	2,435 +5,214	4,853 +2,156	3,589 +3,419	5,218 +1,789
5,997 +1,026	5,289 +1,713	3,698 +3,305	4,756 +2,248	4,248 +2,757	4,658 +2,348
4,853 +2,147	2,216 +4,785	1,157 +6,412	3,720 +3,698	3,612 +3,552	1,687 +5,662

Gearing Up

Add the ones. Regroup.	Add the tens. Regroup.	Add the hundreds. Regroup.	Add the thousands. Regroup.
I	I I	I I I	I I I
7,465 +4,978	7,465 +4,978	7,465 +4,978	7,465 +4,978
3	43	443	I 2,443

Directions: Solve the problems. Colour each answer that has a
3—blue, **4**—red, and **5**—yellow.

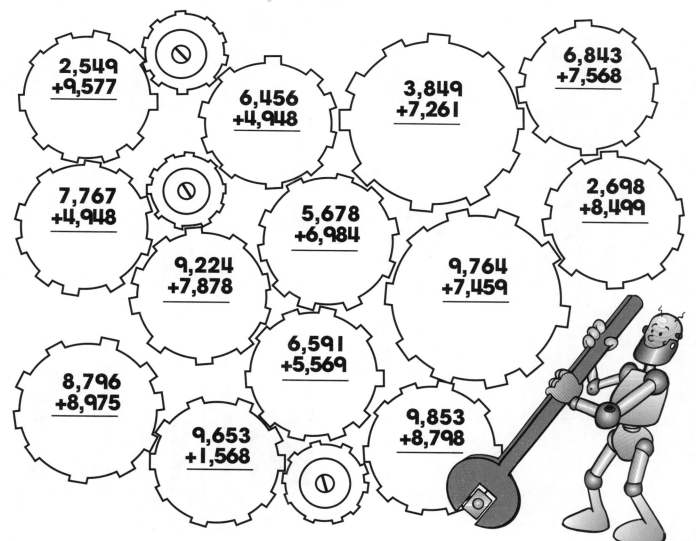

2,549
+9,577

6,456
+4,948

3,849
+7,261

6,843
+7,568

7,767
+4,948

5,678
+6,984

2,698
+8,499

9,224
+7,878

9,764
+7,459

8,796
+8,975

6,591
+5,569

9,653
+1,568

9,853
+8,798

Bubble Math

Directions: Add to solve the problems.

2,647
+3,281

3,426
+2,841

5,642
+1,819

4,629
+1,258

3,690
+2,434

5,942
+1,829

6,241
+2,363

6,843
+2,391

4,826
+2,098

4,625
+1,817

2,648
+1,923

8,465
+1,386

5,642
+2,919

2,641
+6,259

3,142
+2,639

9,124
+1,348

7,205
+1,839

2,643
+7,427

Bubble Blaster 2004

Cotton Pickin' Math

Directions: Solve the problems.

```
  7,215        4,621        6,117        2,481        3,204
     62           35           24        2,514          182
    141        1,318          315            2           23
 +2,015       +    9       +2,136       +   43       +    5
```

```
  8,143           35        7,006          521          496
     60          242          242        3,134        8,172
    235            6            9           64           83
 +1,423       +1,203       +   31       +  243       +  199
```

```
  6,201        5,242        4,162        6,425
    325          342          328           41
     41            8           41          324
 +2,136       +   51       +  503       +    3
```

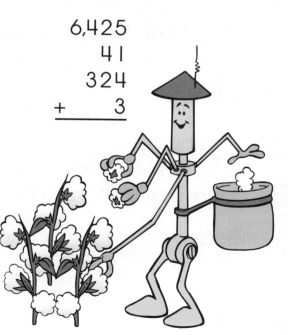

```
  4,205        2,516        5,426
     81          310          310
      3           82          512
 +  414       +    3       +    4
```

Problem Solving

Directions: Solve each problem.

Work Space:

1. Last year there were 44 monkeys on an
   island. There are 8 more monkeys this year.
   How many monkeys are on the island now?

   There were_____ monkeys last year.
   There are _____ more monkeys this year.
   There are _____ monkeys on the island now.

1.

2. There were 72 children and 9 adults in our
   group at the zoo. How many people were
   in our group?

   _____ children were in our group.
   _____ adults were in our group.
   _____ people were in our group.

2.

3. One group of monkeys was fed 6 kilograms
   of fruit. Another group was fed 19 kilograms.
   How much fruit was that in all?

   That was _____ kilograms of fruit in all.

3.

4. The children drank 68 cartons of milk.
   There were 8 cartons left. How many
   cartons of milk were there to start with?

   There were _____ cartons of milk to start
   with.

4.

Problem Solving

Directions: Solve each problem.

Work Space:

1. January has 31 days. February has 29 days this year. How many days are in the two months?

There are _____ days in January.
There are _____ days in February this year.
There are _____ days in January and February.

1.

2. Jeff weighs 46 kilograms. His father is 36 kilograms heavier. How much does Jeff's father weigh?

Jeff weighs _____ kilograms.
His father is_____ kilograms heavier.
His father weighs _____ kilograms.

2.

3. Lauren had 29 points. She earned 13 more. How many points did she have then?

Lauren had _____ points.
She earned _____ more.
She had _____ points then.

3.

4. Adam gained 18 kilograms in the last two years. Two years ago, he weighed 59 kilograms. How much does he weigh today?

Adam weighs _____ kilograms today?

4.

79

Palindrome Sums

A **number palindrome** is similar to a word palindrome in that it reads the same backward or forward.

Examples:
75,457
1,689,861

Directions: Create number palindromes using addition.

Your Number

To do this, choose any number:
652

_____

Then, reverse that number's digits:
256

_____

and add the two numbers together:
652 + 256 = 908

_____

If the sum is not a palindrome, reverse the digits in that sum and add as you did in the first step:
908 + 809 = 1717

_____

Continue in this manner until the sum is a palindrome.
1717 + 7171 = 888

_____

_____

_____

_____

The example required three steps to produce a palindrome. How many steps did it take for you to create a number palindrome?

_____

Subtraction

To subtract the ones, rename 63 as "5 tens and 13 ones."	Subtract the ones.	Subtract the tens.

$$\begin{array}{r} 63 \\ -\ 9 \\ \hline \end{array} \qquad \begin{array}{r} {}^{5\ 13} \\ \cancel{63} \\ -\ 9 \\ \hline \end{array} \qquad \begin{array}{r} {}^{5\ 13} \\ \cancel{63} \\ -\ 9 \\ \hline 4 \end{array} \qquad \begin{array}{r} {}^{5\ 13} \\ \cancel{63} \\ -\ 9 \\ \hline 54 \end{array}$$

Directions: Subtract.

1.
$$\begin{array}{r} 53 \\ -\ 8 \\ \hline \end{array} \qquad \begin{array}{r} 27 \\ -\ 9 \\ \hline \end{array} \qquad \begin{array}{r} 46 \\ -\ 9 \\ \hline \end{array} \qquad \begin{array}{r} 54 \\ -\ 5 \\ \hline \end{array} \qquad \begin{array}{r} 32 \\ -\ 6 \\ \hline \end{array} \qquad \begin{array}{r} 65 \\ -\ 7 \\ \hline \end{array}$$

2.
$$\begin{array}{r} 28 \\ -\ 9 \\ \hline \end{array} \qquad \begin{array}{r} 48 \\ -\ 9 \\ \hline \end{array} \qquad \begin{array}{r} 35 \\ -\ 6 \\ \hline \end{array} \qquad \begin{array}{r} 44 \\ -\ 7 \\ \hline \end{array} \qquad \begin{array}{r} 67 \\ -\ 8 \\ \hline \end{array} \qquad \begin{array}{r} 92 \\ -\ 9 \\ \hline \end{array}$$

3.
$$\begin{array}{r} 52 \\ -\ 6 \\ \hline \end{array} \qquad \begin{array}{r} 62 \\ -\ 4 \\ \hline \end{array} \qquad \begin{array}{r} 61 \\ -\ 6 \\ \hline \end{array} \qquad \begin{array}{r} 73 \\ -\ 5 \\ \hline \end{array} \qquad \begin{array}{r} 50 \\ -\ 9 \\ \hline \end{array} \qquad \begin{array}{r} 42 \\ -\ 5 \\ \hline \end{array}$$

4.
$$\begin{array}{r} 96 \\ -\ 8 \\ \hline \end{array} \qquad \begin{array}{r} 73 \\ -\ 6 \\ \hline \end{array} \qquad \begin{array}{r} 80 \\ -\ 7 \\ \hline \end{array} \qquad \begin{array}{r} 42 \\ -\ 3 \\ \hline \end{array} \qquad \begin{array}{r} 63 \\ -\ 4 \\ \hline \end{array} \qquad \begin{array}{r} 51 \\ -\ 9 \\ \hline \end{array}$$

5.
$$\begin{array}{r} 94 \\ -\ 8 \\ \hline \end{array} \qquad \begin{array}{r} 88 \\ -\ 9 \\ \hline \end{array} \qquad \begin{array}{r} 33 \\ -\ 4 \\ \hline \end{array} \qquad \begin{array}{r} 27 \\ -\ 9 \\ \hline \end{array} \qquad \begin{array}{r} 46 \\ -\ 8 \\ \hline \end{array} \qquad \begin{array}{r} 64 \\ -\ 7 \\ \hline \end{array}$$

6.
$$\begin{array}{r} 23 \\ -\ 9 \\ \hline \end{array} \qquad \begin{array}{r} 76 \\ -\ 8 \\ \hline \end{array} \qquad \begin{array}{r} 40 \\ -\ 4 \\ \hline \end{array} \qquad \begin{array}{r} 41 \\ -\ 6 \\ \hline \end{array} \qquad \begin{array}{r} 53 \\ -\ 7 \\ \hline \end{array} \qquad \begin{array}{r} 25 \\ -\ 7 \\ \hline \end{array}$$

Name _____

Subtraction

To subtract the ones, rename 92 as "8 tens and 12 ones."	Subtract the ones.	Subtract the tens.

$$\begin{array}{r} 92 \\ -\ 38 \end{array}$$

$$\begin{array}{r} {\scriptstyle 8\ 12} \\ \cancel{9}2 \\ -\ 38 \end{array}$$

$$\begin{array}{r} {\scriptstyle 8\ 12} \\ \cancel{9}2 \\ -\ 38 \\ \hline 4 \end{array}$$

$$\begin{array}{r} {\scriptstyle 8\ 12} \\ \cancel{9}2 \\ -\ 38 \\ \hline 54 \end{array}$$

Directions: Subtract.

1.
$$\begin{array}{r} 35 \\ -\ 17 \end{array}$$
$$\begin{array}{r} 27 \\ -\ 19 \end{array}$$
$$\begin{array}{r} 54 \\ -\ 37 \end{array}$$
$$\begin{array}{r} 63 \\ -\ 26 \end{array}$$
$$\begin{array}{r} 84 \\ -\ 59 \end{array}$$
$$\begin{array}{r} 28 \\ -\ 19 \end{array}$$

2.
$$\begin{array}{r} 42 \\ -\ 24 \end{array}$$
$$\begin{array}{r} 56 \\ -\ 39 \end{array}$$
$$\begin{array}{r} 41 \\ -\ 27 \end{array}$$
$$\begin{array}{r} 53 \\ -\ 15 \end{array}$$
$$\begin{array}{r} 86 \\ -\ 78 \end{array}$$
$$\begin{array}{r} 92 \\ -\ 26 \end{array}$$

3.
$$\begin{array}{r} 43 \\ -\ 15 \end{array}$$
$$\begin{array}{r} 37 \\ -\ 29 \end{array}$$
$$\begin{array}{r} 26 \\ -\ 19 \end{array}$$
$$\begin{array}{r} 55 \\ -\ 36 \end{array}$$
$$\begin{array}{r} 43 \\ -\ 27 \end{array}$$
$$\begin{array}{r} 28 \\ -\ 19 \end{array}$$

4.
$$\begin{array}{r} 54 \\ -\ 26 \end{array}$$
$$\begin{array}{r} 35 \\ -\ 18 \end{array}$$
$$\begin{array}{r} 22 \\ -\ 15 \end{array}$$
$$\begin{array}{r} 56 \\ -\ 29 \end{array}$$
$$\begin{array}{r} 38 \\ -\ 19 \end{array}$$
$$\begin{array}{r} 31 \\ -\ 18 \end{array}$$

5.
$$\begin{array}{r} 83 \\ -\ 25 \end{array}$$
$$\begin{array}{r} 94 \\ -\ 16 \end{array}$$
$$\begin{array}{r} 65 \\ -\ 39 \end{array}$$
$$\begin{array}{r} 73 \\ -\ 17 \end{array}$$
$$\begin{array}{r} 80 \\ -\ 28 \end{array}$$
$$\begin{array}{r} 92 \\ -\ 35 \end{array}$$

6.
$$\begin{array}{r} 35 \\ -\ 26 \end{array}$$
$$\begin{array}{r} 90 \\ -\ 55 \end{array}$$
$$\begin{array}{r} 56 \\ -\ 27 \end{array}$$
$$\begin{array}{r} 41 \\ -\ 16 \end{array}$$
$$\begin{array}{r} 50 \\ -\ 38 \end{array}$$
$$\begin{array}{r} 61 \\ -\ 15 \end{array}$$

Subtracting Two-Digit Numbers

With Regrouping

Step 1: Decide whether to regroup. In the ones column, 3 is less than 9 so, regroup 4 tens 3 ones to 3 tens 13 ones.

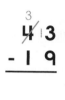
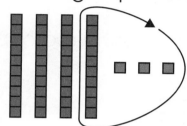

Step 2: Subtract the ones.

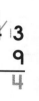
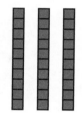

Step 3: Subtract the tens.

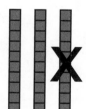

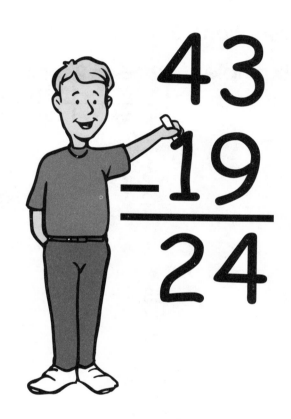

Directions: Subtract to find the difference. Regroup, if needed.

67	85	86	91	44	61
-34	-12	-47	-48	-27	-34

32	97	60	52	71	83
-14	-36	-45	-22	-19	-15

Subtraction: Regrouping

Subtraction means "taking away" or subtracting one number from another to find the difference. For example, 10 - 3 = 7. To regroup is to use one ten to form ten ones, one 100 to form ten tens, and so on.

Directions: Study the example. Subtract using regrouping.

Example:

32	=	2 tens	+	12 ones
-13	=	1 ten	+	3 ones
19	=	1 ten	+	9 ones

$$\begin{array}{r} 33 \\ -\,28 \\ \hline \end{array} \qquad \begin{array}{r} 86 \\ -\,59 \\ \hline \end{array} \qquad \begin{array}{r} 92 \\ -\,37 \\ \hline \end{array} \qquad \begin{array}{r} 71 \\ -\,48 \\ \hline \end{array}$$

$$\begin{array}{r} 63 \\ -\,47 \\ \hline \end{array} \qquad \begin{array}{r} 45 \\ -\,18 \\ \hline \end{array} \qquad \begin{array}{r} 31 \\ -\,22 \\ \hline \end{array} \qquad \begin{array}{r} 55 \\ -\,39 \\ \hline \end{array}$$

82 - 69 = _____   73 - 36 = _____

The Yankees won 85 games.
The Cubs won 69 games.
How many more games
did the Yankees win?   _____

Subtraction: Regrouping

Directions: Regrouping for subtraction is the opposite of regrouping for addition. Study the example. Subtract using regrouping. Then use the code to colour the flowers.

Example:

$$\begin{array}{r} 647 \\ -453 \\ \hline 194 \end{array}$$

Steps:

1. Subtract ones.
2. Subtact tens. Five tens cannot be subtracted from 4 tens.
3. Regroup tens by regrouping 6 hundreds (5 hundreds + 10 tens).
4. Add the 10 tens to the four tens.
5. Subtract 5 tens from 14 tens.
6. Subtract the hundreds.

If the answer has: 1 one, colour it **red**; 8 ones, colour it pink; 5 ones, colour it yellow.

Subtraction: Regrouping

Directions: Study the example. Follow the steps. Subtract using regrouping.

Example:

$$\begin{array}{r} 634 \\ -\ 455 \\ \hline 179 \end{array}$$

Steps:
1. Subtract ones. You cannot subtract 5 ones from 4 ones.
2. Regroup ones by regrouping 3 tens to 2 tens + 10 ones.
3. Subtract 5 ones from 14 ones.
4. Regroup tens by regrouping hundreds (5 hundreds + 10 tens).
5. Subtract 5 tens from 12 tens.
6. Subtract hundreds.

635 - 169	553 - 174	832 - 563	944 - 578
423 - 268	941 - 872	733 - 498	266 - 197
387 - 198	594 - 385	960 - 759	887 - 598

Sue goes to school 185 days a year. Yoko goes to school 313 days a year. How many more days of school does Yoko attend each year?

_____

Subtraction: Regrouping

Directions: Study the example. Follow the steps. Subtract using regrouping. If you have to regroup to subtract ones and there are no tens, you must regroup twice.

Example:

$$\begin{array}{r} 300 \\ -182 \\ \hline 118 \end{array}$$

Steps:
1. Subtract ones. You cannot subtract 2 ones from 0 ones.
2. Regroup. No tens. Regroup hundreds (2 hundreds + 10 tens).
3. Regroup tens (9 tens + 10 ones).
4. Subtract 2 ones from ten ones.
5. Subtract 8 tens from 9 tens.
6. Subtract 1 hundred from 2 hundreds.

602 - 423	306 - 128	600 - 263	807 - 499	703 - 328
800 - 557	206 - 137	400 - 224	508 - 379	909 - 769
207 - 138	604 - 397	308 - 199	700 - 531	900 - 278

Subtraction: Regrouping

Directions: Subtract. Regroup when necessary. The first one is done for you.

$$
\begin{array}{r} 7,354 \\ -\ 5,295 \\ \hline 2,059 \end{array}
\qquad
\begin{array}{r} 4,214 \\ -\ 3,185 \\ \hline \end{array}
\qquad
\begin{array}{r} 8,437 \\ -\ 5,338 \\ \hline \end{array}
\qquad
\begin{array}{r} 6,837 \\ -\ 4,318 \\ \hline \end{array}
$$

$$
\begin{array}{r} 5,735 \\ -\ 3,826 \\ \hline \end{array}
\qquad
\begin{array}{r} 1,036 \\ -\ \ \ 947 \\ \hline \end{array}
\qquad
\begin{array}{r} 6,735 \\ -\ 6,646 \\ \hline \end{array}
\qquad
\begin{array}{r} 3,841 \\ -\ 1,953 \\ \hline \end{array}
$$

Columbus discovered America in 1492. Jacques Cartier discovered Canada in 1534. How many years difference was there between these two dates?

_____

Subtraction: Mental Math

Directions: Try to do these subtraction problems in your head without using paper and pencil.

9 − 3	12 − 6	7 − 6	5 − 1	15 − 5	2 − 0
40 − 20	90 − 80	100 − 50	20 − 20	60 − 10	70 − 40
450 − 250	500 − 300	250 − 20	690 − 100	320 − 20	900 − 600
1,000 − 400	8,000 − 500	7,000 − 900	4,000 − 2,000	9,500 − 4,000	5,000 − 2,000

Hats, Hats, Hats

Directions: Subtract to find the difference. If the bottom number is larger than the top number in a column, you will need to regroup from the column to the left.

Example:

```
    2
  7 3̸ 6        466         837          742
- 6 2 9       -327        -529         -428
  1 0 7
```

```
              784         673                      648
             -565        -458                     -426
```

```
  982                     947          543          928
 -665                    -729         -426         -619
```

```
  847         427         524                       245
 -628        -318        -318                      -126
```

```
  852         545
 -328        -221
```

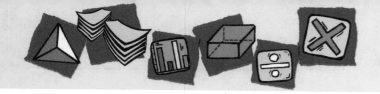

Name _____

Soaring to the Stars

Directions: Connect the dots in order and form two stars. Begin one star with the subtraction problem whose difference is 100 and end with the problem whose difference is 109. Begin the other star with 110 and end with 120. Then, colour the pictures.

953
-839

493
-378

774
-658

364
-247

751
-638

839
-728

844
-726

570
-458

446
-327

384
-279

590
-487

575
-471

653
-547

383
-273

696
-576

493
-386

359
-257

862
-754

190
- 89

359
-259

585
-476

Dino-Code

How is a T-Rex like an explosion?

Directions: To find out, solve the following problems and write the matching letter above each answer on the blanks.

He's . . . ___ ___ ___ ___   ___ ___
195 185 92 92   171 195

___ ___ ___ ___ — ___ ___ ___ ___ ___ !
265 74 183 171   93 74 45 181 191

Remember to regroup when the bottom number is larger than the top number in a column.

F =
$$\begin{array}{r} 348 \\ -153 \\ \hline \end{array}$$

L =
$$\begin{array}{r} 765 \\ -673 \\ \hline \end{array}$$

G =
$$\begin{array}{r} 427 \\ -382 \\ \hline \end{array}$$

T =
$$\begin{array}{r} 637 \\ -446 \\ \hline \end{array}$$

H =
$$\begin{array}{r} 878 \\ -697 \\ \hline \end{array}$$

U =
$$\begin{array}{r} 548 \\ -363 \\ \hline \end{array}$$

O =
$$\begin{array}{r} 824 \\ -653 \\ \hline \end{array}$$

N =
$$\begin{array}{r} 439 \\ -256 \\ \hline \end{array}$$

I =
$$\begin{array}{r} 447 \\ -373 \\ \hline \end{array}$$

M =
$$\begin{array}{r} 568 \\ -475 \\ \hline \end{array}$$

D =
$$\begin{array}{r} 748 \\ -483 \\ \hline \end{array}$$

Paint by Number

Directions: Solve each problem. Colour each shape according to the key below.

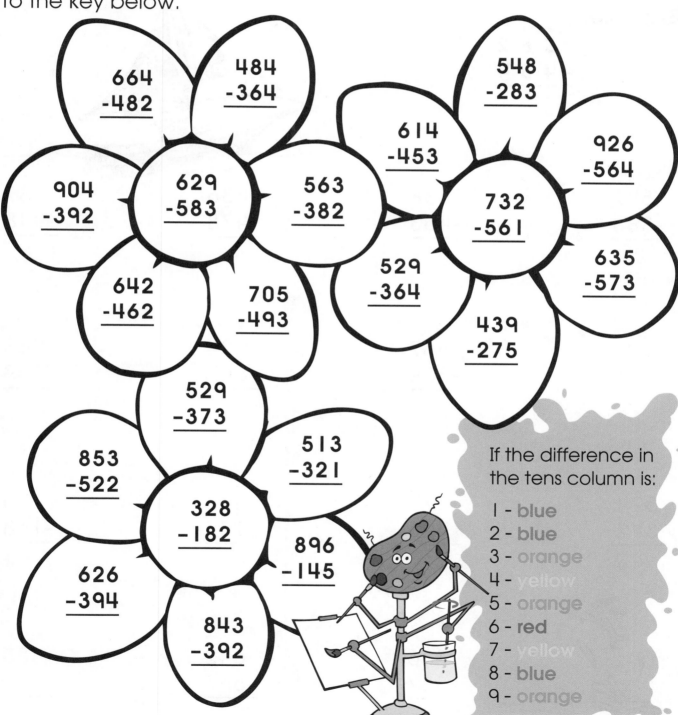

664 −482	484 −364
904 −392	629 −583
	563 −382
642 −462	705 −493
	529 −373
853 −522	513 −321
	328 −182
626 −394	896 −145
	843 −392
548 −283	
614 −453	926 −564
732 −561	
529 −364	635 −573
439 −275	

If the difference in the tens column is:

1 - blue
2 - blue
3 - orange
4 - yellow
5 - orange
6 - red
7 - yellow
8 - blue
9 - orange

Name _____

Sailing Through Subtraction

Directions: Subtract, regrouping when needed.

Example:

```
    7 14
    8 5 12
  - 4 6 4
  -------
    3 8 8
```

```
  542        638        836        737
 -383       -453       -478       -448
```

```
  243        567        984        468
 -154       -384       -643       -399
```

```
  524        674        374        246
 -342       -495       -185       -158
```

```
             736        642        435
            -557       -557       -286
```

Gobble, Gobble

Directions: Solve each problem. Colour the picture according to the key below. If the answer has a **3** in it, colour it orange, **4**—red, **5**—purple, **6**—brown, **7**—yellow, **8**—blue, and **9**—green. Remember to regroup when needed.

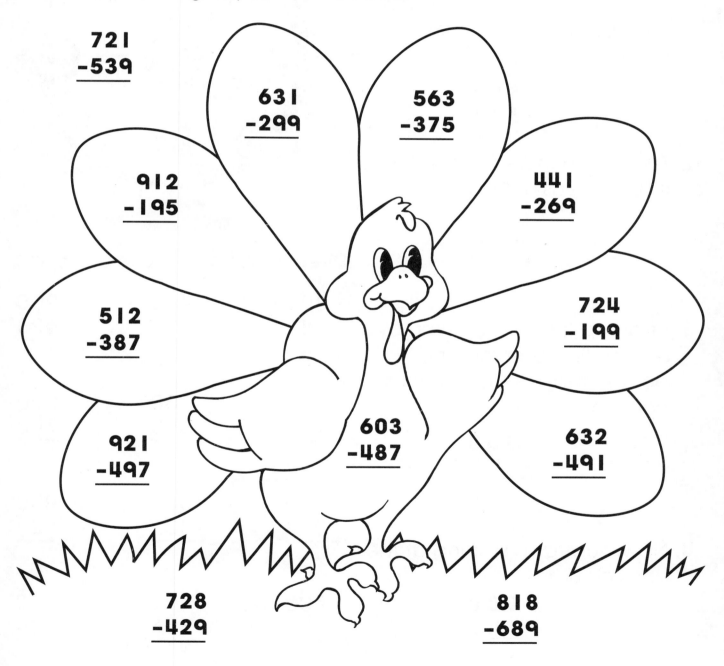

721
−539

631
−299

563
−375

912
−195

441
−269

512
−387

724
−199

921
−497

603
−487

632
−491

728
−429

818
−689

Name _____

Round and Round She Goes

When regrouping with zeros, follow these steps:

1. 7 is larger than 0. Go to the tens column to regroup. Since there is a 0 in that column, you can't regroup. Go to the hundreds column.

```
  2
  ↗  ↘
  3 0 0
- 1 4 7
```

2. Take one hundred away. Move it to the tens column.

```
  2
  ⁄3 ¹0 0
- 1 4 7
```

Directions: Solve these problems.

800 -736	406 -243	900 -623

3. Regroup the tens column by subtracting one ten and adding that ten to the ones column.

```
    2 9
  ⁄3 ⁄0 ¹0
- 1 4 7
```

200 - 82	700 -543	800 -746

400 -278	600 -432	900 -824

4. Now, subtract, starting at the ones column.

```
    2 9
  ⁄3 ⁄0 ¹0
- 1 4 7
─────────
  1 5 3
```

500 -248	400 -365	300 -284

Subtraction: Regrouping

96

Complete Math Grade 3

Name _____

Jungle Math

Directions: Solve these problems.

Across

2. 517
    −228

7. 535
    −248

9. 561
    −247

3. 428
    −249

8. 857
    −389

4. 562
    −274

5. 924
    −348

6. 923
    −346

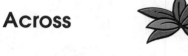

5. 824
    −247

Down

1. 421
    −342

6. 921
    −346

2. 627
    −348

7. 926
    −718

3. 362
    −194

8. 721
    −240

4. 582
    −346

10. 768
     −292

Subtraction: Regrouping

Timely Zeros

Directions: Subtract.

```
  300        803        504
 -189       -324       -362
```

```
  900        800        702
 -648       -724       -561
```

```
  200        600        500        807        406
 -149       -476       -362       -298       -328
```

```
  300        600        700        308        500
 -243       -421       -348       -189       -384
```

```
             302        600        400
            -195       -247       -108
```

```
             205        308
            -148       -189
```

Subtraction Maze

Directions: Solve the problems. Remember to regroup when needed.

4,172 − 1,536	6,723 −2,586	547 −259	834 −463	562 −325	7,146 −3,498
9,427 −6,648	8,149 −5,372	5,389 − 1,652	421 −275	7,456 −3,724	818 −639
772 −586	6,529 −4,538	5,379 −2,835	6,275 −3,761	5,612 − 1,505	8,355 −5,366

Directions: Shade in the answers from above to find the path.

2,514	288	186	3,732	2,989
2,779	156	1,901	2,414	4,137
3,748	3,337	2,777	371	179	1,991
3,048	3,737	146	2,717 →		
679	237	374	4,107 →		
886	2,636	2,544	3,648		

KITTY

High Class Math

Directions: Solve these problems.

			3,270 - 1,529	8,248 - 1,513

7,648 -3,291	4,321 -1,809	8,241 -3,516	3,002 -1,231	9,200 -3,146

| 5,017
-2,408 | 8,254
-3,187 | 7,265
-2,134 | 3,846
-1,359 | 8,006
-3,084 |

| 3,084
-1,926 | 6,265
-4,189 | 4,824
-1,913 | 6,205
-1,054 | 5,253
-4,428 |

| | 9,205
-3,187 | 5,809
-3,913 | 5,642
-2,408 | |

Kite Craze!

Directions: Subtract.

8,794
-6,428
‾‾‾‾‾

9,643
-8,825
‾‾‾‾‾

8,825
-7,436
‾‾‾‾‾

5,648
-3,929
‾‾‾‾‾

7,005
-6,223
‾‾‾‾‾

8,416
-3,509
‾‾‾‾‾

4,162
-2,840
‾‾‾‾‾

6,514
-3,282
‾‾‾‾‾

5,436
-2,924
‾‾‾‾‾

9,246
-8,518
‾‾‾‾‾

4,862
-3,946
‾‾‾‾‾

9,486
-6,294
‾‾‾‾‾

9,085
-6,241
‾‾‾‾‾

8,462
-6,391
‾‾‾‾‾

7,643
-6,521
‾‾‾‾‾

6,430
-4,252
‾‾‾‾‾

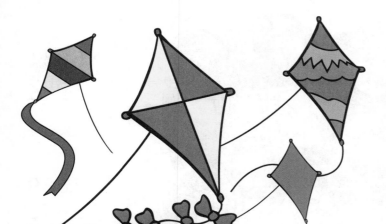

Name _____

Subtraction on Stage!

Directions: Subtract.

```
  5,648          2,148
 -2,425         -  825
```

```
  7,641          7,648          5,408          8,209
 -5,246         -3,289         -1,291         -4,182
```

```
  8,419          6,249          6,428          4,287
 -2,182         -1,526         -4,159         -2,492
```

```
  7,645          2,016          8,247          9,047
 -2,826         -1,021         -6,459         -6,152
```

```
                                               5,231
                                              -1,642
```

```
                                               7,689
                                              -2,845
```

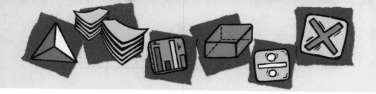

Subtraction Search

Directions: Solve each problem. Find the answer in the chart and circle it. The answers may go in any direction.

6,003 −2,737	5,040 −3,338	9,000 −5,725
7,200 −4,356	3,406 −1,298	5,602 −3,138
7,006 −5,429	3,006 −2,798	3,605 −2,718
5,904 −3,917	5,039 −1,954	8,704 −2,496

2	1	6	3	2	7	5
6	3	3	2	1	0	8
2	2	1	6	3	3	4
0	2	2	6	5	0	6
8	5	4	2	0	8	7
8	9	0	6	1	5	6
3	2	8	4	4	2	1
8	3	4	8	8	5	0
8	1	9	8	7	2	9
3	4	5	8	5	6	7
8	1	3	7	0	4	2
9	3	2	1	7	0	2

4,081 −3,594	6,508 − 399	5,039 −2,467	9,006 − 575	5,001 −2,351
	8,002 −5,686	6,058 −2,175	9,504 −7,368	7,290 −1,801

Problem Solving

Directions: Solve each problem.

Work Space:

1. There were 48 words on a spelling test. Sarah missed 9 of them. How many words did she spell correctly?

There were _____ words on the test.
Sarah missed _____ words.
She spelled _____ words correctly

1.

2. Ryan earned 91 points. Mike earned 5 points less than Ryan. How many points did Mike earn?

Ryan earned _____ points.
Mike earned _____ points less than Ryan.
Mike earned _____ points.

2.

3. Sheila lost 7 of the 45 games she played. How many games did she win?

She won _____ games.

3.

4. Travis had 50 tickets to sell. He sold some and had 6 left. How many tickets did he sell?

Travis sold _____ tickets.

4.

5. Angela's great-grandfather is 82 years old. How old was he 4 years ago?

Four years ago, he was _____ years old.

5.

Problem Solving

Directions: Solve each problem.

Work Space:

1. Joseph weighs 43 kilograms. Zach weighs 12 kilograms less than Joseph. How much does Zach weigh?

   Joseph weighs _____ kilograms.
   Zach weighs _____ kilograms less than Joseph.
   Zach weighs _____ kilograms.

1.

2. There are 73 children in the gym. Forty-five of them are boys. How many girls are in the gym?

   There are _____ children in the gym.
   There are _____ boys in the gym.
   There are _____ girls in the gym.

2.

3. A store has 84 bicycles. They have 45 girls' bicycles. How many boys' bicycles do they have?

   _____ bicycles are boys' bicycles.

3.

4. It takes 50 points to win a prize. Paige has 38 points. How many more points does Paige need to win a prize?

   Paige needs _____ points.

4.

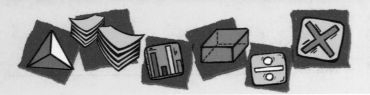

Addition and Subtraction

Directions: Add.

1.
$$53 + 6$$ $$24 + 2$$ $$2 + 35$$ $$8 + 81$$ $$64 + 3$$ $$25 + 2$$

2.
$$36 + 5$$ $$54 + 8$$ $$8 + 39$$ $$2 + 59$$ $$48 + 8$$ $$26 + 7$$

3.
$$42 + 33$$ $$72 + 14$$ $$54 + 23$$ $$61 + 28$$ $$19 + 40$$ $$26 + 52$$

4.
$$54 + 27$$ $$35 + 36$$ $$59 + 38$$ $$54 + 19$$ $$27 + 48$$ $$39 + 39$$

Directions: Subtract.

5.
$$37 - 3$$ $$29 - 4$$ $$54 - 4$$ $$87 - 2$$ $$56 - 5$$ $$89 - 6$$

6.
$$47 - 9$$ $$72 - 5$$ $$45 - 7$$ $$55 - 9$$ $$40 - 5$$ $$34 - 7$$

7.
$$54 - 12$$ $$42 - 30$$ $$75 - 64$$ $$46 - 23$$ $$93 - 81$$ $$89 - 41$$

8.
$$73 - 25$$ $$85 - 49$$ $$92 - 24$$ $$64 - 56$$ $$77 - 48$$ $$88 - 38$$

Name _____

Addition and Subtraction

To check
34 + 19 = 53,
subtract 19
from _____.

$$\begin{array}{r} 34 \\ + 19 \\ \hline 53 \\ - 19 \\ \hline 34 \end{array}$$

These should be the same.

To check
53 - 19 = 34,
add _____
to 34 .

$$\begin{array}{r} 53 \\ - 19 \\ \hline 34 \\ + 19 \\ \hline 53 \end{array}$$

These should be the same.

Directions: Add. Check each answer.

1.
$$\begin{array}{r} 54 \\ + 7 \end{array}$$
$$\begin{array}{r} 46 \\ + 9 \end{array}$$
$$\begin{array}{r} 63 \\ + 18 \end{array}$$
$$\begin{array}{r} 58 \\ + 27 \end{array}$$
$$\begin{array}{r} 21 \\ + 49 \end{array}$$
$$\begin{array}{r} 45 \\ + 46 \end{array}$$

2.
$$\begin{array}{r} 26 \\ + 38 \end{array}$$
$$\begin{array}{r} 37 \\ + 19 \end{array}$$
$$\begin{array}{r} 41 \\ + 9 \end{array}$$
$$\begin{array}{r} 58 \\ + 18 \end{array}$$
$$\begin{array}{r} 67 \\ + 27 \end{array}$$
$$\begin{array}{r} 35 \\ + 38 \end{array}$$

Directions: Subtract. Check each answer.

3.
$$\begin{array}{r} 62 \\ - 8 \end{array}$$
$$\begin{array}{r} 48 \\ - 9 \end{array}$$
$$\begin{array}{r} 35 \\ - 16 \end{array}$$
$$\begin{array}{r} 96 \\ - 29 \end{array}$$
$$\begin{array}{r} 52 \\ - 14 \end{array}$$
$$\begin{array}{r} 43 \\ - 5 \end{array}$$

4.
$$\begin{array}{r} 36 \\ - 18 \end{array}$$
$$\begin{array}{r} 57 \\ - 8 \end{array}$$
$$\begin{array}{r} 67 \\ - 19 \end{array}$$
$$\begin{array}{r} 52 \\ - 17 \end{array}$$
$$\begin{array}{r} 51 \\ - 23 \end{array}$$
$$\begin{array}{r} 60 \\ - 46 \end{array}$$

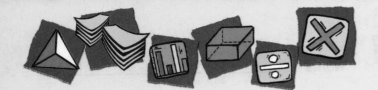

Problem Solving

Directions: Answer each question.

Work Space:

1. This morning, the temperature was 23° degrees.
This afternoon, it was 31° degrees.
How many degrees did it go up?

   Are you to add
       or subtract? _____
   How many degrees did
       the temperature go up? _____

   1.

2. There were 45 people at a meeting. After
28 of them left, how many people were
still at the meeting?

   Are you to add
       or subtract? _____
   How many people
       were still at the meeting? _____

   2.

3. Renée drove 67 kilometres in the morning and
24 kilometres in the afternoon. How far did she
drive?

   Are you to add
       or subtract? _____
   How far did she drive? _____

   3.

4. A clown has 26 orange and 28 blue balloons.
How many balloons is that?

   Are you to add
       or subtract? _____
   How many orange and
       blue balloons are there? _____

   4.

Problem Solving

Directions: Answer each question.

Work Space:

1. Nicholas is on a trip of 170 kilometres. So far, he has gone 90 kilometres. How many kilometres must he go?

   Are you to add
   or subtract? _____
   How many more
   kilometres must he go? _____

1.

2. A school has 20 men teachers. It has 30 women teachers. How many teachers are in the school?

   Are you to add
   or subtract? _____
   How many teachers are in the school? _____

2.

3. Logan weighs 31 kilograms. His older brother weighs 91 kilograms. How many more kilograms does his older brother weigh?

   Are you to add
   or subtract? _____
   How many more kilograms does
   his older brother weigh? _____

3.

4. Jessica has 110 pennies. Emily has 90 pennies. Jessica has how many more pennies than Emily?

   Jessica has _____ more pennies than Emily.

4.

Addition and Subtraction

Directions: Add.

1.	$\begin{array}{r} 5 \\ +\ 6 \\ \hline \end{array}$	$\begin{array}{r} 50 \\ +\ 60 \\ \hline \end{array}$	$\begin{array}{r} 7 \\ +\ 7 \\ \hline \end{array}$	$\begin{array}{r} 70 \\ +\ 80 \\ \hline \end{array}$	$\begin{array}{r} 90 \\ +\ 80 \\ \hline \end{array}$	$\begin{array}{r} 70 \\ +\ 70 \\ \hline \end{array}$
2.	$\begin{array}{r} 53 \\ +\ 95 \\ \hline \end{array}$	$\begin{array}{r} 44 \\ +\ 74 \\ \hline \end{array}$	$\begin{array}{r} 82 \\ +\ 96 \\ \hline \end{array}$	$\begin{array}{r} 67 \\ +\ 70 \\ \hline \end{array}$	$\begin{array}{r} 55 \\ +\ 52 \\ \hline \end{array}$	$\begin{array}{r} 73 \\ +\ 86 \\ \hline \end{array}$
3.	$\begin{array}{r} 63 \\ +\ 78 \\ \hline \end{array}$	$\begin{array}{r} 82 \\ +\ 89 \\ \hline \end{array}$	$\begin{array}{r} 97 \\ +\ 27 \\ \hline \end{array}$	$\begin{array}{r} 56 \\ +\ 75 \\ \hline \end{array}$	$\begin{array}{r} 88 \\ +\ 88 \\ \hline \end{array}$	$\begin{array}{r} 97 \\ +\ 44 \\ \hline \end{array}$
4.	$\begin{array}{r} 26 \\ +\ 53 \\ \hline \end{array}$	$\begin{array}{r} 66 \\ +\ 25 \\ \hline \end{array}$	$\begin{array}{r} 74 \\ +\ 65 \\ \hline \end{array}$	$\begin{array}{r} 39 \\ +\ 87 \\ \hline \end{array}$	$\begin{array}{r} 82 \\ +\ 17 \\ \hline \end{array}$	$\begin{array}{r} 76 \\ +\ 72 \\ \hline \end{array}$

Directions: Subtract.

5.	$\begin{array}{r} 16 \\ -\ 7 \\ \hline \end{array}$	$\begin{array}{r} 160 \\ -\ 70 \\ \hline \end{array}$	$\begin{array}{r} 15 \\ -\ 9 \\ \hline \end{array}$	$\begin{array}{r} 150 \\ -\ 90 \\ \hline \end{array}$	$\begin{array}{r} 140 \\ -\ 60 \\ \hline \end{array}$	$\begin{array}{r} 170 \\ -\ 80 \\ \hline \end{array}$
6.	$\begin{array}{r} 136 \\ -\ 53 \\ \hline \end{array}$	$\begin{array}{r} 165 \\ -\ 74 \\ \hline \end{array}$	$\begin{array}{r} 154 \\ -\ 90 \\ \hline \end{array}$	$\begin{array}{r} 186 \\ -\ 93 \\ \hline \end{array}$	$\begin{array}{r} 179 \\ -\ 82 \\ \hline \end{array}$	$\begin{array}{r} 147 \\ -\ 67 \\ \hline \end{array}$
7.	$\begin{array}{r} 146 \\ -\ 97 \\ \hline \end{array}$	$\begin{array}{r} 158 \\ -\ 69 \\ \hline \end{array}$	$\begin{array}{r} 172 \\ -\ 85 \\ \hline \end{array}$	$\begin{array}{r} 163 \\ -\ 77 \\ \hline \end{array}$	$\begin{array}{r} 125 \\ -\ 58 \\ \hline \end{array}$	$\begin{array}{r} 116 \\ -\ 39 \\ \hline \end{array}$
8.	$\begin{array}{r} 176 \\ -\ 53 \\ \hline \end{array}$	$\begin{array}{r} 184 \\ -\ 35 \\ \hline \end{array}$	$\begin{array}{r} 154 \\ -\ 72 \\ \hline \end{array}$	$\begin{array}{r} 153 \\ -\ 74 \\ \hline \end{array}$	$\begin{array}{r} 146 \\ -\ 32 \\ \hline \end{array}$	$\begin{array}{r} 107 \\ -\ 40 \\ \hline \end{array}$

Name _____

Skipping Through the Tens

Directions: Skip count by tens. Begin with the number on the first line. Write each number that follows.

0, ____ , ____ , ____ , ____ , ____ , ____ , ____ , ____ , ____ , 100

3, ____ , ____ , ____ , ____ , 53 , ____ , ____ , ____ , ____ , 103

1, ____ , ____ , ____ , ____ , ____ , ____ , 81 , ____ , ____

8, ____ , ____ , ____ , ____ , 68 , ____ , ____ , ____ , ____

6, ____ , ____ , ____ , ____ , ____ , ____ , ____ , ____ , ____

4, ____ , ____ , ____ , ____ , ____ , ____ , ____ , ____ , 104

2, ____ , ____ , ____ , ____ , ____ , ____ , ____ , 92 , ____

5, ____ , ____ , 45 , ____ , ____ , ____ , ____ , ____ , ____

7, ____ , ____ , ____ , ____ , ____ , 77 , ____ , ____ , ____

9, ____ , ____ , ____ , ____ , ____ , ____ , ____ , ____ , ____

What is ten more than . . . ?

26 _____   29 _____

44 _____   77 _____

53 _____   91 _____

24 _____   49 _____

66 _____   35 _____

54 _____   82 _____

Counting to 100

Directions: Skip count to 100.

By twos:

		6	8				16			22			
30							44						56
				66						78			
							100						

By threes:

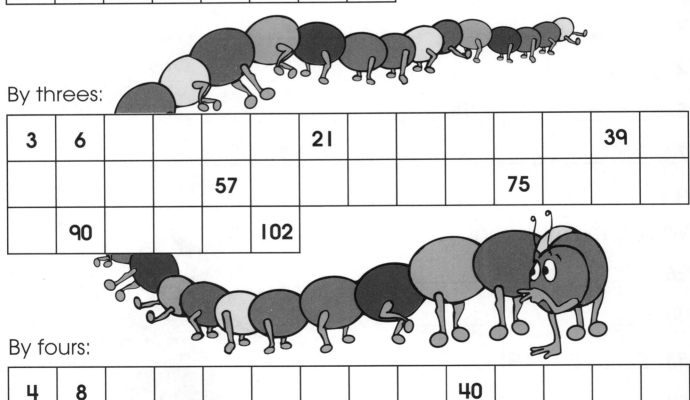

3	6					21						39
					57						75	
	90						102					

By fours:

4	8								40				
60							88			100			

On another sheet of paper, count by fives to 100. Then, count by sixes.

Count the Legs!

Directions: Multiplication is a quick way to add. For example, count the legs of the horses below. They each have 4 legs. You could add 4 + 4 + 4. But it is quicker to say that there are 3 groups of 4 legs. In multiplication, that is 3 x 4.

Multiply to find the number of legs. Write each problem twice.

——— horses x ——— legs = ———

——— x ——— = ———

——— ostriches x ——— legs = ———

——— x ——— = ———

——— insects x ——— legs = ———

——— x ——— = ———

——— stools x ——— legs = ———

——— x ——— = ———

——— cows x ——— legs = ———

——— x ——— = ———

——— birds x ——— legs = ———

——— x ——— = ———

     113   Multiplication

Name _____

Multiplication

Multiplication is a short way to find the sum of adding the same number a certain amount of times. For example, we write $7 \times 4 = 28$ instead of $7 + 7 + 7 + 7 = 28$.

Directions: Study the example. Multiply.

Example:

There are two groups of seashells. There are 3 seashells in each group. How many seashells are there in all?

$2 \times 3 = 6$

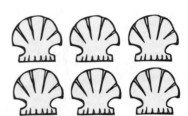

$4 + 4 = $ _____

$2 \times 4 = $ _____

$3 + 3 + 3 = $ _____

$3 \times 3 = $ _____

$$\begin{array}{r} 2 \\ \times 3 \\ \hline \end{array} \qquad \begin{array}{r} 3 \\ \times 5 \\ \hline \end{array} \qquad \begin{array}{r} 4 \\ \times 3 \\ \hline \end{array} \qquad \begin{array}{r} 6 \\ \times 2 \\ \hline \end{array} \qquad \begin{array}{r} 7 \\ \times 3 \\ \hline \end{array}$$

$$\begin{array}{r} 5 \\ \times 2 \\ \hline \end{array} \qquad \begin{array}{r} 6 \\ \times 3 \\ \hline \end{array} \qquad \begin{array}{r} 4 \\ \times 2 \\ \hline \end{array} \qquad \begin{array}{r} 7 \\ \times 2 \\ \hline \end{array} \qquad \begin{array}{r} 8 \\ \times 3 \\ \hline \end{array}$$

$$\begin{array}{r} 5 \\ \times 5 \\ \hline \end{array} \qquad \begin{array}{r} 9 \\ \times 4 \\ \hline \end{array} \qquad \begin{array}{r} 8 \\ \times 5 \\ \hline \end{array} \qquad \begin{array}{r} 6 \\ \times 6 \\ \hline \end{array} \qquad \begin{array}{r} 9 \\ \times 3 \\ \hline \end{array}$$

Multiplication

2 x 3 is read "two times three."
3 x 2 is read "three times two."
4 x 5 is read "four times five."

3 x 6 is read "three times six."

2 x 7 is read "two times seven."

2 x 3 means 3 + 3.
3 x 2 means 2 + 2+ 2.
4 x 5 means 5 + 5 + 5 + 5.

3 x 6 means _____

2 x 7 means _____

Directions: Complete the following as shown.

1. 3 x 2 is read _____

2. 3 x 4 is read _____

3. 5 x 2 is read _____

4. 4 x 8 is read _____

5. 4 x 7 is read _____

Directions: Complete the following as shown.

6. 2 x 4 means _____4 + 4_____

7. 3 x 5 means _____

8. 3 x 7 means _____

9. 4 x 6 means _____

10. 2 x 8 means _____

11. 3 x 9 means _____

4 x 2 means _____2 + 2 + 2 + 2_____

5 x 3 means _____

7 x 3 means _____

6 x 4 means _____

8 x 2 means _____

9 x 3 means _____

Multiplication

3 x 4 means 4 + 4 + 4.   4 x 3 means 3 + 3 + 3 + 3.

```
      4              4                  4              3
                     4                                3
    x 3            + 4                x 3              3
   ----           ----               ----           + 3
    12             12                 12             ----
                                                     12
```

Directions: Add or multiply.

1.
```
    8         8         4         4         5         5
  + 8       x 2       + 4       x 2       + 5       x 2
  ----      ----      ----      ----      ----      ----
```

2.
```
    6         6         7         7         2         2
  + 6       x 2       + 7       x 2       + 2       x 2
  ----      ----      ----      ----      ----      ----
```

3.
```
    9         9         3         3         1         1
  + 9       x 2       + 3       x 2       + 1       x 2
  ----      ----      ----      ----      ----      ----
```

4.
```
    2                   3                   4
    2         2         3         3         4         4
  + 2       x 3       + 3       x 3       + 4       x 3
  ----      ----      ----      ----      ----      ----
```

5.
```
    5                   6                   7
    5         5         6         6         7         7
  + 5       x 3       + 6       x 3       + 7       x 3
  ----      ----      ----      ----      ----      ----
```

6.
```
    8                   9                   1
    8         8         9         9         1         1
  + 8       x 3       + 9       x 3       + 1       x 3
  ----      ----      ----      ----      ----      ----
```

Multiplication: Zero and One

Any number multiplied by zero equals zero. One mutiplied by any number equals that number. Study the example. Multiply.

Example:

How many full sails are there in all?

2 boats x **1** sail on each boat = **2** sails

How many full sails are there now?

2 boats x **0** sails = **0** sails

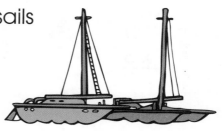

Directions: Multiply.

1 x 5	2 x 1	3 x 0	4 x 1	0 x 6	7 x 0

9 x 1	8 x 0	3 x 1	4 x 0	7 x 1	6 x 1

Multiplication

Name _____

Directions: Multiply.

3 x 5	4 x 6	3 x 8

5 x 5	4 x 8	5 x 4

6 x 7	3 x 9	2 x 8	7 x 6	9 x 4

6 x 8	5 x 6	7 x 7	5 x 3	8 x 9

A riverboat makes 3 trips a day every day.
How many trips does it make in a week? _____

Name _____

Multiplication

$$\begin{array}{r} 1 \\ \times 0 \\ \hline 0 \end{array} \quad \begin{array}{r} 2 \\ \times 0 \\ \hline 0 \end{array} \quad \begin{array}{r} 0 \\ \times 3 \\ \hline 0 \end{array} \quad \begin{array}{r} 0 \\ \times 4 \\ \hline 0 \end{array} \qquad \begin{array}{r} 0 \\ \times 1 \\ \hline 0 \end{array} \quad \begin{array}{r} 1 \\ \times 1 \\ \hline 1 \end{array} \quad \begin{array}{r} 2 \\ \times 1 \\ \hline 2 \end{array} \quad \begin{array}{r} 1 \\ \times 3 \\ \hline 3 \end{array}$$

Directions: Multiply.

1.
$$\begin{array}{r} 0 \\ \times 2 \\ \hline \end{array} \quad \begin{array}{r} 9 \\ \times 1 \\ \hline \end{array} \quad \begin{array}{r} 1 \\ \times 7 \\ \hline \end{array} \quad \begin{array}{r} 6 \\ \times 0 \\ \hline \end{array} \quad \begin{array}{r} 1 \\ \times 5 \\ \hline \end{array} \quad \begin{array}{r} 0 \\ \times 7 \\ \hline \end{array}$$

2.
$$\begin{array}{r} 4 \\ \times 0 \\ \hline \end{array} \quad \begin{array}{r} 8 \\ \times 1 \\ \hline \end{array} \quad \begin{array}{r} 1 \\ \times 4 \\ \hline \end{array} \quad \begin{array}{r} 0 \\ \times 9 \\ \hline \end{array} \quad \begin{array}{r} 7 \\ \times 0 \\ \hline \end{array} \quad \begin{array}{r} 6 \\ \times 1 \\ \hline \end{array}$$

3.
$$\begin{array}{r} 5 \\ \times 0 \\ \hline \end{array} \quad \begin{array}{r} 0 \\ \times 8 \\ \hline \end{array} \quad \begin{array}{r} 5 \\ \times 1 \\ \hline \end{array} \quad \begin{array}{r} 1 \\ \times 6 \\ \hline \end{array} \quad \begin{array}{r} 1 \\ \times 1 \\ \hline \end{array} \quad \begin{array}{r} 8 \\ \times 0 \\ \hline \end{array}$$

4.
$$\begin{array}{r} 1 \\ \times 7 \\ \hline \end{array} \quad \begin{array}{r} 0 \\ \times 4 \\ \hline \end{array} \quad \begin{array}{r} 3 \\ \times 0 \\ \hline \end{array} \quad \begin{array}{r} 9 \\ \times 0 \\ \hline \end{array} \quad \begin{array}{r} 7 \\ \times 1 \\ \hline \end{array} \quad \begin{array}{r} 1 \\ \times 5 \\ \hline \end{array}$$

5.
$$\begin{array}{r} 0 \\ \times 7 \\ \hline \end{array} \quad \begin{array}{r} 1 \\ \times 9 \\ \hline \end{array} \quad \begin{array}{r} 1 \\ \times 6 \\ \hline \end{array} \quad \begin{array}{r} 0 \\ \times 5 \\ \hline \end{array} \quad \begin{array}{r} 1 \\ \times 0 \\ \hline \end{array} \quad \begin{array}{r} 2 \\ \times 1 \\ \hline \end{array}$$

6.
$$\begin{array}{r} 1 \\ \times 4 \\ \hline \end{array} \quad \begin{array}{r} 1 \\ \times 8 \\ \hline \end{array} \quad \begin{array}{r} 4 \\ \times 0 \\ \hline \end{array} \quad \begin{array}{r} 8 \\ \times 1 \\ \hline \end{array} \quad \begin{array}{r} 0 \\ \times 6 \\ \hline \end{array} \quad \begin{array}{r} 0 \\ \times 3 \\ \hline \end{array}$$

7.
$$\begin{array}{r} 0 \\ \times 9 \\ \hline \end{array} \quad \begin{array}{r} 6 \\ \times 1 \\ \hline \end{array} \quad \begin{array}{r} 0 \\ \times 2 \\ \hline \end{array} \quad \begin{array}{r} 9 \\ \times 1 \\ \hline \end{array} \quad \begin{array}{r} 0 \\ \times 1 \\ \hline \end{array} \quad \begin{array}{r} 3 \\ \times 1 \\ \hline \end{array}$$

8.
$$\begin{array}{r} 1 \\ \times 2 \\ \hline \end{array} \quad \begin{array}{r} 6 \\ \times 0 \\ \hline \end{array} \quad \begin{array}{r} 7 \\ \times 0 \\ \hline \end{array} \quad \begin{array}{r} 1 \\ \times 3 \\ \hline \end{array} \quad \begin{array}{r} 4 \\ \times 1 \\ \hline \end{array} \quad \begin{array}{r} 0 \\ \times 0 \\ \hline \end{array}$$

Fact Snacks

Directions: Ask an adult for a paper plate and a couple of snacks, such as popcorn, pretzels, candy corn, or chocolate-covered candies. Arrange the snacks into sets, such as five sets of 5 or nine sets of 3.

Now, add the sets together. Write the related fact. Use the snack manipulatives to answer the following multiplication problems. Group the snacks into sets with the number shown in each set.

$4 \times 2 =$ 4 sets with 2 in each set $= 8$

1. 3 $\times 2$	**2.** 5 $\times 3$	**3.** 1 $\times 7$	**4.** 2 $\times 9$	**5.** 6 $\times 6$
6. 7 $\times 4$	**7.** 8 $\times 5$	**8.** 3 $\times 4$	**9.** 6 $\times 7$	**10.** 10 $\times\ 2$
11. 1 $\times 3$	**12.** 4 $\times 8$	**13.** 9 $\times 2$	**14.** 3 $\times 3$	**15.** 5 $\times 7$

After you answer and check the problems, enjoy the tasty fact snacks.

Name _____

Multiplying

Numbers to be multiplied together are called **factors.** The answer is the **product. Example:** 3 x 6

1. The first factor tells how many groups there are. There are 3 groups.

2. The second factor tells how many are in each group. There are 6 in each group.

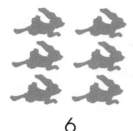  

3 groups of 6 equal 18.

3 x 6 = 18

6 + 6 + 6 = 18

Some helpful hints to remember when multiplying:

- When you multiply by 0, the product is always 0. **Example:** 0 x 7 = 0
- When you multiply by 1, the product is always the factor being multiplied. **Example:** 1 x 12 = 12
- When multiplying by 2, double the factor other than 2. **Example:** 2 x 4 = 8
- The order doesn't matter when multiplying. **Example:** 5 x 3 = 15, 3 x 5 = 15
- When you multiply by 9, the digits in the product add up to 9 (until 9 x 11). **Example:** 7 x 9 = 63, 6 + 3 = 9
- When you multiply by 10, multiply by 1 and add 0 to the product. **Example:** 10 x 3 = 30
- When you multiply by 11, write the factor you are multiplying by twice (until 10). **Example:** 11 x 8 = 88

Directions: Multiply.

2 x9	3 x8	4 x9	2 x11	5 x9	10 x 5	7 x6	11 x 4	9 x7

8 x6	7 x12	8 x5	10 x10	4 x8	5 x5	8 x8	3 x6	7 x8

Factor Fun

When you change the order of the factors, you have the same product.

Directions: Multiply.

7 x 3	3 x 7	6 x 5	5 x 6	2 x 3	3 x 2
4 x 6	6 x 4	2 x 9	9 x 2	8 x 4	4 x 8
7 x 2	2 x 7	3 x 6	6 x 3	9 x 4	4 x 9
8 x 3	3 x 8	5 x 2	2 x 5	9 x 3	3 x 9

Racing to the Finish

Directions: Multiply.

5	2	4	9	7	3
x 3	x 8	x 6	x 3	x 5	x 9

4	6	4	0	3	7
x 2	x 2	x 4	x 6	x 2	x 2

6	3	8	4	5	7
x 5	x 4	x 3	x 5	x 2	x 4

6	4	2	8	3	5
x 3	x 8	x 2	x 5	x 7	x 5

5	9	4	9		
x 9	x 2	x 6	x 4		

Name _____

Climbing Granite Boulders!

Directions: Multiply.

9	6	3
x1	x1	x9

2	8	7	8
x9	x9	x8	x7

3 x 3 = _____

4 x 4 = _____

7	5
x7	x9

6	2
x7	x6

9 x 9 = _____

6 x 6 = _____

9 x 0 = _____

8
x8

5
x7

8 x 6 = _____   3 x 5 = _____

4 x 8 = _____   2 x 8 = _____

7 x 2 = _____   3 x 7 = _____

3 x 6 = _____

6 x 6 = _____

5 x 6 = _____

2 x 2 = _____   4 x 7 = _____

2 x 3 = _____   4 x 6 = _____

6 x 9 = _____   0 x 4 = _____

7 x 9 = _____

5 x 5 = _____

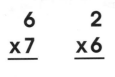

Multiplication

Directions: Time yourself as you multiply. How quickly can you complete this page?

$$\begin{array}{r} 3 \\ \times 2 \\ \hline \end{array}$$
$$\begin{array}{r} 8 \\ \times 7 \\ \hline \end{array}$$
$$\begin{array}{r} 1 \\ \times 0 \\ \hline \end{array}$$
$$\begin{array}{r} 1 \\ \times 6 \\ \hline \end{array}$$
$$\begin{array}{r} 3 \\ \times 4 \\ \hline \end{array}$$
$$\begin{array}{r} 0 \\ \times 4 \\ \hline \end{array}$$

$$\begin{array}{r} 4 \\ \times 1 \\ \hline \end{array}$$
$$\begin{array}{r} 4 \\ \times 4 \\ \hline \end{array}$$
$$\begin{array}{r} 2 \\ \times 5 \\ \hline \end{array}$$
$$\begin{array}{r} 9 \\ \times 3 \\ \hline \end{array}$$
$$\begin{array}{r} 9 \\ \times 9 \\ \hline \end{array}$$
$$\begin{array}{r} 5 \\ \times 3 \\ \hline \end{array}$$

$$\begin{array}{r} 0 \\ \times 8 \\ \hline \end{array}$$
$$\begin{array}{r} 2 \\ \times 6 \\ \hline \end{array}$$
$$\begin{array}{r} 9 \\ \times 6 \\ \hline \end{array}$$
$$\begin{array}{r} 8 \\ \times 5 \\ \hline \end{array}$$
$$\begin{array}{r} 7 \\ \times 3 \\ \hline \end{array}$$
$$\begin{array}{r} 4 \\ \times 2 \\ \hline \end{array}$$

$$\begin{array}{r} 3 \\ \times 5 \\ \hline \end{array}$$
$$\begin{array}{r} 2 \\ \times 0 \\ \hline \end{array}$$
$$\begin{array}{r} 4 \\ \times 6 \\ \hline \end{array}$$
$$\begin{array}{r} 1 \\ \times 3 \\ \hline \end{array}$$
$$\begin{array}{r} 0 \\ \times 0 \\ \hline \end{array}$$
$$\begin{array}{r} 3 \\ \times 3 \\ \hline \end{array}$$

Multiplication Table

Directions: Complete the multiplication table. Use it to practise your multiplication facts.

X	0	1	2	3	4	5	6	7	8	9	10
0	0										
1		1									
2			4								
3				9							
4					16						
5						25					
6							36				
7								49			
8									64		
9										81	
10											100

Multiplication

Factors are the numbers multiplied together in a multiplication problem. The answer is called the product. If you change the order of the factors, the product stays the same.

Example:

There are 4 groups of fish.
There are 3 fish in each group.
How many fish are there in all?

$\quad$ 4 $\quad$ x $\quad$ 3 $\quad$ = 12

factor x factor = product

Directions: Draw 3 groups of 4 fish.

$\quad$ 3 x 4 = 12

Compare your drawing and answer with the example. What did you notice?

Directions: Fill in the missing numbers. Multiply.

$\quad$ 5 x 4 = ____ $\qquad$ 3 x 6 = ____ $\qquad$ 4 x 2 = ____

$\quad$ 4 x 5 = ____ $\qquad$ 6 x 3 = ____ $\qquad$ 2 x 4 = ____

| $\begin{array}{r}3\\ \times 7\\ \hline\end{array}$ | $\begin{array}{r}7\\ \times 3\\ \hline\end{array}$ | $\begin{array}{r}2\\ \times 9\\ \hline\end{array}$ | $\begin{array}{r}9\\ \times 2\\ \hline\end{array}$ | $\begin{array}{r}8\\ \times 4\\ \hline\end{array}$ | $\begin{array}{r}4\\ \times 8\\ \hline\end{array}$ |

| $\begin{array}{r}5\\ \times 2\\ \hline\end{array}$ | $\begin{array}{r}2\\ \times 5\\ \hline\end{array}$ | $\begin{array}{r}6\\ \times 3\\ \hline\end{array}$ | $\begin{array}{r}3\\ \times 6\\ \hline\end{array}$ | $\begin{array}{r}5\\ \times 6\\ \hline\end{array}$ | $\begin{array}{r}6\\ \times 5\\ \hline\end{array}$ |

Name _____

Double Trouble

Directions: Solve each multiplication problem. Below each answer, write the letter from the code that matches the answer. Read the coded question and write the answer in the space provided.

1	4	9	16	25	36	49	64	81	100	121	144
E	G	H	I	N	O	S	T	U	W	X	Y

10 x10	3 x3	6 x6

4 x4	7 x7

7 x7	4 x4	8 x8	8 x8	4 x4	5 x5	2 x2

5 x5	1 x1	11 x11	8 x8

8 x8	6 x6

12 x12	6 x6	9 x9

?

Answer: _____

On the Right Track

Preparation: Glue the gameboard on page 131 onto poster board. Make a spinner, using the pattern below. Use a brass fastener to attach a paper clip to the centre of the spinner so the clip spins freely.

Directions: This game involves two players. Players spin the spinner. The player with the highest number goes first. Players start at the station. Player One spins and moves his or her marker to the first space on the track that has a multiple of the number he or she spun. A multiple is the product or answer you would get when you multiply the number on the spinner by another number. If no multiple remains, Player One loses his or her turn. If a player puts his or her marker on a wrong multiple or skips a multiple, he or she must go back to the station. The first player to reach the end of the line is the winner.

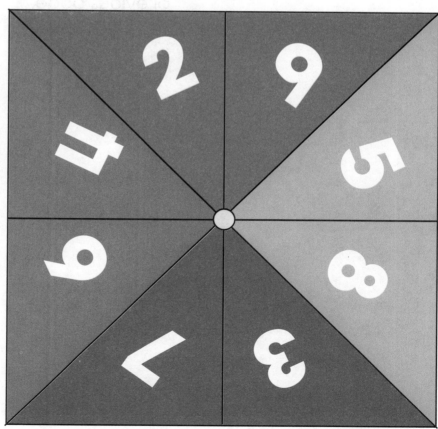

Complete Math Grade 3   **129**   Multiplication

This page was left intentionally
blank for cutting activity on
previous page.

On the Right Track Gameboard

63 56 36 72

15 20

28 32

18 14

45 24

48

16 12

21 81

54

Station 42

End of the Line 27

This page was left intentionally
blank for cutting activity on
previous page.

Crossword Number Fun

Directions: Write the word form of each product in the puzzle.

Across

3. 9 x 4 = _____

8. 10 x 5 = _____

9. 2 x 9 = _____

10. 3 x 12 = _____

12. 7 x 11 = _____

14. 4 x 10 = _____

15. 6 x 5 = _____

16. 0 x 7 = _____

Down

1. 7 x 8 = _____

2. 6 x 1 = _____

4. 2 x 5 = _____

5. 11 x 3 = _____

6. 5 x 1 = _____

7. 5 x 4 = _____

11. 12 x 8 = _____

13. 3 x 8 = _____

Name _____

Wacky Waldo's Snow Show

Wacky Waldo's Snow Show is an exciting and fantastic sight. Waldo has trained whales and bears to skate together on the ice. There is a hockey game between a team of sharks and a pack of wolves. Elephants ride sleds down steep hills. Horses and buffaloes ski swiftly down mountains.

Directions: Write each problem and its answer.

1. Wacky Waldo has 4 ice-skating whales. He has 4 times as many bears who ice skate. How many bears can ice skate? _____ X _____ = _____	**4.** The Wolves' hockey team has 4 grey wolves. It has 8 times as many red wolves. How many red wolves does it have? _____ X _____ = _____
2. Waldo's Snow Show has 4 shows on Thursday, but it has 6 times as many on Saturday. How many shows are there on Saturday? _____ X _____ = _____	**5.** Waldo taught 6 buffaloes to ski. He was able to teach 5 times as many horses to ski. How many horses did he teach? _____ X _____ = _____
3. The Sharks' hockey team has 3 great white sharks. It has 6 times as many tiger sharks. How many tiger sharks does it have? _____ X _____ = _____	**6.** Buff, a skiing buffalo, took 7 nasty spills when he was learning to ski. His friend Harry Horse fell down 8 times as often. How many times did Harry fall? _____ X _____ = _____

Problem Solving

Directions: Solve each problem.

Work Space:

I. Ashley wants to buy 5 erasers. They cost 9 cents each. How much will she have to pay?

Ashley wants to buy _____ erasers.
One eraser costs _____ cents.
Ashley will have to pay _____ cents.

I.

2 There are 5 rows of mailboxes. There are 7 mailboxes in each row. How many mailboxes are there in all?

There are _____ mailboxes in each row.
There are _____ rows of mailboxes.
There are _____ mailboxes in all.

2.

3. Milton, the pet monkey, eats 4 meals every day. How many meals does he eat in a week?

There are _____ days in a week.
Milton eats _____ meals every day.
Milton eats _____ meals in a week.

3.

4. In a baseball game each team gets 3 outs per inning. How many outs does each team get in a 5-inning game?

There are _____ innings in the game.
Each team gets _____ outs per inning.
The team gets _____ outs in the 5-inning game.

4.

Problem Solving

Directions: Solve each problem.   **Work Space:**

1. Neal has 6 books. Each book weighs 1 kilogram.
What is the weight of all the books?

Neal has _____ books.
Each book weighs _____ kilogram.
The six books weigh _____ kilograms.

2. A basketball game has 4 time periods.
Kate's team is to play 8 games. How
many periods will her team play?

Kate's team is to play _____ games.
Each game has _____ time periods.
Kate's team will play _____ time periods in all.

3. Meagan works 8 hours every day. How
many hours does she work in 5 days?

She works _____ hours in 5 days.

4. Shane can ride his bicycle 5 kilometres in an hour.
At that speed how far could he ride in 2 hours?

Shane could ride _____ kilometres in 2 hours.

5. Calvin bought 5 bags of balloons. Each
bag had 6 balloons. How many balloons
did he buy?

Calvin bought _____ balloons in all.

1.

2.

3.

4.

5.

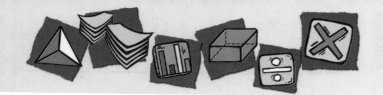

Problem Solving

Directions: Solve each problem.

Work Space:

1. There are 6 rows of cactus plants. Each row has 4 plants. How many cactus plants are there in all?

   There are _____ rows of cactus plants.
   There are _____ cactus plants in each row.
   There are _____ cactus plants in all.

   I.

2. There are 8 marigold plants in each row. There are 6 rows. How many marigold plants are there?

   There are _____ marigold plants in each row.
   There are _____ rows of marigold plants.
   There are _____ marigold plants in all.

   2.

3. There are 6 rosebushes in each row. There are 9 rows. How many rosebushes are there?

   There are _____ rosebushes in each row.
   There are _____ rows of rosebushes.
   There are _____ rosebushes in all.

   3.

Problem Solving

Directions: Solve each problem.

Work Space:

1. In Tori's building there are 7 floors. There are 9 apartments on each floor. How many apartments are in the building?

   There are _____ floors in this building.
   There are _____ apartments on each floor.
   There are _____ apartments in this building.

   1.

2. The science club meets 4 times each month. The club meets for 7 months. How many meetings will the science club have?

   The science club meets _____ times each month.
   The club meets for _____ months.
   The club will have _____ meetings in all.

   2.

3. Each bag of corn weighs 8 kilograms. There are 7 bags. How much do the bags weigh in all?

   Each bag weighs _____ kilograms.
   There are _____ bags.
   The bags weigh _____ kilograms in all.

   3.

4. There are 7 days in a week. How many days are there in 5 weeks?

   There are _____ days in 5 weeks.

   4.

Problem Solving

Directions: Solve each problem.

Work Space:

1. There are 8 chairs around each table. There are 9 tables. How many chairs are around all the tables?

There are _____ chairs around each table.
There are _____ tables.
There are _____ chairs around all the tables.

1.

2 Workers are eating lunch at 9 tables. Each table has 9 workers. How many workers are eating lunch?

There are _____ tables .
_____ workers are at each table.
_____ workers are eating lunch.

2.

3. The workers drink 9 litres of milk each day. They are at work 5 days a week. How many litres of milk do they drink in 5 days?

They drink _____ litres of milk in 5 days.

3.

4. A bowling league bowls 4 times each month. How many times will the league bowl in 9 months?

The bowling league will bowl _____ times.

4.

5. A regular baseball game is 9 innings long. How many innings are in 7 regular games?

There are _____ innings in 7 regular games.

5.

Problem Solving

Directions: Solve each problem.

Work Space:

1. Some students formed 5 teams. There were 8 students on each team. How many students were there?
There were _____ teams.
There were _____ students on each team.
There were _____ students in all.

1.

2. The waiter put 9 napkins on each table. There were 9 tables. How many napkins did the waiter use?
The waiter put _____ napkins on each table.
There were _____ tables.
The waiter used _____ napkins in all.

2.

3. Dr. Mede rides her bicycle 6 kilometres every day. How far would she ride in 9 days?
Dr. Mede rides _____ kilometres every day.
She rides for each of _____ days.
She would ride _____ kilometres in all.

3.

4. Mr. Brown works 7 hours each day. How many hours will he work in 6 days?
Mr. Brown will work _____ hours in 6 days.

4.

5. There are 8 hot dogs in each package. How many hot dogs are there in 9 packages?
There are _____ hot dogs in 9 packages.

5.

Backward Multiplication

Division problems are like multiplication problems—just turned around. As you solve 8 ÷ 4, think, "How many groups of 4 make 8?" or "What number 'times' 4 is eight?"

2 x 4 = 8, so 8 ÷ 4 = **2**.

Directions: Use the pictures to help you solve these division problems.

9 ÷ 3 =

6 ÷ 2 =

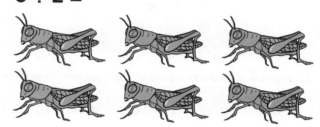

16 ÷ 4 =

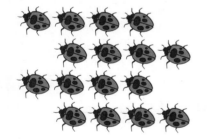

10 ÷ 5 =

20 ÷ 1 =

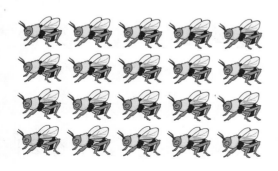

18 ÷ 3 =

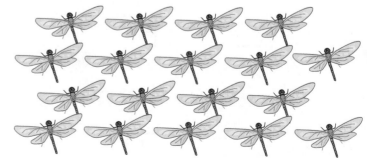

What Exactly Is Division?

In division, you begin with an amount of something (the dividend), separate it into small groups (the divisor), then find out how many groups are created (the quotient).

Dividend Divisor Quotient
$15 \div 3 = 5$ sets
in all   in each set

$$\overset{5\ sets}{3\overline{)15}}\ \text{in all}$$
in each set

Directions: Solve these division problems.

$21 \div 3 =$ _____ $3\overline{)21}$ $18 \div 3 =$ _____ $3\overline{)18}$

$20 \div 5 =$ _____ $5\overline{)20}$ $16 \div 4 =$ _____ $4\overline{)16}$

$14 \div 7 =$ _____ $7\overline{)14}$ $12 \div 2 =$ _____ $2\overline{)12}$

$18 \div 2 =$ _____ $2\overline{)18}$ $24 \div 6 =$ _____ $6\overline{)24}$

Division

Division is a way to find out how many times one number is contained in another number. For example, 28 ÷ 4 = 7 means that there are seven groups of four in 28.

Directions: Study the example. Divide.

Example:

There are 6 oars.
Each canoe needs 2 oars.
How many canoes can be used?

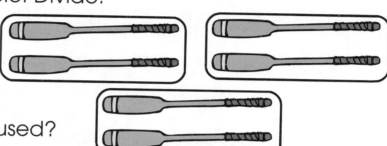

Circle groups of 2.
There are 3 groups of 2.

6	÷	2	=	3
oars		number of oars needed per canoe		canoes

9 ÷ 3 = _____   8 ÷ 2 = _____   16 ÷ 4 = _____

15 ÷ 5 = _____   18 ÷ 2 = _____   20 ÷ 4 = _____

21 ÷ 7 = _____   24 ÷ 6 = _____   12 ÷ 2 = _____

Division

÷ and ⌐‾‾ mean divide.

6 ÷ 2 = 3 is read "6 divided by 2 is equal to 3."

8 ÷ 2 = 4 is read "____ divided by 2 is equal to ____."

$2\overline{)6}$ with 3 above is read "6 divided by 2 is equal to 3."

$2\overline{)8}$ with 4 above is read "____divided by 2 is equal to ____."

divisor ------→ $2\overline{)8}$ ←----- dividend, with 4 above ←----- quotient

In $2\overline{)8}$ (with 4 above), the divisor is ____, the dividend is ____, and the quotient is ____.

Directions: Complete each sentence.

1. 10 ÷ 2 = 5 is read "_____ divided by 2 is equal to _____."

2. 21 ÷ 3 = 7 is read "_____ divided by 3 is equal to _____."

3. 4 ÷ 2 = 2 is read "_____ divided by 2 is equal to _____."

4. $3\overline{)18}$ (with 6 above) is read "_____ divided by 3 is equal to _____."

5. $2\overline{)18}$ (with 9 above) is read "_____ divided by 2 is equal to _____."

6. $3\overline{)24}$ (with 8 above) is read "_____ divided by 3 is equal to _____."

7. In $3\overline{)21}$ (with 7 above), the divisor is ____, the dividend is ____, and the quotient is ____.

8. In $2\overline{)4}$ (with 2 above), the divisor is ____, the dividend is ____, and the quotient is ____.

9. In $2\overline{)10}$ (with 5 above), the divisor is ____, the dividend is ____, and the quotient is ____.

Division

6 ✖'s in all
2 ✖'s in each group.
How many groups?

6 ÷ 2 = __3__

There are __3__ groups

6 ✖'s in all
3 groups of ✖'s
How many ✖'s in each group

6 ÷ 3 = _____

There are _____ ✖'s in each group

Directions: Complete the following.

1. 10 ★'s in all.
2 ★'s in each group.
How many groups?

10 ÷ 2 = _____

There are _____ groups.

10 ★'s in all.
5 groups of ★'s.
How many ★'s in each group?

10 ÷ 5 = _____

There are _____ ★'s in each group.

2. 8 ■'s in all.

____ ■'s in each group.
How many groups?

8 ÷ 2 = _____

There are _____ groups.

_____ ■'s in all.

4 groups of ■'s.
How many ■'s in each group?

8 ÷ 4 = _____

There are_____ ■'s in each group.

3. ____ ◯'s in all.

____ ◯'s in each group.
How many groups?

4 ÷ 2 = _____

There are _____ groups.

_____ ◯'s in all.

_____ groups of ◯'s.
How many ◯'s in each group?

4 ÷ 2 = _____

There are _____ ◯'s in each group.

Division

Directions: Divide. Draw a line from the boat to the sail with the correct answer.

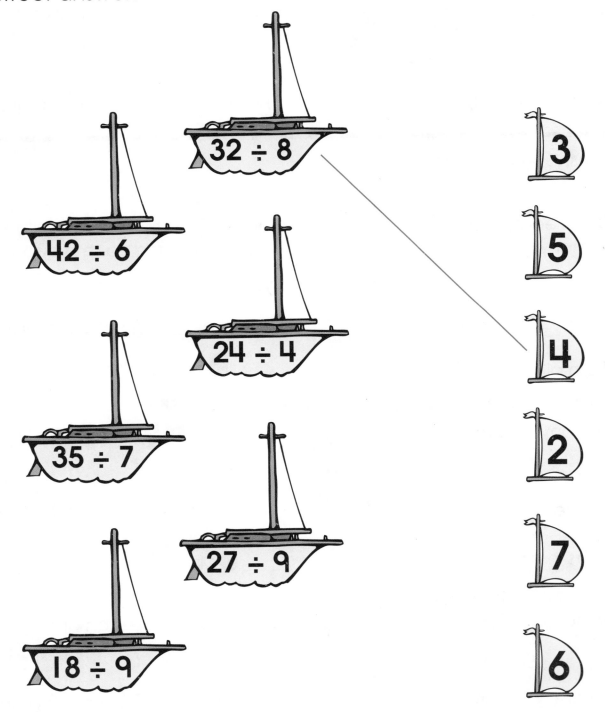

Division

Name _____

Division is a way to find out how many times one number is contained in another number. The ÷ sign means "divided by." Another way to divide is to use ⌐ . The **dividend** is the larger number that is divided by the smaller number, or **divisor**. The answer of a division problem is called the **quotient**.

Directions: Study the example. Divide.

Example:

$$20 \div 4 = 5$$

dividend   divisor   quotient

quotient

$$4\overline{)20}$$

divisor   dividend

$$35 \div 7 = \underline{\quad} \qquad 7\overline{)35} \qquad 42 \div 6 = \underline{\quad} \qquad 6\overline{)42}$$

$$2\overline{)12} \qquad 3\overline{)18} \qquad 4\overline{)36} \qquad 5\overline{)50}$$

$$6\overline{)24} \qquad 7\overline{)21} \qquad 8\overline{)32} \qquad 9\overline{)27}$$

$$36 \div 6 = \underline{\quad} \qquad 28 \div 4 = \underline{\quad} \qquad 15 \div 5 = \underline{\quad} \qquad 12 \div 2 = \underline{\quad}$$

A tree farm has 36 trees. There are 4 rows of trees. How many trees are there in each row? _____

Division: Zero and One

Directions: Study the rules of division and the examples. Divide, then write the number of the rule you used to solve each problem.

Examples:

Rule 1: $1\overline{)5}$ (quotient 5)   Any number divided by 1 is that number.

Rule 2: $5\overline{)5}$ (quotient 1)   Any number except 0 divided by itself is 1.

Rule 3: $7\overline{)0}$ (quotient 0)   Zero divided by any number is zero.

Rule 4: $0\overline{)7}$ You cannot divide by zero.

$1\overline{)6}$ Rule _____ $4 \div 1 =$ _____   Rule _____

ZERO

$7\overline{)7}$ Rule _____ $9 \div 9 =$ _____   Rule _____

ONE

$9\overline{)0}$ Rule _____ $7 \div 1 =$ _____   Rule _____

$1\overline{)4}$ Rule _____ $6 \div 0 =$ _____   Rule _____

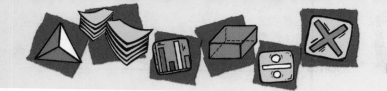

Blastoff!

Directions: Divide.

1 ⟌ 6　　　20 ⟌ 0

2 ⟌ 12　　　2 ⟌ 14

2 ⟌ 16　　9 ⟌ 0　　2 ⟌ 2　　2 ⟌ 8　　15 ⟌ 0

1 ⟌ 19　　2 ⟌ 18　　7 ⟌ 0　　2 ⟌ 10　　1 ⟌ 35

1 ⟌ 23　　1 ⟌ 17　　1 ⟌ 7　　2 ⟌ 4　　12 ⟌ 0

　　　　　　　　　2 ⟌ 6　　1 ⟌ 11　　1 ⟌ 5

Carrier Math Messengers

Directions: Divide.

3⟌12   8⟌48   2⟌18

5⟌25   9⟌72   4⟌24

9⟌72

6⟌42   8⟌40   2⟌4   7⟌56   9⟌63

9⟌45   7⟌7   3⟌15   2⟌8   7⟌63

8⟌48

3⟌24   6⟌30   9⟌54

9⟌81   7⟌28   4⟌32

Name _____

Lizzy the Lizard Bags Her Bugs

Directions: Lizzy the Lizard separates her bugs into separate bags so that her lunch is ready for the week. Help her decide how to divide the bugs.

1. Lizzy caught 45 cockroaches. She put 5 into each bag. How many bags did she use?

    _____ ÷ _____ = _____

2. Lizzy found 32 termites. She put 4 into each bag. How many bags did she need?

    _____ ÷ _____ = _____

3. Lizzy captured 49 stinkbugs. She put them into 7 bags. How many stinkbugs were in each bag?

    _____ ÷ _____ = _____

4. Lizzy bagged 27 horn beetles. She used 3 bags. How many beetles went into each bag?

    _____ ÷ _____ = _____

5. Lizzy lassoed 36 butterflies. She put 9 into each bag. How many bags did she need?

    _____ ÷ _____ = _____

6. Lizzy went fishing and caught 48 water beetles. She used 6 bags for her catch. How many beetles went into each bag?

    _____ ÷ _____ = _____

Problem Solving

Directions: Solve each problem.   **Work Space:**

1. Twenty-four people are at work. They work in 3 departments. The same number of people work in each department. How many people work in each department?

   There are _____ people.
   They work in _____ departments.
   There are _____ people in each department.

2. Dan put 8 books into 2 stacks. Each stack had the same number of books. How many books were in each stack?

   There were _____ books in all.
   They were put into _____ stacks.
   There were _____ books in each stack.

3. Janice put 16 litres of water into 2 jars. She put the same number of litres into each jar. How many litres of water did she put into each jar?

   Janice put _____ litres of water into jars.
   She used _____ jars.
   Janice put _____ litres of water into each jar.

4. Kim has 27 apples. She wants to put the same number of apples in each of 3 boxes. How many apples should she put in each box?

   She should put _____ apples in each box.

Work Space:

1.

2.

3.

4.

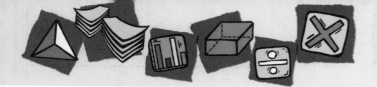

Problem Solving

Directions: Solve each problem.

Work Space:

1. A loaf of bread has 24 slices. Mrs. Spencer uses 4 slices each day. How long will a loaf of bread last her?

   A loaf of bread has _____ slices.
   Mrs. Spencer uses _____ slices a day.
   The loaf of bread will last _____ days.

   1.

2. A football team played 28 quarters. There are 4 quarters in a game. How many games did they play?

   The football team played _____ quarters.
   There are _____ quarters in each game.
   The football team played _____ games.

   2.

3. A basketball game is 32 minutes long. The game is separated into 4 periods. Each period has the same number of minutes. How long is each period?

   A basketball game is _____ minutes long.
   The game is separated into _____ period.
   Each period is _____ minutes long.

   3.

4. Emma worked 25 problems. She worked 5 problems on each sheet of paper. How many sheets of paper did she use?

   She used _____ sheets of paper.

   4.

Problem Solving

Directions: Solve each problem.

Work Space:

1. Dana bought 16 rolls. The rolls came in 2 packs. The same number of rolls were in each pack. How many rolls were in each pack?

Dana bought _____ rolls.
These rolls filled _____ packs.
There were _____ rolls in each pack.

1.

2. There are 9 families in an apartment building. There are 3 families on each floor. How many floors are in the building?

There are _____ families in the building.
There are _____ families on each floor.
There are _____ floors in the building.

2.

3. Arlene put 36 oranges in bags. She put 4 oranges in each bag. How many bags did she fill?

Arlene put _____ oranges in bags.
She put _____ oranges in each bag.
Arlene filled _____ bags with oranges.

3.

4. Marcos read 35 pages of science in 5 days. He read the same number of pages each day. How many pages did he read each day?

Marcos read _____ pages each day.

4.

Fraction Bars

This page was left intentionally
blank for cutting activity on
previous page.

The Parts Equal the Whole

The one long Fraction Bar on page 165 is a whole. Each bar thereafter is broken up into equal parts.

Directions: Name what part of the whole each bar is. Write its fraction on it.

Colour the whole bar yellow, the halves blue, the thirds green, the fourths red, and the sixths orange. Then, cut the bars apart carefully on the lines. Store the pieces in an envelope.

Show relationships between the bar, such as the number of fourths in a whole or the number of sixths in a third, etc.

Use the fraction bars to answer the following questions:

1. How many sixths are in a whole? _____

2. Name four fractions that equal $\frac{1}{2}$. _____

3. What fractions equal $\frac{1}{3}$? _____

4. How many fourths are in $\frac{1}{2}$? _____

    How many sixths? _____

    How many eighths? _____

    How many tenths? _____

5. Which is larger, $\frac{3}{4}$ or $\frac{4}{6}$? _____

6. Which is larger, $\frac{1}{3}$ or $\frac{1}{2}$? _____

7. Which is smaller, $\frac{2}{3}$ or $\frac{4}{4}$? _____

8. Which is smaller, $\frac{1}{2}$ or $\frac{3}{4}$? _____

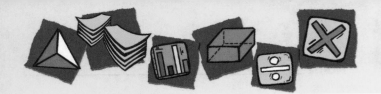

Doing Decimals

Just as a fraction stands for part of a whole number, a **decimal** also shows part of a whole number. And with decimals, the number is always broken into ten or a power of ten (hundred, thousand, etc.) parts. These place values are named tenths, hundredths, thousandths, etc.

A **decimal point** is a dot placed between the ones place and the tenths place.

0.2 is read as "two tenths."

 0.4 is four tenths.

Directions: Write the answer as a decimal for the shaded parts.

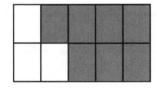   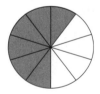   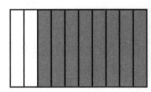

_____   _____   _____

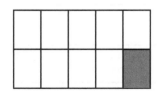   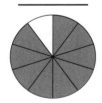   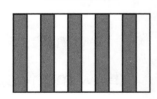

_____   _____   _____

Directions: Colour the parts that match the decimal numbers.

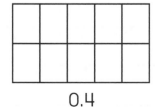   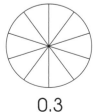   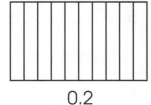

0.4   0.3   0.2

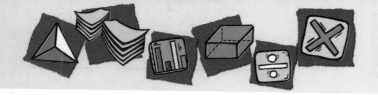

Decimals

A decimal is a number with one or more numbers to the right of a decimal point. A decimal point is a dot placed between the ones place and the tens place of a number, such as 2.5.

Example:

$\frac{3}{10}$ can be written as .3.   They are both read as three-tenths.

Directions: Write the answer as a decimal for the shaded parts.

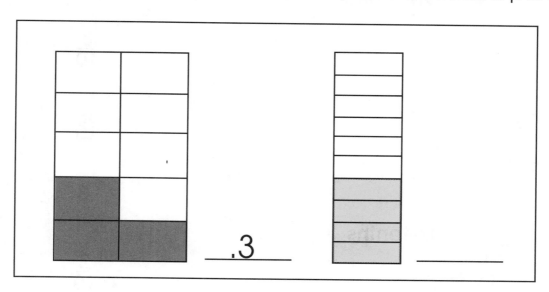

.3 _____   _____

Directions: Colour parts of each object to match the decimals given.

.7   .6   .5

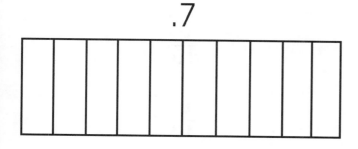      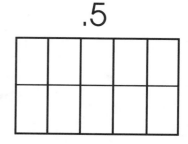

Decimals

A decimal is a number with one or more numbers to the right of a decimal point, such as 6.5 or 2.25. **Equivalent** means numbers that are equal.

Directions: Draw a line between the equivalent numbers.

.8

five-tenths

$\dfrac{5}{10}$

$\dfrac{8}{10}$

.7

$\dfrac{6}{10}$

.4

.3

six-tenths

$\dfrac{2}{10}$

three-tenths

$\dfrac{7}{10}$

.2

$\dfrac{9}{10}$

nine-tenths

$\dfrac{4}{10}$

Decimals Greater Than 1

Directions: Write the decimal for the part that is shaded.

Example: $2\frac{4}{10}$

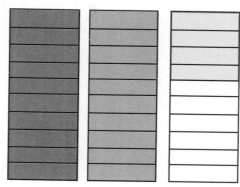

Write: 2.4   Read: two and four-tenths

$1\frac{2}{10}$ = ____

$3\frac{6}{10}$ = ____

$2\frac{3}{10}$ = ____

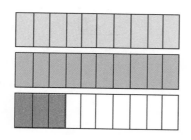

$2\frac{7}{10}$ = ____

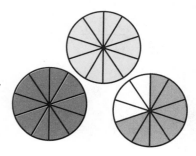

Directions: Write each number as a decimal.

four and two-tenths = ____   seven and one-tenth = ____

$3\frac{4}{10}$ = ____ $6\frac{9}{10}$ = ____ $8\frac{3}{10}$ = ____ $7\frac{5}{10}$ = ____

Decimals: Addition and Subtraction

Decimals are added and subtracted in the same way as other numbers. Simply carry down the decimal point to your answer.

Directions: Add or subtract.

Examples:

$$\begin{array}{r} \overset{1}{1}.3 \\ + 2.8 \\ \hline 4.1 \end{array}$$

$$\begin{array}{r} 4.5 \\ - 2.2 \\ \hline 2.3 \end{array}$$

$$\begin{array}{r} 1.3 \\ + 2.2 \\ \hline \end{array}$$

$$\begin{array}{r} 4.6 \\ - 3.4 \\ \hline \end{array}$$

$$\begin{array}{r} 5.1 \\ + 8.8 \\ \hline \end{array}$$

$$\begin{array}{r} 6.7 \\ - 4.3 \\ \hline \end{array}$$

$$\begin{array}{r} 7.9 \\ - 3.7 \\ \hline \end{array}$$

$$\begin{array}{r} 6.4 \\ + 8.7 \\ \hline \end{array}$$

$$\begin{array}{r} 11.4 \\ - 9.5 \\ \hline \end{array}$$

$$\begin{array}{r} 0.5 \\ + 3.6 \\ \hline \end{array}$$

9.3 + 1.2 = ____   2.5 – 0.7 = ____   1.2 + 5.0 = ____

Bob jogs around the school every day. The distance for one time around is 0.7 of a kilometre. If he jogs around the school two times, how many kilometres does he jog each day? ____

Decimal Divisions

Decimals are often used with whole numbers.

Examples: 2.8

3.5

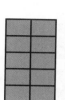 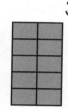 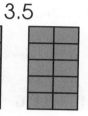 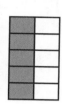

Directions: Write the decimal for each picture.

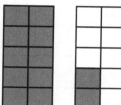   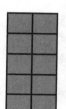 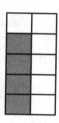 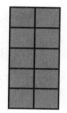

_____   _____   _____

Directions: Shade in the picture to show the decimal number.

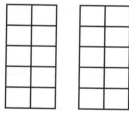   

1.9   3.5   0.4   4.1

When reading decimals with whole numbers, say "point" or "and" for the decimal point.

Directions: Write the word names for each decimal from above.

1.9 _____   0.4 _____

3.5 _____   4.1 _____

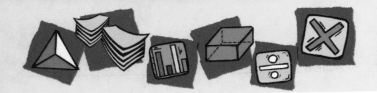

Name _____

How Hot Are You?

Directions: Write the number for each word name. Cross off the number in the cloud. The number that is left is your body temperature. Hint: Remember to add a zero to hold any place value not given.

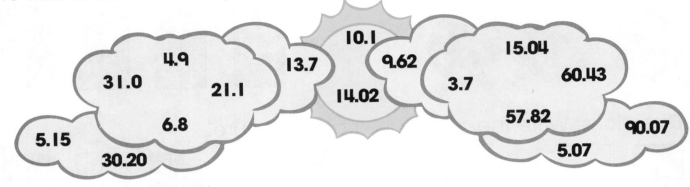

10.1
13.7   9.62
14.02
15.04
60.43
3.7
57.82   90.07
31.0   4.9   21.1
6.8
5.15   5.07
30.20

1. six and eight tenths _____
2. four and nine tenths _____
3. thirteen and seven tenths _____
4. twenty-one and one tenth _____
5. five and fifteen hundredths _____
6. nine and sixty-two hundredths _____
7. fifteen and four hundredths _____
8. fifty-seven and eighty-two hundredths _____
9. three and seven tenths _____
10. sixty and forty-three hundredths _____
11. ninety and seven hundredths _____
12. fourteen and two hundredths _____
13. five and seven hundredths _____
14. ten and one tenth _____
15. thirty and twenty hundredths _____

Your body temperature is: _____

Get the Point

When you add or subtract decimals, remember to include the decimal point.

Add.
```
  3.6
+ 3.3
-----
  6.9
```

Subtract.
```
  6.8
- 2.6
-----
  4.2
```

Directions: Solve these problems.

```
  4.2          6.4          3.1          4.7          4.9          4.2 7
+ 5.2        + 1.4        + 7.8        + 3.2        + 2.0        + 5.5 2
```

```
  5.9          6.7          7.8          5.8          3.9          4.8 6
- 3.2        - 5.6        - 2.5        - 3.3        - 1.5        - 1.7 6
```

```
  0.2 3        0.4 3        0.2 6        0.6 4        0.6 8        6.7 3
+ 0.2 5      + 0.1 6      + 0.4 2      + 0.1 5      + 0.3 1      + 1.1 5
```

```
  0.8 7        0.9 8        0.7 9        0.8 7        0.8 3        5.8 6
- 0.4 2      - 0.3 5      - 0.1 5      - 0.6 7      - 0.1 2      - 3.8 3
```

```
  3.1 3        4.7 2        6.8 7        4.9 8        5.9 7        6.9 8
+ 2.2 6      + 1.1 5      + 2.1 1      - 2.3 2      - 2.5 4      - 1.4 5
```

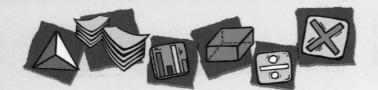

Name _____

Geometry

Geometry is the branch of mathematics that has to do with points, lines, and shapes.

   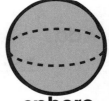

cube   **rectangular prism**   **cone**   **cylinder**   **sphere**

Directions: Use the code to colour the picture.

Colour:
cubes — **blue**
rectangular prisms — **red**
cones — **green**
cylinders — **yellow**
spheres — **orange**

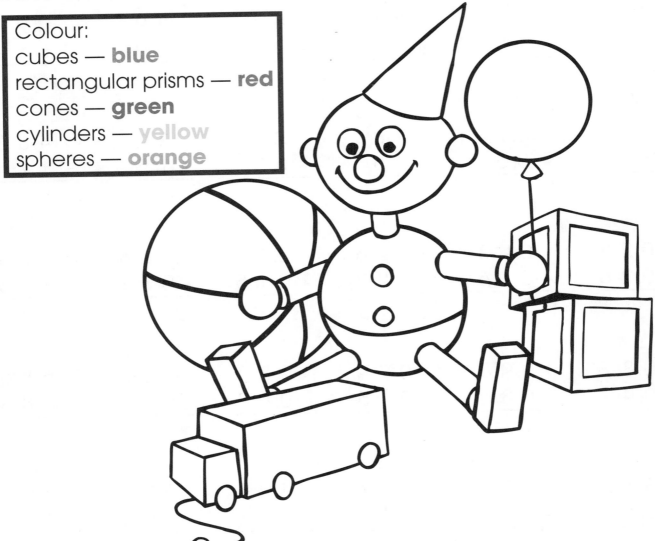

Geometric Colouring

Directions: Colour the geometric shapes in the box below.

Name _____

Name _____

Geometry Match-Ups

A **polygon** is a closed shape with straight sides.

Directions: Cut out each polygon on the next page. To make them more durable, glue them onto cardboard or oaktag. Use the shapes to fill out the table below. (Keep the shapes for other activities as well.)

Game: Play this game with a partner. Put the shapes in a bag or cover them with a sheet of paper. Player One pulls out a shape and tells how many sides and angles it has. Without showing the shape, he/she puts the polygon back. Player Two should name the shape. Then, Player Two puts his/her hand in the bag and, without looking, tries to find the polygon from the description. Then, switch roles. Continue the game until all the polygons have been identified.

When you finish playing, complete the chart below.

Drawing of the shape (or polygon)	Shape name	Number of sides	Number of angles (or corners)
	triangle		
	square		
	pentagon		
	rectangle		
	hexagon		

Geometry

Complete Math Grade 3

Shapes

hexagon

pentagon

square

triangle

rectangle

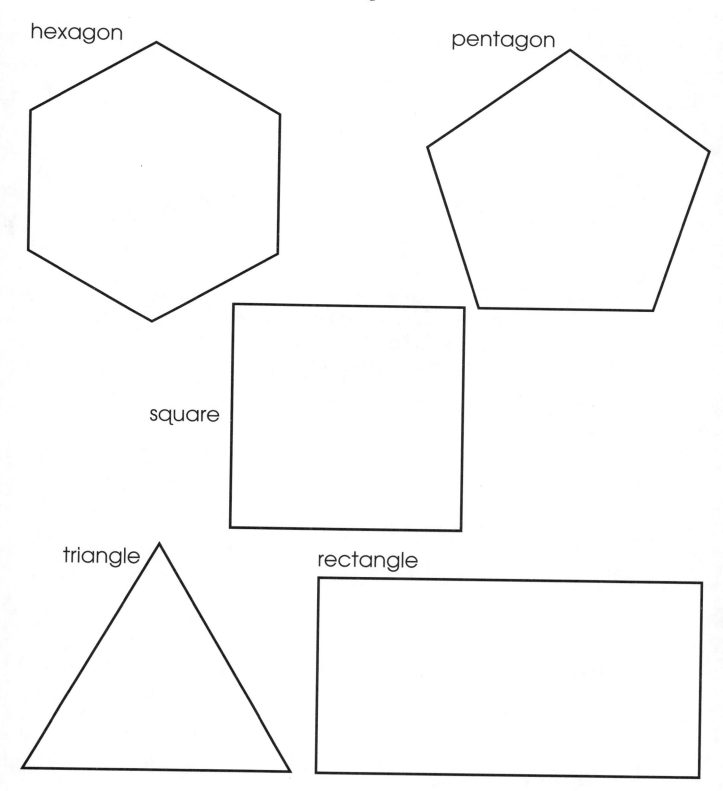

This page was left intentionally blank for cutting activity on previous page.

Geometry: Lines, Segments, Rays, Angles

Geometry is the branch of mathematics that has to do with points, lines, and shapes.

A **line** goes on and on in both directions. It has no end points.

 Line CD

A **segment** is part of a line. It has two end points.

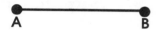 Segment AB

A **ray** has a line segment with only one end point. It goes on and on in the other direction.

 Ray EF

An **angle** has two rays with the same end point.

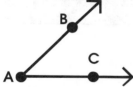 Angle BAC

Directions: Write the name for each figure.

 <u> line </u>

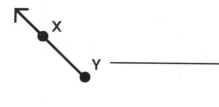 _____

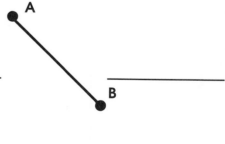 _____

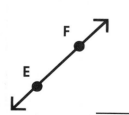 _____

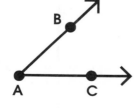 _____

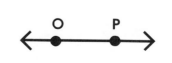 _____

Name _____

Look At the World From a Different Angle

Lines come together in many different ways. The point where two lines meet is called an **angle.** You may have to look at the things around you in a different way to find these angles.

Use the table below to record your observations from around the house. Look for objects that illustrate each category on the chart. Draw a sketch of each object and label it. Find as many objects for each category as possible.

acute

perpendicular

Directions: Look around the house and find one object that illustrates all five geometric categories. Sketch the object and label the various types of angles, lines, or shapes that it has.

∟ right	< acute	⌐ obtuse	— straight	+ perpendicular

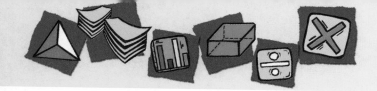

Geometry Game

Directions: 1. Cut out the cards at the bottom of the page. Put them in a pile.

2. Cut out the game boards on the next page.

3. Take turns drawing cards.

4. If you have the figure that the card describes on your game board, cover it.

5. The first one to get three in a row, wins.

cube	point	angle
cylinder	rectangular prism	line
square	cone	circle
sphere	triangle	segment
rectangle	tangram	ray

This page was left intentionally
blank for cutting activity on
previous page.

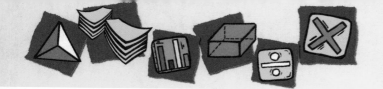

Geometry Game Boards

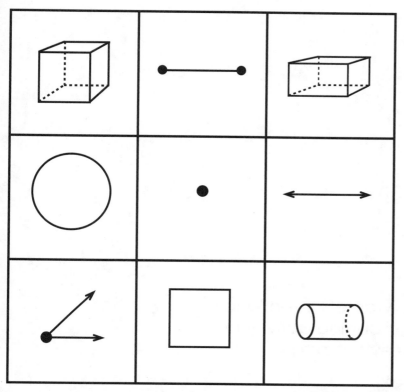

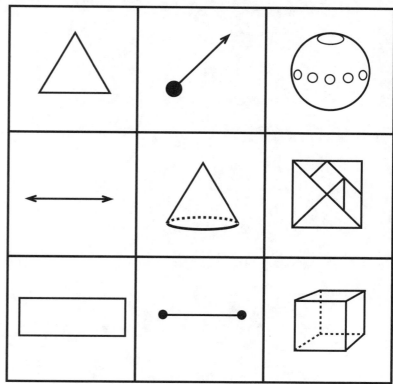

This page was left intentionally
blank for cutting activity on
previous page.

Geometry: Perimeter

The **perimeter** is the distance around an object. Find the perimeter by adding the lengths of all the sides.

Directions: Find the perimeter for each object (m = metre).

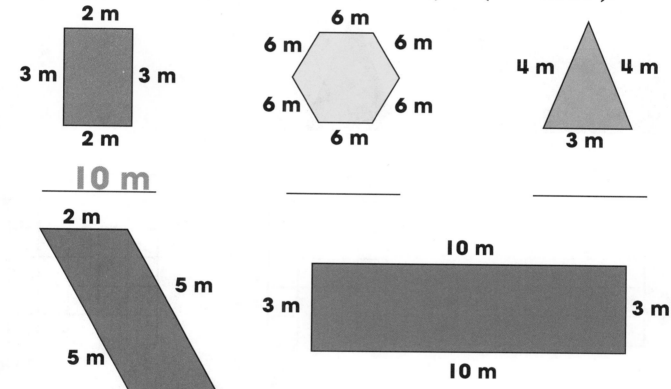

2 m
3 m   **3 m**
2 m

6 m
6 m   **6 m**
6 m   **6 m**
6 m

4 m   **4 m**
3 m

10 m
_____

_____

_____

2 m
5 m
5 m
2 m

10 m
3 m   **3 m**
10 m

_____

_____

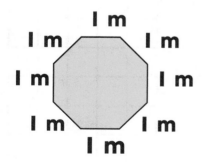

1 m
1 m   **1 m**
1 m   **1 m**
1 m   **1 m**
1 m

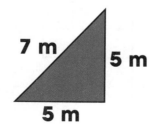

7 m   **5 m**
5 m

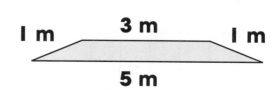

3 m
1 m   **1 m**
5 m

_____

_____

_____

Perimeter Problems

The perimeter is the distance around the outside of a shape. Find the perimeters for the figures below by adding the lengths of all the sides.

Examples:

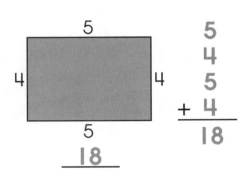

5
4
5
+ 4
18

18

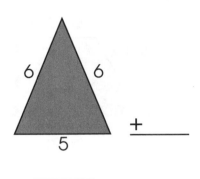

+ _____

_____

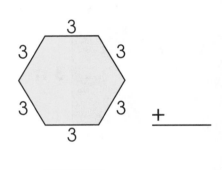

+ _____

_____

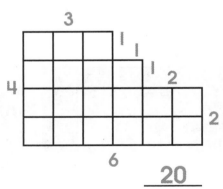

20

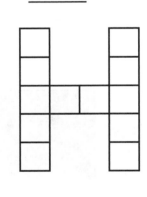

_____

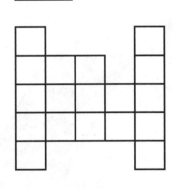

_____

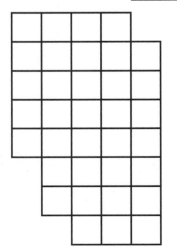

_____

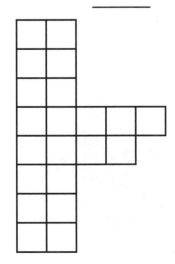

_____

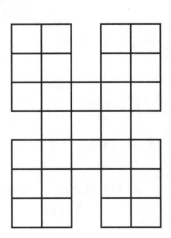

_____

Map Skills: Scale

A **map scale** shows how far one place is from another. This map scale shows that 1 centimetre on this page equals 1 kilometre at the real location.

Directions: Use a ruler and the map scale to find out how far it is from Ann's house to other places. Round to the nearest centimetre.

Map Scale:
1 cm = 1 km

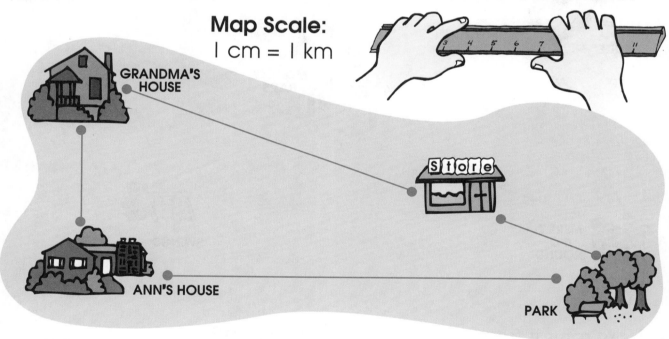

1. How far is it from Ann's house to the park? _____

2. How far is it from Ann's house to Grandma's house? _____

3. How far is it from Grandma's house to the store? _____

4. How far did Ann go when she went from her house to Grandma's and then to the store? _____

Name _____

Map Skills: Scale

Directions: Use a ruler and the map scale to measure the map and answer the questions. Round to the nearest metre.

Map Scale
1 cm = 10 m

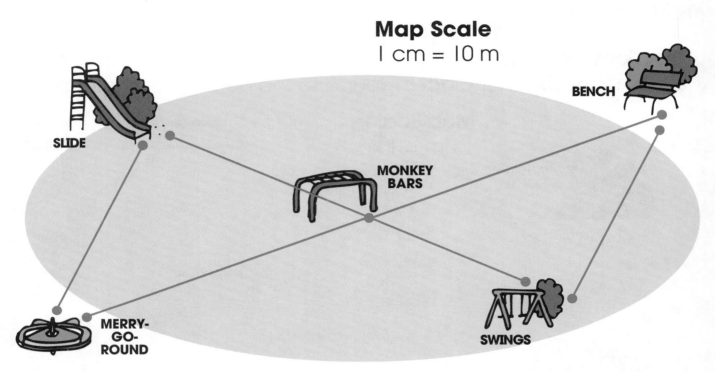

1. How far is it from the bench to the swings? _____

2. How far is it from the bench to the monkey bars? _____

3. How far is it from the monkey bars to the merry-go-round? _____

4. How far is it from the bench to the merry-go-round? _____

5. How far is it from the merry-go-round to the slide? _____

6. How far is it from the slide to the swings? _____

Map Skills and Coordinates   190   Complete Math Grade 3

Coordinates

Directions: Locate the points on the grid and colour in each box.

What animal did you form? _____

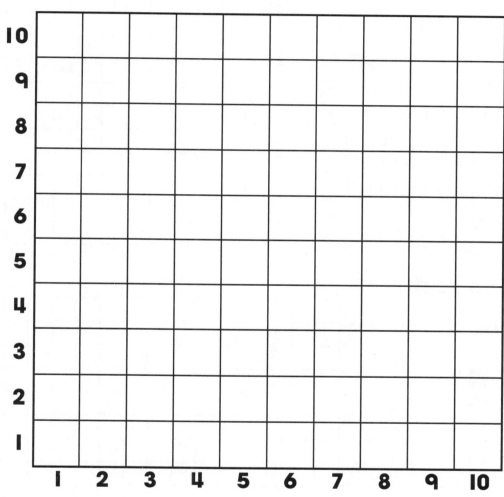

(across, up)

(4, 7)	(4, 1)	(7, 1)	(3, 5)	(2, 8)	(8, 6)	(4, 8)	(3, 7)
(5, 4)	(6, 5)	(5, 5)	(6, 6)	(7, 3)	(8, 5)	(10, 5)	(4, 3)
(7, 6)	(4, 6)	(1, 8)	(6, 4)	(7, 2)	(4, 5)	(9, 6)	(4, 9)
(3, 6)	(7, 5)	(5, 6)	(4, 2)	(4, 4)	(7, 4)	(2, 7)	(3, 8)

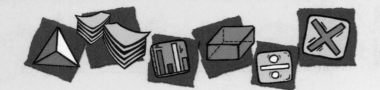

Gliding Graphics

Directions: Draw the lines as directed from point to point for each graph.

Draw a line from:

- F, 7 to D, 1
- D, 1 to I, 6
- I, 6 to N, 8
- N, 8 to M, 3
- M, 3 to F, 1
- F, 1 to G, 4
- G, 4 to E, 4
- E, 4 to B, 1
- B, 1 to A, 8
- A, 8 to D, 11
- D, 11 to F, 9
- F, 9 to F, 7
- F, 7 to I, 9
- I, 9 to I, 6
- I, 6 to F, 7

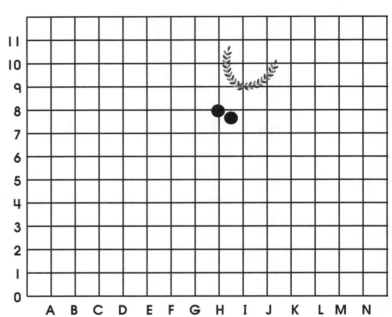

Draw a line from:

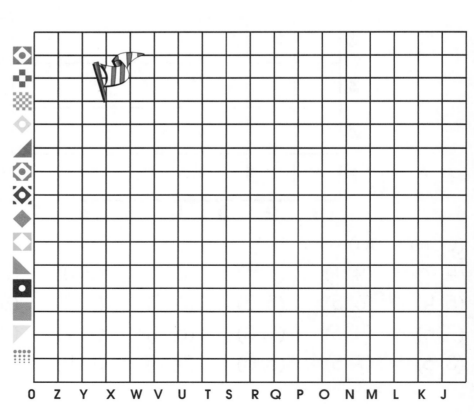

- J, ◉ to N, ◣
- N, ◣ to U, ◣
- U, ◣ to Z, ■
- Z, ■ to X, ✛
- X, ✛ to U, ◣
- U, ◣ to S, ◈
- S, ◈ to N, ◣
- N, ◣ to N, ◉
- N, ◉ to J, ◉
- J, ◉ to L, ▦
- L, ▦ to Y, ▦
- Y, ▦ to Z, ■
- Z, ■ to L, ■
- L, ■ to J, ◉

Graphs

A **graph** is a drawing that shows information about numbers.

Directions: Colour the picture. Then tell how many there are of each object by completing the graph.

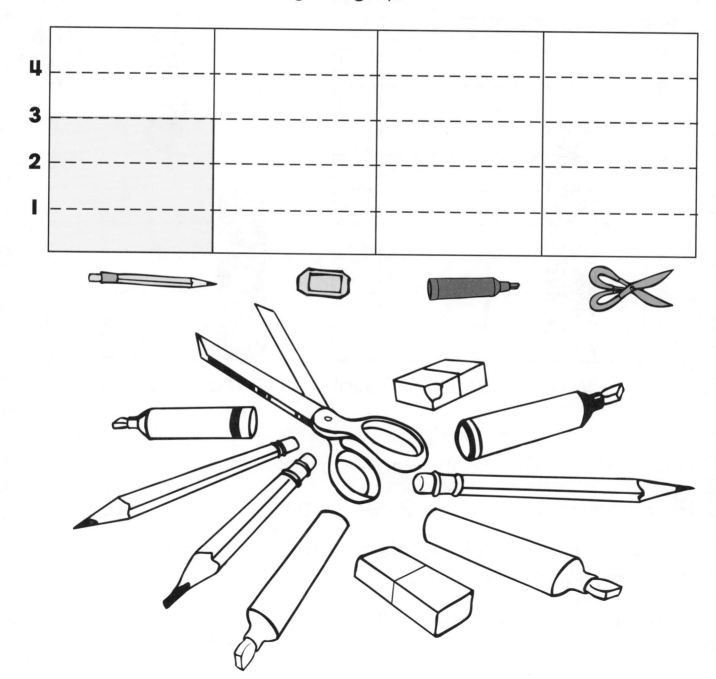

Graphs

Directions: Answer the questions about the graph.

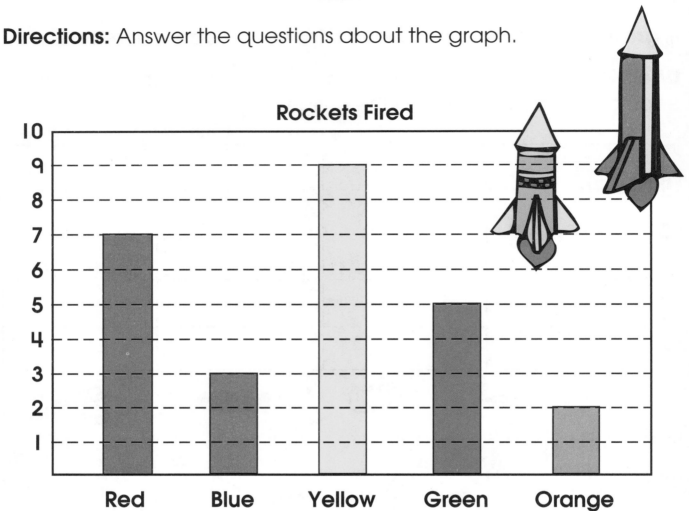

Rockets Fired

How many rockets did the Red Club fire? _____

How many rockets did the Green Club fire? _____

The Yellow Club fired 9 rockets. How many more rockets
did it fire than the Blue Club? _____

How many rockets were fired in all? _____

Name _____

Flower Graph

A **pictograph** is a graph using pictures to give information. Cut out the flowers and glue them onto the pictograph. Each picture stands for 2 flowers.

Daisies					
Sunflowers					
Tulips					
Roses					

How many tulips?_____
        sunflowers?_____
        roses?_____
        daisies?_____
How many more tulips than roses?_____
How many more daisies than sunflowers?____
How many sunflowers and tulips? _____
How many roses and daisies?_____

This page was left intentionally
blank for cutting activity on
previous page.

Frog Bubbles

Directions: Complete the line graph to show how many bubbles each frog blew.

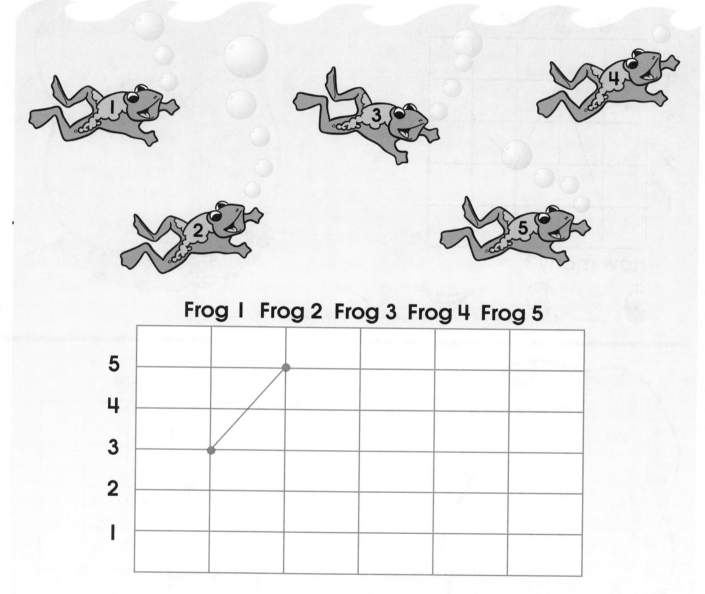

How many bubbles? Frog 1:____ 2:____ 3:____ 4:____ 5:____

Which frog blew the most bubbles?_____

Which frog blew the fewest?_____

Potato Face

Directions: Read the line graphs to draw the potato faces.

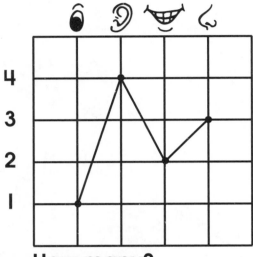

How many?

 s ___  s ___  s ___ 〜 s ___

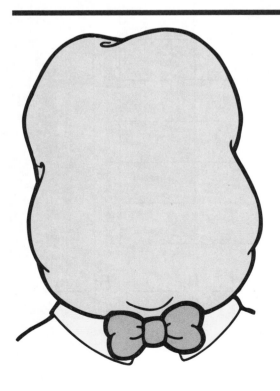

How many?

◉ s ___ ⟆ s ___ 😁 s ___ 〜 s ___

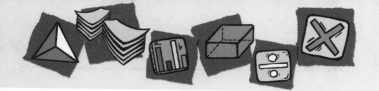

Vote for Me!

Middletown School had an election to choose the new members of the Student Council. Grace, Bernie, Laurie, Sherry, and Sam all ran for the office of president. On the chart below are the five students' names with the number of the votes each received.

Grace	21	36	39
Bernie	47	32	26
Laurie	25	44	38
Sherry	34	37	40
Sam	48	33	29

Directions: Use the information and the clues below to see who became president and how many votes he or she received. After each clue, cross out the numbers that do not apply.

- The winning number of votes was an even number.
- The winning number of votes was between 30 and 40.
- The two digits added together are greater than 10.

_____ became the president of the Student

Council with _____ votes.

Who would have become president if the winning number was **odd** and the other clues remained the same?

_____

Name _____

School Statistics

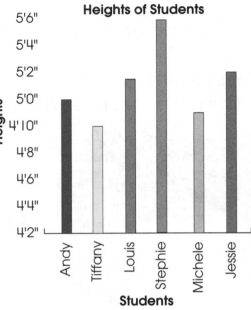

Heights of Students

Directions: Read each graph and follow the directions.

List the names of the students from the shortest to the tallest.

1. _____   4. _____

2. _____   5. _____

3. _____   6. _____

Lunches Bought

List how many lunches the students bought each day, from the greatest amount to the least.

1. _____   4. _____

2. _____   5. _____

3. _____

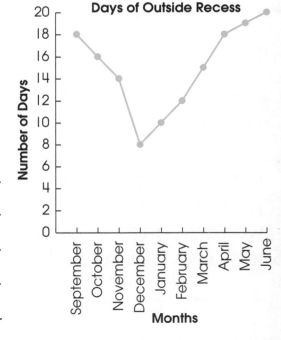

Days of Outside Recess

List the months in the order of the most number of outside recesses to the least number.

1. _____   6. _____

2. _____   7. _____

3. _____   8. _____

4. _____   9. _____

5. _____   10. _____

Candy Sales

Every year the students at Lincoln Elementary sell candy as a fund-raising project. These are the results of the sales for this year.

Grade Level	Number of Sales
Kindergarten	40
First	70
Second	50
Third	80
Fourth	85
Fifth	75

Directions: Colour the bar graph to show the number of sales made at each grade level.

Number of Sales

90						
85						
80						
75						
70						
65						
60						
55						
50						
45						
40						
35						
30						
25						
20						
15						
10						
5						
	K	1	2	3	4	5

Grade Level

Directions: Write the grade levels in order starting with the one that sold the most.

1. _____
2. _____
3. _____

4. _____
5. _____
6. _____

Hot Lunch Favourites

The cooks in the cafeteria asked each third- and fourth-grade class to rate the hot lunches. They wanted to know which food the children liked the best.

The table shows how the students rated the lunches.
Key: Each 🧍 equals 2 students.

Food	Number of students who liked it best
hamburgers	🧍 🧍 🧍 🧍 🧍 🧍
hot dogs	🧍 🧍 🧍 🧍 🧍 🧍 🧍
tacos	🧍 🧍 🧍 🧍 🧍
chili	
soup and sandwiches	🧍
spaghetti	🧍 🧍
fried chicken	🧍 🧍 🧍 🧍
fish sticks	🧍 🧍 🧍

Directions: Colour the bar graph to show the information on the table. Remember that each 🧍 equals 2 people. The first one is done for you.

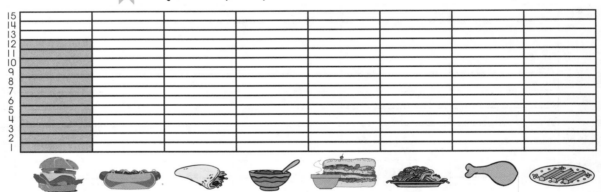

Number of Students

15 14 13 12 11 10 9 8 7 6 5 4 3 2 1

Directions: Write the food in order starting with the one that students liked most.

1. _____
2. _____
3. _____
4. _____

5. _____
6. _____
7. _____
8. _____

Name _____

Measurement: Ounce and Pound

Ounces and **pounds** are measurements of weight in the standard measurement system. The ounce is used to measure the weight of very light objects. The pound is used to measure the weight of heavier objects. 16 ounces = 1 pound.

Example:

8 ounces   15 pounds

Directions: Decide if you would use ounces or pounds to measure the weight of each object. Circle your answer.

ounce   pound   ounce   pound

ounce   pound   ounce   pound

a chair: ounce   pound   **a table:**   ounce   pound

a shoe: ounce   pound   **a shirt:**   ounce   pound

Measurement: Centimetre

A **centimetre** is a unit of length in the metric system.

Directions: Use a centimetre ruler to measure each object to the nearest half of a centimetre. Write **cm** to stand for centimetre.

Example:

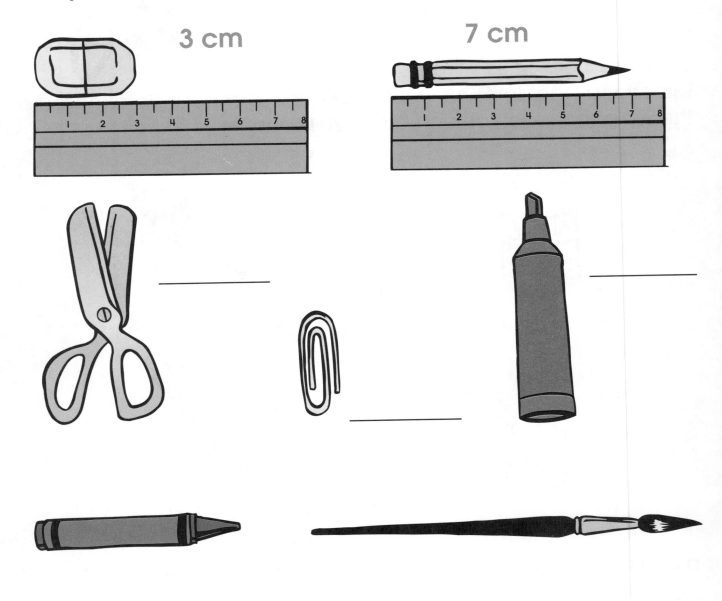

3 cm

7 cm

Measurement: Inches

An **inch** is a unit of length in the standard measurement system.

Directions: Use a ruler to measure each object to the nearest $\frac{1}{4}$ inch. Write **in.** to stand for inch.

Example:

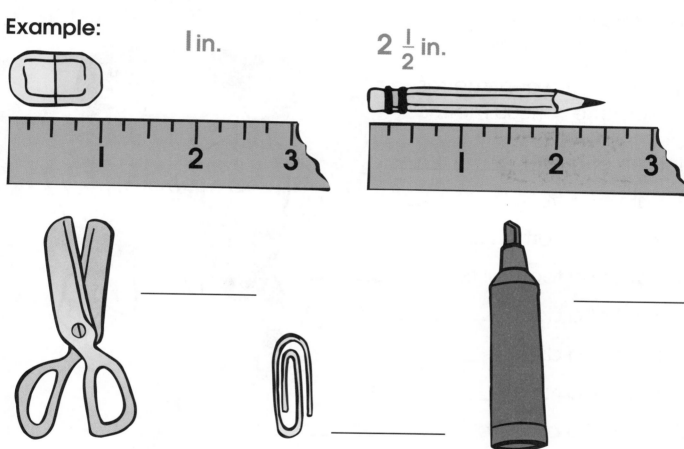

1 in.

$2\frac{1}{2}$ in.

_____

_____

_____

_____   _____

Measurement: Metre and Kilometre

Metres and **kilometres** are units of length in the metric system. A metre is equal to 39.37 inches. A kilometre is equal to about $\frac{5}{8}$ of a mile.

Directions: Decide whether you would use metre or kilometres to measure each object.

1 metre = 100 centimetres
1 kilometre = 1,000 metres

length of a river __**kilometre**__

height of a tree _____

width of a room _____

length of a football field _____

height of a door _____

length of a dress _____

length of a race _____

height of a basketball pole _____

width of a window _____

distance a plane travels _____

Directions: Solve the problem.

Tara races Tom in the 100-metre dash. Tara finishes 10 metres in front of Tom. How many centimetres did Tara finish in front of Tom?

_____

Measurement: Foot, Yard, Mile

Directions: Decide whether you would use foot, yard, or mile to measure each object.

1 foot = 12 inches
1 yard = 36 inches or 3 feet
1 mile = 1,760 yards

length of a river ___miles___

height of a tree _____

width of a room _____

length of a football field _____

height of a door _____

length of a dress _____

length of a race _____

height of a basketball hoop _____

width of a window _____

distance a plane travels _____

Directions: Solve the problem.

Tara races Tom in the 100-yard dash. Tara finishes
10 yards in front of Tom. How many feet did Tara finish
in front of Tom?

_____

How Does Your Home Measure Up?

Directions: Take a "measuring journey" through your house. To begin, brainstorm a list of various destinations around your house. Then, list five objects found in each room and write them on the left-hand side of a sheet of paper.

Example:
Kitchen
stove
teaspoon
cookbook
can opener
box of cereal

Bathroom
toothbrush
hairbrush
soap
mirror
bandage

Bedroom
books
desk/table
pillow
clock
hanger

Read through the objects on the list and write estimations of their measurements. Decide on a unit of measurement to use and whether to measure length, width, or both. Then, measure the objects. (A tape measure or string may be used to measure the size or circumference of any oddly shaped objects.) Finally, compare your estimations with the actual measurements.

Object	Estimate	Actual

Growing String Beans

Bar Graph

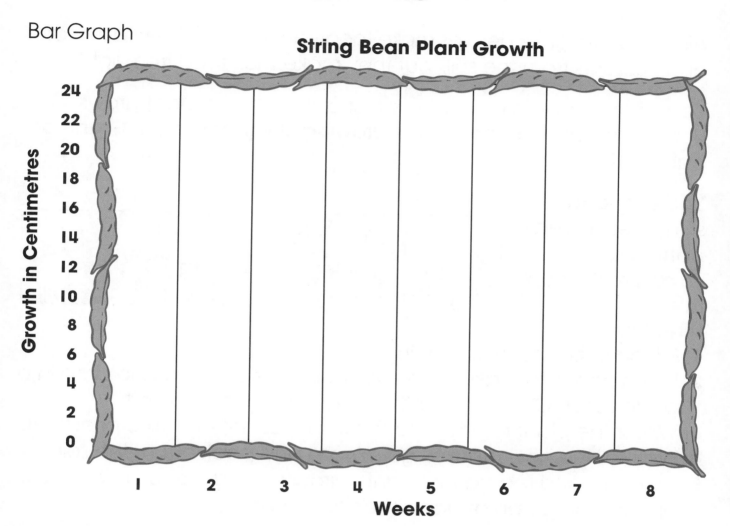

String Bean Plant Growth

Growth in Centimetres

24
22
20
18
16
14
12
10
8
6
4
2
0

1   2   3   4   5   6   7   8

Weeks

Other Ideas:

1. Try growing a few other interesting plants like:
   Carrot tops cut off and placed in a pie tin filled with water.
   Plain popcorn seeds from the store (not oiled or treated). Plant
   them in the ground.

2. Go to your local plant nursery or hardware store and look at the
   selection of plant seeds available.

3. Plant a young tree in your yard and measure its growth each year.

Complete Math Grade 3   209   Measurement

Growing String Beans

All plants with green leaves make food from the sun. They take water and nutrients from the soil, but they make their food from light.

You will measure in inches how fast a string bean plant grows. Record this information on the **Growing String Beans Bar Graph** on page 209.

You will need:
string bean seeds
potting soil
16 oz. plastic cup
ruler

Directions:
1. Fill the cup $\frac{3}{4}$ full with potting soil.
2. Use a pencil to make a hole 2.5 centimetres deep and drop in a bean seed. Gently cover the seed and lightly water it.
3. Water the plant regularly so the soil does not become dried out.
4. Wait for the new plant to germinate and peek out of the soil.
5. Measure and record the plant's growth using the ruler. Record it on the bar graph at each specified interval.
6. When it has grown, enjoy the delicious string beans as a treat!

How To Measure: Place the ruler next to the plant, resting it on the soil. Measure from the top of the plant down to the soil.

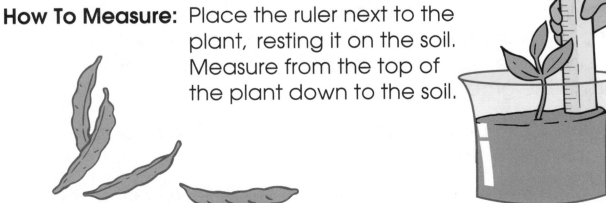

Hand–Foot–Ruler

Directions:

1. Measure the span of your hand by stretching your thumb and little finger as far apart as possible. Lay your hand on a ruler to find out this length (span). Record the centimetres of the span on the record sheet below.

2. Measure the length of your pace by taking one step forward and holding it. Have someone put the edge of a yardstick next to the heel of your back foot and measure to the back of the heel on your forward foot. Record the pace distance in centimetres on the record sheet.

3. Using a ruler or yardstick, measure the distances listed on the record sheet. Record all findings in centimetres.

Hand Span _____   Pace _____

Length of Table:
Hand Span _____   Ruler _____

Length of Room:
Pace _____   Yardstick _____

Height of Bookcase:
Hand Span _____   Ruler _____

Width of Kitchen:
Pace _____   Yardstick _____

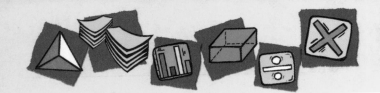

A Measurement of Our Own

Create your own new system of measurement. Brainstorm ideas on what and how you should base the new unit. For example, you may use the length of your finger, the length of a juice box, the length of your backpack, etc. as a base.

Next, create a ruler using your new unit of measurement. A metre is made of centimetres and a foot is made of inches. Break your standard unit into smaller units and add these to the ruler. When the ruler is complete, fill out the form below.

Directions: Answer the questions below.

1. What is the name of your unit of measurement?_____

2. What would your unit of measurement be best suited for measuring— long distances or microscopic organisms?_____

   Why?_____

3. Would you rather use your new unit of measurement versus the metric unit? _____ Why or why not?_____

4. Measure an object using your new ruler.
   What did it measure? _____
   If you were to tell someone that the object you measured was that long, do you think that person would be able to picture its length?_____ Why or why not? _____

5. Why do you think everyone in the entire country uses the exact same unit of measurement?

   _____

212

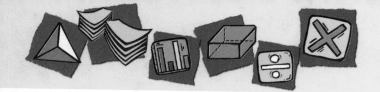

Name _____

Make a Tape Measure

Directions:

1. Cut out the rectangle pattern below on the solid lines.

2. Cut the rectangle into six strips by cutting on the dotted lines.   Put a little glue on the shaded end of one strip and glue it to the end of another strip. Press the strips together. Repeat this step until all the strips are joined to make one long strip.

4. Cut off the one leftover shaded end. You now have a tape measure.

5. Lay your tape measure out flat. Starting from the left side, mark off centimetres and $\frac{1}{2}$ centimetres. Number the centimetres.

6. Reinforce your tape measure by putting clear tape on the back of it.

This page was left intentionally blank for cutting activity on previous page.

Roman Numerals

Another way to write numbers is to use Roman numerals.

I	1	VII	7
II	2	VIII	8
III	3	IX	9
IV	4	X	10
V	5	XI	11
VI	6	XII	12

Directions: Fill in the Roman numerals on the watch.

What time is it on the watch?

_____ o'clock

Roman Numerals

I	1	VII	7
II	2	VIII	8
III	3	IX	9
IV	4	X	10
V	5	XI	11
VI	6	XII	12

Directions: Write the number.

V _____   VII _____

X _____   IX _____

II _____   XII _____

Directions: Write the Roman numeral.

4 _____   5 _____

10 _____   8 _____

6 _____   3 _____

Roman Numerals

I means I.   V means 5.   X means 10.

II   means I + I or 2.   III   means I + I + I or 3.
VI   means 5 + I or 6.   IV   means 5 – I or 4.
XXV   means 10 + 10 + 5 or 25   IX   means 10 – I or 9.

VII   means 5 + I + ____ or ____.   XXI   means 10 + ____ + I or ____.

XIV   means ____ + 4 or ____.   XIX   means ____ + 9 or ____.

Directions: Complete the following as shown.

1.   XXIV = ____   XX = ____   XXII = ____   VIII = ____

2.   IV = ____   XXVI = ____   XVII = ____   XXXI = ____

3.   XXXVI = ____   XXIX = ____   XI = ____   XXXIII = ____

4.   XVIII = ____   IX = ____   XXXIV = ____   XIII = ____

5.   V = ____   XXV = ____   VI = ____   XXI = ____

6.   XXXVIII = ____   XXXV = ____   XXVII = ____   XVI = ____

7.   XXIII = ____   XXXVII = ____   XIV = ____   XXXII = ____

Directions: Write a Roman numeral for each of the following.

8.   3 = _____   7 = _____   15 = _____

9.   19 = _____   22 = _____   28 = _____

10.   30 = _____   20 = _____   39 = _____

Time: Hour, Half-Hour, Quarter-Hour, 5 Min. Intervals

Directions: Write the time shown on each clock.

Example:

7:15

7:00

_____

_____

_____

_____

_____

_____

_____

_____

_____

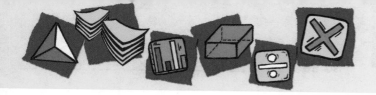

Time: A.M. and P.M.

In telling time, the hours between 12:00 midnight and 12:00 noon are A.M. hours. The hours between 12:00 noon and 12:00 midnight are P.M. hours.

Directions: Draw a line between the times that are the same.

Example:

7:30 in the morning

7:30 A.M.
half-past seven A.M.
seven thirty in the morning

9:00 in the evening

9:00 P.M.
nine o'clock at night

six o'clock in the evening   8:00 A.M.

3:30 A.M.   six o'clock in the morning

4:15 P.M.   6:00 P.M.

eight o'clock in the morning   eleven o'clock in the evening

quarter past five in the evening   three thirty in the morning

11:00 P.M.   four fifteen in the evening

6:00 A.M.   5:15 P.M.

Time: Minutes

A minute is a measurement of time. There are sixty seconds in a minute and sixty minutes in an hour.

Directions: Write the time shown on each clock.

Example:

Each mark is one minute.
The hand is at mark number 6.

Write: 5:06

Read: six minutes after five.

_____

_____

_____

_____

_____

_____

_____

_____

_____

_____

_____

_____

Time on My Hands

Draw the hour and minute hands to show each time below.

Example:

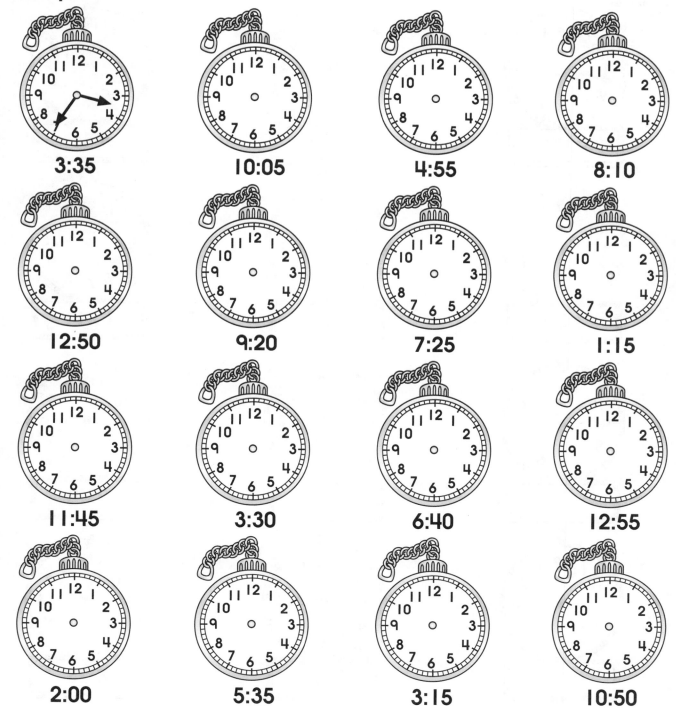

3:35	10:05	4:55	8:10
12:50	9:20	7:25	1:15
11:45	3:30	6:40	12:55
2:00	5:35	3:15	10:50

Name _____

Minute Men

Directions: Draw the hour and minute hands on these clocks.

Example: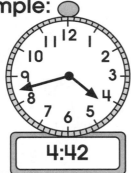

4:42

9:03

6:51

1:24

7:33

10:11

3:58

12:01

2:49

4:17

5:36

8:23

Take Time for These

Directions: Write the time shown on these clocks.

Example:

6:47 _____ _____ _____ _____

_____ _____ _____ _____

_____ _____ _____ _____

Father Time Teasers

Directions: Write the times below.

Example:

25 minutes ago

5:35

10 minutes later

_____

40 minutes ago

_____

35 minutes ago

_____

50 minutes later

_____

15 minutes ago

_____

20 minutes later

_____

45 minutes ago

_____

5 minutes ago

_____

30 minutes later

_____

55 minutes later

_____

25 minutes ago

_____

Time "Tables"

Name _____

Directions: Draw the hands on these clocks.

10 minutes before
12:17

36 minutes after
8:19

8 minutes before
1:05

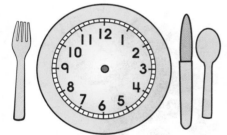

21 minutes after
8:40

16 minutes before
4:30

46 minutes after
10:11

32 minutes before
5:25

11 minutes after
3:16

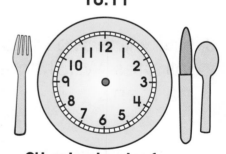

24 minutes before
12:30

17 minutes after
1:31

43 minutes before
2:01

18 minutes after
6:45

Monkeying Around

Directions: Nat can't tell time. He needs your help to solve these problems.

1. Nat is supposed to be at school in 10 minutes. What time should he get there?

_____

2. Nat started breakfast at 7:10 A.M. It took him 15 minutes to eat. Mark the time he finished.

3. Nat will leave school in 5 minutes. What time will it be then?

_____

5. It is now 6:45 P.M. Nat must start his homework in 5 minutes. Mark the starting time on the clock.

4. Nat's family will eat dinner in 15 minutes. When will that be?

_____

6. Nat will go to the park in 15 minutes. It is now 1:25 P.M. Mark the time he will go to the park.

Name _____

Money: Coins and Dollars

dollar = 100¢ or $1.00

 penny =
1¢ or $.01

 nickel =
5¢ or $.05

 quarter =
25¢ or $.25

 dime =
10¢ or $.10

Directions: Write the amount for each group of money shown. Use a dollar sign and decimal point. The first one is done for you.

 **$.07** _____

 _____

 _____

 _____

 _____

 _____

Garage Sale

Directions: Use the fewest number of coins possible to equal the amount shown in each box. Write or draw the coins you would use in each box.

17¢

98¢

24¢

63¢

58¢

35¢

Money

I penny	I nickel	I dime	I quarter	I dollar
I cent	5 cents	10 cents	25 cents	100 cents
I¢ or $0.01	5¢ or $0.05	10¢ or $0.10	25¢ or $0.25	$1.00

25 pennies have a value of ___25___ cents or ___I___ quarter.

5 pennies have a value of _____ cents or _____ nickel.

$2.57 means ___2___ dollars and ___57___ cents.

$3.45 means _____ dollars and _____ cents.

Directions: Complete the following.

1.   5 pennies have a value of _____ cents or _____ nickel.

2.   10 pennies have a value of _____ cents or _____ dime.

3.   20 pennies have a value of _____ cents or _____ dimes.

4.   15 pennies have a value of _____ cents or _____ nickels.

5.   20 pennies have a value of _____ cents or _____ nickels.

Directions: Complete the following as shown.

6. $14.05 means _____ dollars and _____ cents.

7. $12.07 means _____ dollars and _____ cents.

8. $8.14 means _____ dollars and _____ cents.

9. $0.65 means _____ dollars and _____ cents.

10. $10.01 means _____ dollars and _____ cents.

Name _____

Your Answer's Safe With Me

Directions: Find the right "combination" to open each safe. Draw the bills and coins needed to make each amount.

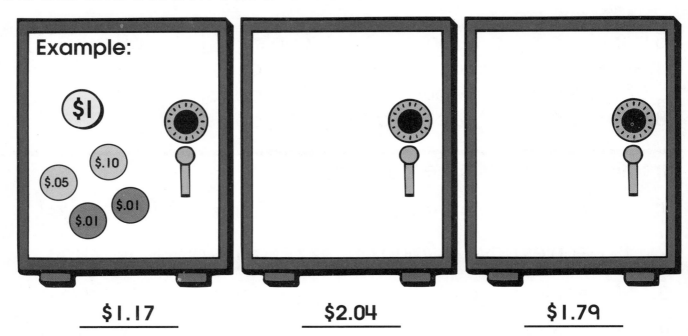

Example:

$1 $.10 $.05 $.01 $.01

____$1.17____   ____$2.04____   ____$1.79____

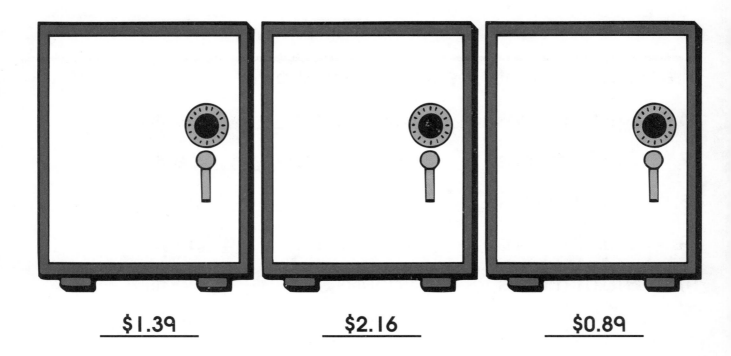

____$1.39____   ____$2.16____   ____$0.89____

Complete Math Grade 3

Easy Street

Directions: What is each house worth? Count the money in each house on Easy Street. Write the amount on the line below it.

Example:

$2.40

_____   _____   _____   _____

_____   _____   _____   _____

A Collection of Coins

Directions: Write the number of coins needed to make the amount shown.

Money	Quarters	Dimes	Nickels	Pennies
76¢				
45¢				
98¢				
40¢				
84¢				
62¢				
31¢				
$1.42				
$1.98				

Monetary Message

Directions: What's the smartest thing to do with your money? To find out, solve the following problems and write the matching letter above the answer.

___ ___ ___ ___   ___ ___ ,
$42.71 $33.94 $50.42 $100.73 $45.70 $2.39

___ ___ ___   ___ ___   ___ ___ ___ ___
$33.94 $26.13 $88.02 $45.70 $2.39 $51.12 $45.70 $11.01 $11.01

___ ___ ___   ___ ___ !
$33.94 $88.02 $88.02 $55.76 $42.79

$$V = \begin{array}{r} \$42.13 \\ +\ \ 8.29 \\ \hline \end{array} \qquad A = \begin{array}{r} \$\ 4.56 \\ +\ 29.38 \\ \hline \end{array} \qquad N = \begin{array}{r} \$\ 4.65 \\ +\ 21.48 \\ \hline \end{array} \qquad S = \begin{array}{r} \$23.46 \\ +\ 19.25 \\ \hline \end{array}$$

$$P = \begin{array}{r} \$\ 9.31 \\ +\ 33.48 \\ \hline \end{array} \qquad L = \begin{array}{r} \$\ 6.73 \\ +\ \ 4.28 \\ \hline \end{array} \qquad E = \begin{array}{r} \$81.49 \\ +\ 19.24 \\ \hline \end{array} \qquad T = \begin{array}{r} \$\ \ .42 \\ 1.94 \\ +\ \ \ .03 \\ \hline \end{array}$$

$$U = \begin{array}{r} \$50.84 \\ +\ \ 4.92 \\ \hline \end{array} \qquad I = \begin{array}{r} \$\ 7.49 \\ +\ 38.21 \\ \hline \end{array}$$

$$D = \begin{array}{r} \$\ 3.04 \\ +\ 84.98 \\ \hline \end{array} \qquad W = \begin{array}{r} \$\ 1.89 \\ +\ 49.23 \\ \hline \end{array}$$

Name _____

Add 'Em Up!

Directions: Write the prices, then add. Regroup, when needed.

$29.32 $0.69 $0.84 $2.41 $34.99 $3.84 $3.84 $8.43 $43.09 $29.32 $3.09 $4.37

1. _____ skateboard
    + _____ hat

2. _____ dictionary
    + _____ radio

3. _____ wallet
    + _____ goldfish

4. _____ hot dog
    + _____ watch

5. _____ dictionary
    + _____ kite

6. _____ in-line skates
    + _____ trumpet

7. _____ hot dog
    + _____ rocket

8. _____ skateboard
    + _____ goldfish

9. _____ hat
    + _____ kite

10. _____ radio
    + _____ trumpet

11. _____ rocket
    + _____ goldfish

12. _____ skateboard
    + _____ in-line skates

Money

Complete Math Grade 3

Making Change

When you do not have the exact change to buy something at a store, the clerk must give you change. The first amount of money is what you give the clerk. The second amount is what the item costs.

Directions: In the box, list the fewest number of coins and bills you will receive in change.

	Amount I Have	Cost of Item	Change
1	$3.75	$3.54	
2	$10.00	$5.63	
3	$7.00	$6.05	
4	$7.25	$6.50	
5	$7.50	$6.13	
6	$0.75	$0.37	
7	$7.00	$6.99	
8	$15.00	$12.75	

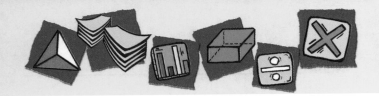

Money: Counting Change

Directions: Subtract the money using decimals to show how much change a person would receive in each of the following.

Example:

Bill had 3 dollars.
He bought a baseball for $2.83.
How much change did he receive?

$3.00
-$2.83
$ .17

Paid 2 dollars.

_____

Paid 1 dollar.

_____

Paid 5 dollars.

_____

Paid 10 dollars.

_____

Paid 4 dollars.

_____

Paid 7 dollars.

_____

Money: Five-Dollar Bill and Ten-Dollar Bill

Directions: Write the amount for each group of money shown. Use a dollar sign and decimal point. The first one is done for you.

Five-dollar bill =
5 one-dollar bills

Ten-dollar bill =
2 five-dollar bills or
10 one-dollar bills

$15.00

_____

_____

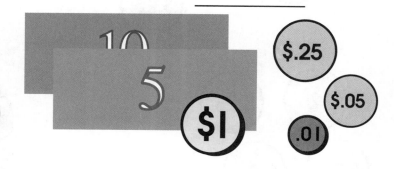

_____

7 one-dollar bills, 2 quarters _____

2 five-dollar bills, 3 one-dollar bills, half-dollar _____

3 ten-dollar bills, 1 five-dollar bill, 3 quarters _____

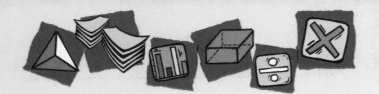

Money: Comparing

Directions: Compare the amount of money in the left column with the price of the object in the right column. Is the amount of money in the left column enough to purchase the object in the right column? Circle yes or no.

Example:

Alice has 2 dollars. She wants to buy a jump rope for $1.75. Does she have enough money?

(**Yes**) No

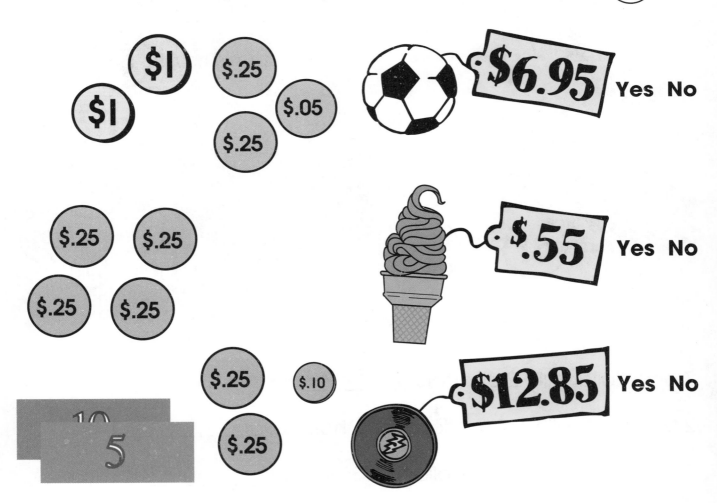

Yes No

Yes No

Yes No

Money

```
          $12.00
$9.05      0.45        45¢      $0.75      $14.08      $13.00
+ 6.98    + 3.16      + 38¢    + 0.38      - 7.25      - 6.05
$16.03    $15.61       83¢      $1.13       $6.83       $6.95
```

Add or subtract as usual.

Put a decimal point (.) and a $ or ¢ in the answer.

Be sure to line up the decimal points.

Directions: Add or subtract.

1.
```
$ 0.36      $3.75      $ 1.36       37¢       $4.35
+ 12.40     + 1.46     + 40.00     + 68¢      + 0.07
```

2.
```
$5.20       $12.64     $3.00        88¢       $24.42
- 3.18      - 5.38     - 0.54      - 76¢      - 1.08
```

3.
```
$ 4.23      $7.25      $ 8.05       47¢       $ 0.08
16.90       0.40       12.16        18¢        3.67
+ 0.89      + 4.42     + 0.58      + 25¢      + 14.37
```

4.
```
$15.40      $5.70      $11.30       91¢       $17.20
- 3.62      - 2.08     - 0.86      - 75¢      - 4.06
```

5.
```
$27.00      $65.21     $0.12        47¢       $3.00
- 13.45     + 3.80     + 1.88      - 19¢      - 1.78
```

6.
```
$16.49      $40.60     $5.00        38¢       $8.75
+ 28.98     - 7.56     - 2.72      + 35¢      + 0.64
```

Match the Sale

Directions: Which item did each child purchase? Calculate the amount. Write each purchase price below.

Jessica:

$17.43
-
$9.14

Tammy:

$43.21
-
$34.86

Heather:

$10.06
-
$1.64

Mark:

$52.46
-
$14.17

Eva:

$65.04
-
$36.94

Monica:

$6.99
-
$3.56

Katelyn:

$9.06
-
$5.24

David:

$15.25
-
$6.82

Curt:

$63.45
-
$46.16

Michele:

$32.45
-
$13.50

Gwen:

$19.24
-
$6.38

Thomas:

$9.43
-
$5.59

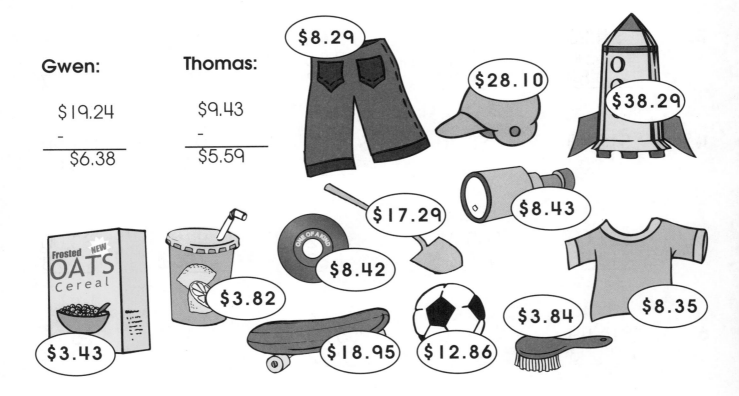

$8.29

$28.10

$38.29

$17.29

$8.43

$8.42

$3.82

$8.35

$3.43

$18.95

$12.86

$3.84

Problem Solving

Directions: Solve each problem.

Work Space:

1. Caitlin's mother bought a dress for $22.98 and a blouse for $17.64. How much did these items cost altogether?

   They cost _____altogether.

2. Find the total cost of a basketball at $18.69, a baseball at $8.05, and a football at $24.98.

   The total cost is _____.

3. Jeremy has $2.50. Landon has $1.75. Jeremy has how much more money than Landon?

   Jeremy has _____ more than Landon.

4. In problem **2,** how much more does the basketball cost than the baseball? How much more does the football cost than the basketball?

   The basketball costs _____ more than the baseball.

   The football costs _____ more than the basketball.

5. Alexandra saved $4.20 one week, $0.90 the next week, and $2.05 the third week. How much money did she save during these 3 weeks?

   Alexandra saved _____ in 3 weeks.

1.

2.

3.

4.

5.

Spending Spree

Directions: Use the clues to figure out what each person bought. Then, subtract to find out how much change each had left.

$12.49

$9.31

Clue:

1. David began with: $40.25
   -_____

   He loves things that zoom into the sky!

2. Mark started with: $50.37
   -_____

   He likes to travel places with his hands free and a breeze in his face!

   $21.52

3. Eva started with: $14.84
   -_____

   She loves to practice her jumping and exercise at the same time!

   $13.45

   $15.29

4. Bill brought: $61.49
   -_____

   He wants to see the heavens for himself!

   $2.43

5. Michelle brought: $40.29
   -_____

   Fuzzy companions make such great friends!

   $3.95

   $52.28

6. Cheryl started with: $16.80
   -_____

   She loves to hear music that is soft and beautiful!

   $32.51

7. Heather arrived with: $20.48
   -_____

   She loves to put it down on paper for everyone to see!

   $47.29

242

Foxy Felix's Shop

Directions: Solve these problems.

SALE
10% off
50% off
on all CDs

1. Mighty Man comics cost $0.13 at Foxy Felix's. You buy 4 of these comics. How much should you pay?

2. Your best friend bought 9 marbles at Foxy Felix's. Each marble cost $0.19. How much money did he spend?

3. Baseball cards are $0.11 each at Foxy Felix's. How much will it cost you for 8 cards?

4. Your sister decides to buy 2 CDs of the latest hit single by the Bird Brains. Each CD costs $0.89. How much will she pay?

5. Crazy stickers cost $0.21 each at Foxy Felix's. You buy 7 of them. How much should you pay?

6. Stinky Stickers have a skunk odour. Your best friend bought 7 Stinky Stickers, which cost $0.18 each. How much did he spend?

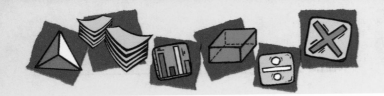

Glossary

Addition: "Putting together" or adding two or more numbers to find the sum.

Angle: Two rays with the same end point.

Centimetre: A measurement of length in the metric system. There are 2.54 centimetres in an inch.

Compare: To discuss how things are similar.

Coordinates: Points on a grid. They are named with numbers across, then down.

Decimal: A number with one or more places to the right of a decimal point, such as 6.5 or 3.78. Money amounts are written with two places to the right of a decimal point, such as $1.30.

Denominator: The bottom number of a fraction.

Difference: The answer in a subtraction problem.

Digit: The symbols used to write numbers: 0, 1, 2, 3, 4, 5, 6, 7, 8 and 9.

Dividend: The larger number that is divided by the smaller number, or divisor, in a division problem. In the problem $28 \div 7 = 4$, 28 is the dividend.

Division: An operation to find out how many times one number is contained in another number. For example, $28 \div 4 = 7$ means that there are seven groups of four in 28.

Divisor: The smaller number that is divided into the dividend in a division problem. In the problem $28 \div 7 = 4$, 7 is the divisor.

Dollar: A dollar is equal to one hundred cents. It is written $1.00.

Factors: The numbers multiplied together in a multiplication problem.

Fraction: A number that names part of a whole, such as $\frac{1}{2}$ or $\frac{3}{4}$.

Front-End Estimation: The process of using only the first digit in a number and replacing every other place value with a zero to round a number.

Geometry: The branch of mathematics that has to do with points, lines, and shapes.

Graph: A drawing that shows information about numbers.

Kilometre: A measurement of distance in the metric system. There are 1,000 metres in a kilometre.

Line Segment: A part of a line with two end points.

Map Scale: Part of a map that shows how far one place is from another.

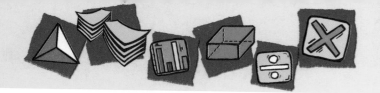

Metre: A measurement of length in the metric system. A metre is equal to 39.37 inches.

Mile: A measurement of distance in the standard measurement system. A mile is equal to 1,760 yards or 5,280 feet.

Multiplication: A short way to find the sum of adding the same number a certain amount of times. For example, 7 x 4 = 28 instead of 7 + 7 + 7 + 7 = 28.

Number Palindrome: A number that reads the same backward or forward.

Numerator: The top number of a fraction.

Ounce: A measurement of weight in the standard measurement system. There are 16 ounces in a pound.

Perimeter: The distance around an object. Find the perimeter by adding the lengths of the sides.

Pictograph: A graph using pictures to give information.

Place Value: The value of a digit, or numeral, shown by where it is in the number.

Polygon: A closed shape with straight sides.

Product: The answer of a multiplication problem.

Quotient: The answer of a division problem.

Ray: A line segment with only one end point. It goes on and on in the other direction.

Regroup: To use ten ones to form one ten, ten tens to form 100, and so on.

Remainder: The number left over in the quotient of a division problem.

Roman Numerals: Another way to write a number. The system uses Roman letters rather than standard digits.

Rounding: Estimating a number by figuring a number using the closest "10" (or "100," "1,000," etc.).

Subtraction: "Taking away" or subtracting one number from another to find the difference.

Yard: A measurement of distance in the standard measurement system. There are 3 feet in a yard.

Page 4

Addition Facts

Directions: Add.

1. 3+1=4; 8+2=10; 1+6=7; 4+7=11; 6+3=9; 2+8=10; 4+5=9; 7+9=16
2. 6+4=10; 8+8=16; 3+9=12; 2+1=3; 5+0=5; 0+2=2; 9+1=10; 3+2=5
3. 2+7=9; 6+9=15; 8+4=12; 3+9=12; 2+2=4; 8+0=8; 0+4=4; 7+1=8
4. 5+2=7; 8+3=11; 1+5=6; 7+8=15; 6+2=8; 4+6=10; 5+4=9; 9+4=13
5. 2+3=5; 4+0=4; 4+3=7; 2+9=11; 1+1=2; 8+8=16; 3+5=8; 5+7=12
6. 8+9=17; 3+3=6; 9+5=14; 6+6=12; 3+8=11; 0+6=6; 7+3=10; 2+6=8
7. 7+7=14; 4+1=5; 3+6=9; 8+7=15; 0+0=0; 9+8=17; 4+2=6; 7+5=12
8. 2+4=6; 0+3=3; 5+8=13; 2+5=7; 1+9=10; 1+0=1; 5+9=14; 8+4=12

Page 5

Addition Facts

Directions: Add.

1. 8+2=10; 7+0=7; 0+1=1; 1+1=2; 6+4=10; 5+2=7; 4+9=13; 2+7=9
2. 1+0=1; 6+3=9; 3+0=3; 2+3=5; 7+1=8; 8+1=9; 6+5=11; 1+9=10
3. 0+5=5; 1+2=3; 6+6=12; 3+5=8; 9+5=14; 5+7=12; 7+6=13; 3+8=11
4. 4+2=6; 6+8=14; 8+5=13; 2+6=8; 8+5=13; 9+8=17; 0+0=0; 4+4=8
5. 7+9=16; 9+7=16; 0+8=8; 4+7=11; 7+9=16; 5+9=14; 3+3=6; 5+4=9
6. 1+3=4; 9+0=9; 2+2=4; 5+1=6; 7+7=14; 6+0=6; 8+6=14; 9+4=13
7. 4+8=12; 9+3=12; 1+4=5; 2+9=11; 8+3=11; 7+3=10; 7+3=10; 0+9=9
8. 2+0=2; 2+8=10; 8+4=12; 4+0=4; 8+7=15; 1+9=10; 4+3=7; 5+5=10

Page 6

Addition

2 → Find the 2 - row.
+6 → Find the 6 - column.
8 → The sum is named where the 2-row and 6-column meet.

Directions: Add.

1. 2+4=6; 3+1=4; 1+2=3; 7+0=7; 0+4=4; 4+1=5; 5+2=7; 3+3=6
2. 2+0=2; 6+3=9; 4+4=8; 3+0=3; 5+3=8; 1+6=7; 0+5=5; 8+1=9
3. 2+6=8; 1+0=1; 1+5=6; 2+2=4; 3+2=5; 2+1=3; 5+4=9; 1+7=8
4. 9+0=9; 5+1=6; 0+3=3; 4+1=5; 4+5=9; 4+8=12; 8+0=8; 4+3=7
5. 0+0=0; 2+3=5; 7+0=7; 0+9=9; 4+2=6; 0+2=2; 0+7=7; 1+1=2

Page 7

Addition

5 → Find the 5 - row.
+7 → Find the 7 - column.
→ The sum is named where the 5-row and 7-column meet.

Directions: Add.

1. 6+5=11; 7+3=10; 2+7=9; 8+4=12; 9+2=11; 6+3=9; 2+6=8
2. 8+2=10; 3+9=12; 3+5=8; 5+2=7; 6+4=10; 5+5=10; 1+9=10
3. 5+3=8; 9+3=12; 6+6=12; 3+7=10; 4+7=11; 9+1=10; 3+8=11
4. 5+7=12; 8+1=9; 5+6=11; 2+8=10; 2+5=7; 7+5=12; 7+1=8
5. 3+4=7; 4+5=9; 4+6=10; 2+9=11; 8+3=11; 4+8=12; 7+4=11

Page 8

Addition

6 → Find the 6 - row.
+7 → Find the 7 - column.
→ The sum is named where the 6-row and 7-column meet.

9 → Find the 9 - row.
+8 → Find the 8 - column.
→ The sum is named where the 9-row and 8-column meet.

Directions: Add.

1. 7+5=12; 8+7=15; 7+4=11; 9+7=16; 4+9=13; 8+8=16; 9+5=14
2. 8+6=14; 9+4=13; 6+8=14; 5+2=7; 6+4=10; 8+7=15; 6+6=12
3. 6+9=15; 5+5=10; 6+7=13; 9+2=11; 8+6=14; 4+6=10; 2+9=11
4. 5+7=12; 8+9=17; 9+6=15; 5+6=11; 9+4=13; 9+9=18; 4+8=12
5. 7+9=16; 8+2=10; 8+9=17; 8+5=13; 9+1=10; 4+7=11; 7+7=14

Page 9

Addition

Directions: Add.

Example:

Add the ones.
26
+21
7

Add the tens.
26
+21
47

18+11=29; 24+35=59; 38+21=59; 49+50=99; 52+33=85

75+12=87; 83+16=99; 67+32=99; 44+25=69; 28+41=69

68 + 20 = 88   54 + 25 = 79   71 + 17 = 88

The Lions scored 42 points. The Clippers scored 21 points. How many points were scored in all? ___63

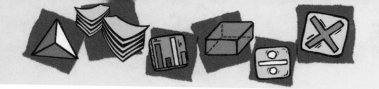

Page 10

Addition

	Add the ones.	Add the tens.		Add the ones.	Add the tens.
36 +2	36 +2 8	36 +2 38	6 +41	6 +41 7	6 +41 47

Directions: Add.

1. 3 +5 8	23 +5 28	2 +3 5	42 +3 45	5 +1 6	25 +1 26
2. 3 +4 7	3 +64 67	4 +5 9	4 +55 59	2 +5 7	2 +85 87
3. 2 +4 6	12 +4 16	22 +4 26	32 +4 36	42 +4 46	52 +4 56
4. 5 +63 68	6 +31 37	24 +3 27	92 +2 94	57 +1 58	2 +41 43
5. 41 +3 44	21 +2 23	3 +63 66	2 +84 86	21 +6 27	4 +14 18
6. 8 +51 59	62 +4 66	25 +3 28	6 +33 39	2 +51 53	5 +43 48
7. 36 +2 38	42 +5 47	2 +51 53	60 +8 68	5 +21 26	34 +2 36

Page 11

Addition

	Add the ones.	Add the tens.		26 +61 87	Add the ones. Add the tens.
36 +43	36 +43 9	36 +43 79			

Directions: Add.

1. 23 +45 68	63 +21 84	45 +22 67	61 +30 91	42 +35 77	60 +25 85
2. 48 +41 89	52 +14 66	32 +54 86	63 +20 83	21 +38 59	45 +52 97
3. 34 +22 56	41 +25 66	36 +22 58	51 +40 91	83 +12 95	42 +30 72
4. 23 +24 47	30 +58 88	27 +12 39	44 +23 67	62 +14 76	35 +53 88
5. 24 +31 55	52 +32 84	42 +27 69	51 +33 84	16 +20 36	43 +23 66
6. 34 +25 59	64 +23 87	18 +41 59	54 +24 78	41 +27 68	14 +32 46

Page 12

Magic Squares

The ancient Chinese believed that these number squares really were magic. To many people, the mystery of having each row, column, and diagonal be the same sum seemed like magic.

Example:
Magic Square for 12

7	0	5
2	4	6
3	8	1

Directions: Make a Magic Square for 15. Find the missing numbers for this magic square. The sum of each row, column, and diagonal must equal 15.

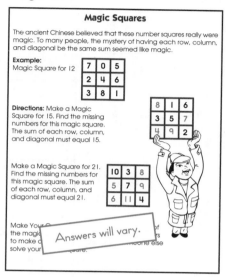

8	1	6
3	5	7
4	9	2

Make a Magic Square for 21. Find the missing numbers for this magic square. The sum of each row, column, and diagonal must equal 21.

10	3	8
5	7	9
6	11	4

Make Your Own ... the magic ... to make ... solve your ...

Answers will vary.

Page 13

Dial - A - Word

Directions: Use the phone pad to calculate the "value" of the words.

Example: PHONE = 74663
PHONE = 7 + 4 + 6 + 6 + 3 = 26

(your name) = *Answers will vary.* = *Answers will vary.*

CALCULATOR = 2 + 2 + 5 + 2 + 8 +5 + 2 + 8 + 6 + 7 = 47

DICTIONARY = 3 + 4 + 2 + 8 + 4 +6 + 6 + 2 + 7 + 9 = 51

PET TRICKS = 7 + 3 + 8 + 8 + 7 +4 + 2 + 5 + 7 = 51

BASEBALL GAME = 2 + 2 + 7 + 3 + 2 +2 + 5 + 5 + 4 + 2 + 6 + 3 = 43

COMPUTERS = 2 + 6 + 6 + 7 + 8 +8 + 3 + 7 + 7 = 54

TENNIS SHOES = 8 + 3 + 6 + 6 + 4 + 7 +7 + 4 + 6 + 3 + 7 = 61

ADDITION = 2 + 3 + 3 + 4 + 8 +4 + 6 + 6 = 36

MENTAL MATH = 6 + 3 + 6 + 8 + 2 +5 + 6 + 2 + 8 + 4 = 50

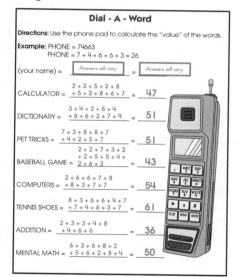

Page 14

Problem Solving

Directions: Solve each problem.

1. Andy played 2 games today. He played 9 games yesterday. How many games did he play in all?

Andy played __2__ games today.

Andy played __9__ games yesterday.

He played __11__ games in all.

2. Jenna rode her bicycle 8 kilometres yesterday. She rode 4 kilometres today. How many kilometres did she ride in all?

Jenna rode __8__ kilometres yesterday.

Jenna rode __4__ kilometres today.

Jenna rode __12__ kilometres in all.

3. Paul hit the ball 7 times. He missed 4 times. How many times did he swing at the ball?

Paul hit the ball __7__ times.

Paul missed the ball __4__ times.

Paul swung at the ball __11__ times.

Work Space:
1.

2.

3.

Page 15

Problem Solving

Directions: Solve each problem.

1. Luciana worked 9 hours Monday. She worked 7 hours Tuesday. How many hours did she work in all on those two days?

She worked __9__ hours Monday.

She worked __7__ hours Tuesday.

She worked __16__ hours in all on those two days.

2. Alex has 6 windows to wash. Nadia has 9 windows to wash. How many windows do they have to wash in all?

Alex has __6__ windows to wash.

Nadia has __9__ windows to wash.

Together they have __15__ windows to wash.

3. Seven cars are in the first row. Six cars are in the second row. How many cars are in the first two rows?

__13__ cars are in the first two rows.

4. There are 9 men and 8 women at work. How many people are at work?

There are __17__ people at work.

Work Space:
1.

2.

3.

4.

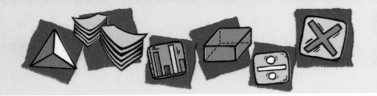

Page 16

Problem Solving

Directions: Solve each problem.

Work Space:

1. John has 32 red marbles and 5 green marbles. How many red and green marbles does he have?

   John has ___37___ red and green marbles.

2. Su-Lee had 5 paper cups. She bought 24 more. How many paper cups did she have then?

   She then had ___29___ paper cups.

3. On the way to work, Michael counted 41 cars and 7 trucks. How many cars and trucks did he count?

   Michael counted ___48___ cars and trucks.

4. Mark worked all the problems on a test. He had 24 right answers and 4 wrong ones. How many problems were on the test?

   There were ___28___ problems on the test.

5. Shea works with 12 women and 6 men. How many people does she work with?

   Shea works with ___18___ people.

Page 17

Six Hundred Silkworms

Sally had hundreds of silkworm eggs in the spring. She couldn't wait for them to hatch. She loved watching them grow, spin cocoons, and hatch into moths.

But once they all hatched, she had 600 silkworms to take care of. Soon she was running out of room to keep them all. She had silkworms in her bedroom. She had silkworms in the family room. She even tried to put silkworms in the kitchen. That's when her mother couldn't take it anymore! "Sally," she said, "600 silkworms are just too many! You have to start giving some of them away."

So Sally took the silkworms to school to give away. The first day, she gave away 20 silkworms. The second day, she gave away 40 more. The third day, she gave away 60 silkworms. How many silkworms did Sally give away by the seventh day?

Directions: Fill in the table. Look for a pattern. It can help you solve the mystery.

Day	Silkworms Given Away	Total Number Given Away
1	20	20
2	40	60
3	60	120
4	80	200
5	100	300
6	120	420
7	140	560

Write Your Own Mystery: Think of something else a person might have to give away. Write some clues. Let someone else solve your mystery.

Page 18

Using Number Concepts

Directions: Cut out the set of cards on the next page.

Use them to form number sentences that answer the questions below.   2 7 5 4 8

1. Use two cards to list each way that you can make the sum of 10.

2. Use two cards to list each way that you can make the sum of 13.

3. Use two cards to list each way that you can make the sum of 16.

4. Use two cards to list each way that you can make the sum of 12.

5. Use two cards to list each way that you can make the sum of 15.

6. Use two cards to list each way that you can make the sum of 17.

7. How did you know you found all the ways?

Answers will vary.

Extension: Repeat this exercise using three cards to make each sum.

Page 21

Subtraction Facts

Directions: Subtract.

1. 11−3=8 | 8−4=4 | 5−5=0 | 12−3=9 | 2−1=1 | 10−9=1 | 4−3=1 | 11−9=2
2. 10−5=5 | 3−3=0 | 6−3=3 | 11−4=7 | 7−1=6 | 10−6=4 | 9−2=7 | 12−4=8
3. 16−7=9 | 9−0=9 | 5−4=1 | 13−7=6 | 10−2=8 | 15−9=6 | 8−8=0 | 14−5=9
4. 13−8=5 | 4−2=2 | 7−7=0 | 12−9=3 | 2−0=2 | 17−9=8 | 6−1=5 | 11−7=4
5. 18−9=9 | 9−8=1 | 6−4=2 | 11−5=6 | 3−1=2 | 15−7=8 | 9−9=0 | 10−8=2
6. 12−6=6 | 8−7=1 | 3−2=1 | 13−9=4 | 10−4=6 | 14−6=8 | 7−5=2 | 12−7=5
7. 15−8=7 | 8−3=5 | 9−5=4 | 12−8=4 | 8−6=2 | 16−9=7 | 5−3=2 | 12−7=5
8. 14−7=7 | 7−1=6 | 6−5=1 | 11−8=3 | 4−1=3 | 10−7=3 | 1−1=0 | 10−3=7

Page 22

Subtraction Facts

Directions: Subtract.

1. 4−2=2 | 13−7=6 | 3−2=1 | 10−1=9 | 6−5=1 | 8−1=7 | 14−5=9 | 10−7=3
2. 8−2=6 | 12−5=7 | 6−3=3 | 10−8=2 | 2−1=1 | 11−9=2 | 14−8=6 | 11−2=9
3. 4−0=4 | 11−3=8 | 9−1=8 | 15−6=9 | 5−0=5 | 7−1=6 | 13−8=5 | 10−9=1
4. 6−4=2 | 13−9=4 | 1−0=1 | 9−2=7 | 7−3=4 | 12−8=4 | 15−7=8 | 5−4=1
5. 0−0=0 | 12−3=9 | 8−4=4 | 14−6=8 | 8−5=3 | 10−4=6 | 16−9=7 | 11−6=5
6. 9−9=0 | 10−2=8 | 3−2=1 | 15−9=6 | 5−1=4 | 12−9=3 | 14−9=5 | 10−3=7
7. 7−5=2 | 12−7=5 | 7−0=7 | 14−7=7 | 7−3=4 | 11−4=7 | 16−7=9 | 11−5=6
8. 4−4=0 | 13−6=7 | 5−2=3 | 16−8=8 | 9−4=5 | 10−5=5 | 13−4=9 | 6−0=6

Page 23

Subtraction

8 → Find 8 in
−6 → the 6 column.
2 → The difference is named in the [   ] at the end of this row.

Directions: Subtract.

1. 5−4=1 | 3−2=1 | 7−7=0 | 1−0=1 | 8−2=6 | 9−7=2 | 4−3=1
2. 7−2=5 | 2−2=0 | 7−6=1 | 8−7=1 | 9−3=6 | 8−1=7 | 4−1=3
3. 0−0=0 | 7−1=6 | 3−0=3 | 6−2=4 | 4−2=2 | 6−2=4 | 9−5=4
4. 9−9=0 | 8−4=4 | 9−1=8 | 7−5=2 | 6−3=3 | 7−6=1 | 2−0=2
5. 5−5=0 | 2−1=1 | 5−0=5 | 8−3=5 | 9−0=9 | 6−3=3 | 7−0=7

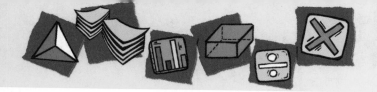

Page 24

Subtraction

11 → Find 11 in
- 4 → the [4] - column.
← The difference is named in the ▨ at the end of this row.

4-column

(grid chart 0-9)

Directions: Subtract.

1. 11−7=4 10−4=6 10−8=2 12−3=9 8−5=3 11−2=9 7−3=4
2. 10−1=9 11−8=3 7−4=3 11−6=5 12−3=9 9−6=3 10−3=7
3. 12−7=5 10−7=3 9−3=6 11−9=2 12−4=8 10−5=5 12−5=7
4. 8−6=2 12−8=4 9−5=4 10−6=4 11−5=6 8−8=0 8−3=5
5. 12−6=6 10−9=1 9−8=1 7−6=1 11−4=7 9−7=2 11−3=8

Page 25

Subtraction

13 → Find 13 in
- 8 → the [8] - column.
← The difference is named in the ▨ at the end of this row.

15 → Find 15 in
- 6 → the [6] - column.
← The difference is named in the ▨ at the end of this row.

6-column   8-column

(grid chart 0-9)

Directions: Subtract.

1. 13−5=8 14−8=6 16−7=9 10−9=1 12−5=7 14−6=8 15−7=8
2. 17−8=9 13−7=6 12−4=8 14−5=9 15−8=7 13−6=7 10−3=7
3. 11−7=4 18−9=9 15−6=9 11−8=3 14−7=7 13−9=4 17−8=9
4. 16−8=8 10−5=5 12−7=5 13−4=9 12−6=6 14−5=9 11−6=5
5. 13−8=5 12−9=3 10−1=9 15−9=6 11−8=3 10−7=3 16−9=7

Page 26

Subtraction

Subtraction means "taking away" or subtracting one number from another to find the difference. For example, 10 − 3 = 7.

Directions: Subtract.

Example: Subtract the ones. Subtract the tens.

39 − 24   39−24=5   39−24 = 15

48−35=13   95−22=73   87−16=71   55−43=12

37−14=23   69−57=12   44−23=21   99−78=21

66 − 44 = 22   57 − 33 = 24

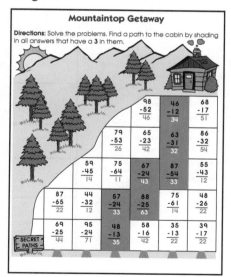

The yellow car traveled 87 kilometres per hour. The orange car traveled 66 kilometres per hour. How much faster was the yellow car traveling?   21

Page 27

Subtraction

	Subtract the ones.	Subtract the tens.		Subtract the ones.	Subtract the tens.
47 − 2	47 − 2 = 5	47 − 2 = 45	64 − 23	64 − 23 = 1	64 − 23 = 41

Directions: Subtract.

1. 9−3=6 49−3=46 5−2=3 35−2=33 7−1=6 87−1=86
2. 8−2=6 78−2=76 4−3=1 64−3=61 9−9=0 89−9=80
3. 45−3=42 36−4=32 78−5=73 42−2=40 38−8=30 65−4=61
4. 49−26=23 37−16=21 58−23=35 49−31=18 78−45=33 73−20=53
5. 58−27=31 69−31=38 42−21=21 49−19=30 84−23=61 78−64=14
6. 78−21=57 67−31=36 40−20=20 56−36=20 45−23=22 92−21=71

Page 28

Subtraction

To check 37 − 24 = 13, add 24 to ___ .
37 − 24 = 13, +24 = 37

To check 59 − 29 = 30, add to 30.
59 − 29 = 30, +29 = 59   These should be the same.

Directions: Subtract. Check each answer.

1. 59−34=25 (+34=59) 27−14=13 (+14=27) 85−23=62 (+23=85) 78−23=55 (+23=78) 47−24=23 (+24=47) 59−26=33 (+26=59)
2. 85−25=60 (+25=85) 48−32=16 (+32=48) 56−24=32 (+24=56) 96−35=61 (+35=96) 40−30=10 (+30=40) 92−81=11 (+81=92)
3. 74−23=51 (+23=74) 58−26=32 (+26=58) 75−24=51 (+24=75) 38−23=15 (+23=38) 45−35=10 (+35=45) 88−35=53 (+35=88)
4. 67−24=43 (+24=67) 87−24=63 (+24=87) 59−36=23 (+36=59) 58−24=34 (+24=58) 79−54=25 (+54=79) 84−23=61 (+23=84)

Page 29

Mountaintop Getaway

Directions: Solve the problems. Find a path to the cabin by shading in all answers that have a **3** in them.

98−52=46   46−12=34   68−17=51
79−53=26   65−23=42   63−31=32   86−32=54
59−45=14   75−64=11   67−24=43   87−54=33   55−43=12
87−65=22   44−32=12   57−24=33   88−25=63   75−61=14   48−26=22
69−25=44   95−24=71   48−13=35   58−16=42   35−13=22   39−17=22

SECRET PATHS

Page 30

Problem Solving

Directions: Solve each problem.

Work Space:

1. There were 12 nails in a box. David used 3 of them. How many nails are still in the box?

   __12__ nails were in a box.
   __3__ nails were used.
   __9__ nails are still in the box.

2. There are 11 checkers on a board. Eight of them are black. The rest are red. How many red checkers are on the board?

   __11__ checkers are on a board.
   __8__ checkers are black and the rest are red.
   __3__ red checkers are on the board.

3. Marty is 10 years old. Her brother Larry is 7. Marty is how many years older than Larry?

   Marty's age is __10__ years.
   Larry's age is __7__ years.
   Marty is __3__ years older than Larry.

4. Twelve people are in a room. Five of them are men. How many are women?

   __7__ women are in the room.

1.

2.

3.

4.

Page 31

Problem Solving

Directions: Solve each problem.

Work Space:

1. Matt wants to collect 13 cars. He now has 5 cars. How many more cars does he need?

   Matt wants __13__ cars.
   He now has __5__ cars.
   He needs __8__ cars.

2. Susan bought 18 valentines. She mailed 9 of them. How many valentines does she have left?

   Susan bought __18__ valentines.
   She mailed __9__ of them.
   She has __9__ valentines left.

3. Courtney had 16 stamps. She used some, and had 7 left. How many stamps did she use?

   Courtney used __9__ stamps.

4. Bret is 14 years old. Amy is 7. Bret is how much older than Amy?

   Bret is __7__ years older than Amy.

5. Fifteen bolts and nuts were on the table. Seven were bolts. How many were nuts?

   There were __8__ nuts.

1.

2.

3.

4.

5.

Page 32

Problem Solving

Directions: Solve each problem.

Work Space:

1. Beth worked 27 problems. She got 6 wrong answers. How many answers did she get right?

   Beth got __21__ answers right.

2. There were 96 parts in a box. Four parts were broken. How many parts were not broken?

   __92__ parts were not broken.

3. At noon the temperature was 28 degrees Celsius. At nine o'clock in the evening, it was 14 degrees Celsius. How many degrees did the temperature drop?

   The temperature dropped __14__ degrees.

4. Clark had 75 cents. Then he spent 25 cents for some paper. How many cents did he have left?

   Clark had __50__ cents left.

5. There are 72 houses in Kyle's neighbourhood. Kyle delivers papers to all but 21 of them. How many houses does he deliver papers to?

   He delivers papers to __51__ houses.

1.

2.

3.

4.

5.

Page 33

Problem Solving

Directions: Solve each problem.

Work Space:

1. Mr. Ming wants to build a fence 58 metres long. He has 27 metres of fence completed. How much of the fence is left to build?

   __31__ metres of fence is left to build.

2. Mrs. Boyle is taking an 89-kilometre trip. She has traveled 64 kilometres. How much farther must she travel?

   Mrs. Boyle must travel __25__ more miles.

3. Sean had 95 cents. Then he spent 45 cents. How many cents did he have left?

   Sean had __50__ cents left.

4. Kevin scored 62 points and Bianca scored 78 points. How many more points did Bianca score than Kevin?

   Bianca scored __16__ more points.

5. Darien lives 38 blocks from the ball park. Kelly lives 25 blocks from the park. How much farther from the ball park does Darien live than Kelly?

   Darien lives __13__ blocks farther than Kelly.

1.

2.

3.

4.

5.

Page 34

Addition and Subtraction

To check
5 + 6 = 11,
subtract 6
from 11.

```
  5
 +6
 ——
 11
 -6
 ——
  5
```
These should be the same.

To check
13 - 4 = 9,
add 4
to __9__.

```
 13
 -4
 ——
  9
 +4
 ——
 13
```
These should be the same.

Directions: Add. Check each answer.

1.
```
 9      8      7      3      1      6
+2     +4     +3     +8     +9     +6
——     ——     ——     ——     ——     ——
11     12     10     11     10     12
```

2.
```
 9      5      4      5      7      9
+3     +6     +8     +5     +4     +1
——     ——     ——     ——     ——     ——
12     11     12     10     11     10
```

Directions: Subtract. Check each answer.

3.
```
10     12     11     10     11     10
-8     -7     -3     -4     -7     -7
——     ——     ——     ——     ——     ——
 2      5      8      6      4      3
```

4.
```
11     12     11     12     10     10
-9     -8     -8     -5     -6     -3
——     ——     ——     ——     ——     ——
 2      4      3      7      4      7
```

Page 35

Addition and Subtraction

To check
6 + 8 = 14,
subtract 8
from 14.

```
  6
 +8
 ——
 14
 -8
 ——
  6
```
These should be the same.

To check
13 - 6 = 7,
add __
to 7.

```
 13
 -6
 ——
  7
 +6
 ——
 13
```
These should be the same.

Directions: Add. Check each answer.

1.
```
 5      9      6      7      9      3
+9     +7     +6     +4     +8     +7
——     ——     ——     ——     ——     ——
14     16     12     11     17     10
```

2.
```
 6      9      6      4      6      8
+7     +3     +9     +9     +4     +6
——     ——     ——     ——     ——     ——
13     12     15     13     10     14
```

Directions: Subtract. Check each answer.

3.
```
14     18     13     15     16     12
-8     -9     -5     -6     -8     -7
——     ——     ——     ——     ——     ——
 6      9      8      9      8      5
```

4.
```
13     12     13     16     15     13
-6     -4     -4     -9     -7     -8
——     ——     ——     ——     ——     ——
 7      8      9      7      8      5
```

Page 36

Addition and Subtraction

Directions: Add.

1. $\begin{array}{r} 3 \\ +6 \\ \hline 9 \end{array}$ $\begin{array}{r} 43 \\ +6 \\ \hline 49 \end{array}$ $\begin{array}{r} 1 \\ +4 \\ \hline 5 \end{array}$ $\begin{array}{r} 51 \\ +4 \\ \hline 55 \end{array}$ $\begin{array}{r} 2 \\ +5 \\ \hline 7 \end{array}$ $\begin{array}{r} 82 \\ +5 \\ \hline 87 \end{array}$

2. $\begin{array}{r} 57 \\ +2 \\ \hline 59 \end{array}$ $\begin{array}{r} 26 \\ +1 \\ \hline 27 \end{array}$ $\begin{array}{r} 44 \\ +3 \\ \hline 47 \end{array}$ $\begin{array}{r} 23 \\ +4 \\ \hline 27 \end{array}$ $\begin{array}{r} 42 \\ +3 \\ \hline 45 \end{array}$ $\begin{array}{r} 21 \\ +5 \\ \hline 26 \end{array}$

3. $\begin{array}{r} 4 \\ +31 \\ \hline 35 \end{array}$ $\begin{array}{r} 5 \\ +43 \\ \hline 48 \end{array}$ $\begin{array}{r} 4 \\ +62 \\ \hline 66 \end{array}$ $\begin{array}{r} 3 \\ +43 \\ \hline 46 \end{array}$ $\begin{array}{r} 5 \\ +12 \\ \hline 17 \end{array}$ $\begin{array}{r} 7 \\ +20 \\ \hline 27 \end{array}$

4. $\begin{array}{r} 54 \\ +31 \\ \hline 85 \end{array}$ $\begin{array}{r} 26 \\ +12 \\ \hline 38 \end{array}$ $\begin{array}{r} 45 \\ +33 \\ \hline 78 \end{array}$ $\begin{array}{r} 67 \\ +21 \\ \hline 88 \end{array}$ $\begin{array}{r} 42 \\ +33 \\ \hline 75 \end{array}$ $\begin{array}{r} 22 \\ +13 \\ \hline 35 \end{array}$

Directions: Subtract.

5. $\begin{array}{r} 7 \\ -4 \\ \hline 3 \end{array}$ $\begin{array}{r} 37 \\ -4 \\ \hline 33 \end{array}$ $\begin{array}{r} 5 \\ -2 \\ \hline 3 \end{array}$ $\begin{array}{r} 45 \\ -2 \\ \hline 43 \end{array}$ $\begin{array}{r} 8 \\ -6 \\ \hline 2 \end{array}$ $\begin{array}{r} 38 \\ -6 \\ \hline 32 \end{array}$

6. $\begin{array}{r} 38 \\ -4 \\ \hline 34 \end{array}$ $\begin{array}{r} 27 \\ -6 \\ \hline 21 \end{array}$ $\begin{array}{r} 54 \\ -3 \\ \hline 51 \end{array}$ $\begin{array}{r} 29 \\ -7 \\ \hline 22 \end{array}$ $\begin{array}{r} 68 \\ -2 \\ \hline 66 \end{array}$ $\begin{array}{r} 26 \\ -3 \\ \hline 23 \end{array}$

7. $\begin{array}{r} 54 \\ -23 \\ \hline 31 \end{array}$ $\begin{array}{r} 69 \\ -24 \\ \hline 45 \end{array}$ $\begin{array}{r} 37 \\ -21 \\ \hline 16 \end{array}$ $\begin{array}{r} 88 \\ -24 \\ \hline 64 \end{array}$ $\begin{array}{r} 93 \\ -21 \\ \hline 72 \end{array}$ $\begin{array}{r} 87 \\ -37 \\ \hline 50 \end{array}$

8. $\begin{array}{r} 28 \\ -13 \\ \hline 15 \end{array}$ $\begin{array}{r} 54 \\ -34 \\ \hline 20 \end{array}$ $\begin{array}{r} 87 \\ -26 \\ \hline 61 \end{array}$ $\begin{array}{r} 54 \\ -21 \\ \hline 33 \end{array}$ $\begin{array}{r} 50 \\ -40 \\ \hline 10 \end{array}$ $\begin{array}{r} 37 \\ -10 \\ \hline 27 \end{array}$

Page 37

Addition and Subtraction

To check 43 + 14 = 57, subtract 14 from _____. $\begin{array}{r} 43 \\ +14 \\ \hline 57 \end{array}$ $\begin{array}{r} 57 \\ -14 \\ \hline 43 \end{array}$ These should be the same.

To check 57 − 14 = 43, add _____ to 43 . $\begin{array}{r} 57 \\ -14 \\ \hline 43 \end{array}$ $\begin{array}{r} 43 \\ +14 \\ \hline 57 \end{array}$ These should be the same.

Directions: Add. Check each answer.

1. $\begin{array}{r} 27 \\ +31 \\ \hline 58 \end{array}$ $\begin{array}{r} 42 \\ +51 \\ \hline 93 \end{array}$ $\begin{array}{r} 26 \\ +30 \\ \hline 56 \end{array}$ $\begin{array}{r} 14 \\ +52 \\ \hline 66 \end{array}$ $\begin{array}{r} 23 \\ +72 \\ \hline 95 \end{array}$ $\begin{array}{r} 65 \\ +22 \\ \hline 87 \end{array}$

2. $\begin{array}{r} 44 \\ +24 \\ \hline 68 \end{array}$ $\begin{array}{r} 31 \\ +27 \\ \hline 58 \end{array}$ $\begin{array}{r} 64 \\ +14 \\ \hline 78 \end{array}$ $\begin{array}{r} 32 \\ +20 \\ \hline 52 \end{array}$ $\begin{array}{r} 42 \\ +36 \\ \hline 78 \end{array}$ $\begin{array}{r} 46 \\ +23 \\ \hline 69 \end{array}$

Directions: Subtract. Check each answer.

3. $\begin{array}{r} 78 \\ -23 \\ \hline 55 \end{array}$ $\begin{array}{r} 48 \\ -13 \\ \hline 35 \end{array}$ $\begin{array}{r} 27 \\ -16 \\ \hline 11 \end{array}$ $\begin{array}{r} 58 \\ -26 \\ \hline 32 \end{array}$ $\begin{array}{r} 67 \\ -24 \\ \hline 43 \end{array}$ $\begin{array}{r} 38 \\ -16 \\ \hline 22 \end{array}$

4. $\begin{array}{r} 75 \\ -61 \\ \hline 14 \end{array}$ $\begin{array}{r} 46 \\ -26 \\ \hline 20 \end{array}$ $\begin{array}{r} 39 \\ -10 \\ \hline 29 \end{array}$ $\begin{array}{r} 45 \\ -23 \\ \hline 22 \end{array}$ $\begin{array}{r} 67 \\ -41 \\ \hline 26 \end{array}$ $\begin{array}{r} 38 \\ -15 \\ \hline 23 \end{array}$

Page 38

Stay on Track

Directions: Add or subtract. Write each answer in the puzzle.

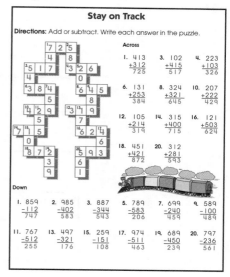

Across

1. $\begin{array}{r} 413 \\ +312 \\ \hline 725 \end{array}$ 3. $\begin{array}{r} 102 \\ +415 \\ \hline 517 \end{array}$ 4. $\begin{array}{r} 223 \\ +103 \\ \hline 326 \end{array}$

6. $\begin{array}{r} 131 \\ +253 \\ \hline 384 \end{array}$ 8. $\begin{array}{r} 324 \\ +321 \\ \hline 645 \end{array}$ 10. $\begin{array}{r} 207 \\ +222 \\ \hline 429 \end{array}$

12. $\begin{array}{r} 105 \\ +214 \\ \hline 319 \end{array}$ 14. $\begin{array}{r} 315 \\ +400 \\ \hline 715 \end{array}$ 16. $\begin{array}{r} 121 \\ +503 \\ \hline 624 \end{array}$

18. $\begin{array}{r} 451 \\ +421 \\ \hline 872 \end{array}$ 20. $\begin{array}{r} 312 \\ +281 \\ \hline 593 \end{array}$

Down

1. $\begin{array}{r} 859 \\ -112 \\ \hline 747 \end{array}$ 2. $\begin{array}{r} 985 \\ -402 \\ \hline 583 \end{array}$ 3. $\begin{array}{r} 887 \\ -344 \\ \hline 543 \end{array}$ 5. $\begin{array}{r} 789 \\ -583 \\ \hline 206 \end{array}$ 7. $\begin{array}{r} 699 \\ -240 \\ \hline 459 \end{array}$ 9. $\begin{array}{r} 589 \\ -100 \\ \hline 489 \end{array}$

11. $\begin{array}{r} 767 \\ -512 \\ \hline 255 \end{array}$ 13. $\begin{array}{r} 497 \\ -321 \\ \hline 176 \end{array}$ 15. $\begin{array}{r} 259 \\ -151 \\ \hline 108 \end{array}$ 17. $\begin{array}{r} 974 \\ -511 \\ \hline 463 \end{array}$ 19. $\begin{array}{r} 689 \\ -450 \\ \hline 239 \end{array}$ 20. $\begin{array}{r} 797 \\ -236 \\ \hline 561 \end{array}$

Page 39

Problem Solving

Directions: Answer each question.

Work Space:

1. Ben had some marbles. He gave 2 of them away and had 9 left. How many marbles did he start with?

   Are you to add or subtract? **Add**
   How many marbles did he start with? **11**

2. A full box has 10 pieces of chalk. This box has only 8 pieces. How many pieces are missing?

   Are you to add or subtract? **Subtract**
   How many pieces are missing? **2**

3. Noah is 11 years old today. How old was he 4 years ago?

   Are you to add or subtract? **Subtract**
   How old was Noah 4 years ago? **7**

4. Nine boys were playing ball. Then 3 more boys began to play. How many boys were playing ball then?

   Are you to add or subtract? **Add**
   How many boys were playing ball? **12**

5. Tricia invited 12 people to her party. Seven came. How many people that were invited did not come?

   Are you to add or subtract? **Subtract**
   How many people did not come? **5**

Page 40

Problem Solving

Directions: Answer each question.

Work Space:

1. Penny worked 9 addition problems. She worked 7 subtraction problems. How many problems did she work?

   Are you to add or subtract? **Add**
   How many problems did she work? **16**

2. Six people were in the room. Then 8 more people came in. How many people were in the room then?

   Are you to add or subtract? **Add**
   How many people were in the room then? **14**

3. There were 18 chairs in a room. Nine of them were being used. How many were not being used?

   Are you to add or subtract? **Subtract**
   How many chairs were not being used? **9**

4. Mr. Noe and Miss Leikel had 17 students absent. Mr. Noe had 9 absent. How many did Miss Leikel have absent?

   Are you to add or subtract? **Subtract**
   How many students were absent from Miss Leikel's class? **8**

Page 41

Problem Solving

Directions: Solve each problem.

Work Space:

1. There are 12 boys and 13 girls in Jean's class. How many students are in her class?

   There are **25** students in her class.

2. Emily scored 32 baskets. She missed 23 times. How many times did she try to score?

   Emily tried to score **55** times.

3. One store ordered 52 bicycles. Another store ordered 45 bicycles. How many bicycles did both stores order?

   Both stores ordered **97** bicycles.

4. One bear cub weighs 64 kilograms. Another bear cub is 22 kilograms heavier. How much does the heavier cub weigh?

   The heavier bear cub weighs **86** kilograms.

5. 43 women and 35 men came to the meeting. How many people came to the meeting?

   78 people came to the meeting.

6. 68 seats were filled, and 21 were empty. How many seats were there?

   There were **89** seats.

Page 42

Problem Solving

Directions: Solve each problem.

Work Space:

1. Mrs. Dial weighs 55 kilograms. Her son weighs 32 kilograms. How much more than her son does Mrs. Dial weigh?

   She weighs __23__ kilograms more.

2. Mitzi planted 55 flower seeds. Only 23 of them grew. How many did not grow?

   __32__ seeds did not grow.

3. A city has 48 mail trucks. Twelve are not being used today. How many mail trucks are being used?

   __36__ mail trucks are being used.

4. A mail carrier delivered 38 letters and picked up 15. How many more letters were delivered than were picked up?

   The carrier delivered __23__ more letters.

5. A city has 89 mail carriers. One day 77 carriers were at work. How many carriers were not at work?

   __12__ carriers were not at work.

1.
2.
3.
4.
5.

Page 43

Outstanding Elephant Math

Directions: Connect the dots in order from least to greatest.

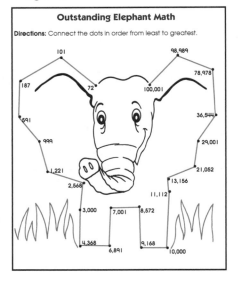

Page 44

Place Value Riddles

Directions: Using the clues below, choose the number each riddle describes. As you read, draw an X on each number that does not fit the clue. After you have read all the clues for each riddle, there should be only one number left.

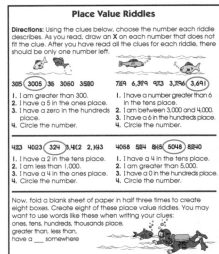

305 (3005) 35 3060 35⬚0

1. I am greater than 300.
2. I have a 5 in the ones place.
3. I have a zero in the hundreds place.
4. Circle the number.

7⬚9 6,3⬚9 9⬚3 3,7⬚6 (3,691)

1. I have a number greater than 6 in the tens place.
2. I am between 3,000 and 4,000.
3. I have a 6 in the hundreds place.
4. Circle the number.

4⬚3 40⬚3 (324) 3,4⬚2 2,1⬚3

1. I have a 2 in the tens place.
2. I am less than 1,000.
3. I have a 4 in the ones place.
4. Circle the number.

4058 5⬚4 8⬚5 (5048) 8⬚40

1. I have a 4 in the tens place.
2. I am greater than 5,000.
3. I have a 0 in the hundreds place.
4. Circle the number.

Now, fold a blank sheet of paper in half three times to create eight boxes. Create eight of these place value riddles. You may want to use words like these when writing your clues: ones, tens, hundreds, thousands place, greater than, less than, have a ___ somewhere

Page 45

4 - 3 - 2 - 1- Blast Off!

Directions: Colour these spaces red:
- three thousand five
- 1,000 less than 3,128
- six thousand eight hundred eighty-nine
- 100 more than 618,665
- 10 less than 2,981
- fifty-nine thousand two

Directions: Colour these spaces blue:
- 10 less than 4,786
- eight thousand six hundred two
- 1,000 less than 638,961
- two thousand four hundred fifty-one
- 100 more than 81,136
- 10,000 less than 48,472

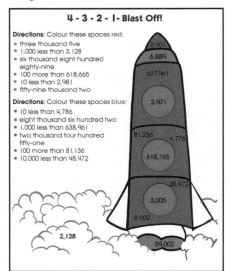

Page 46

Place Value Puzzles

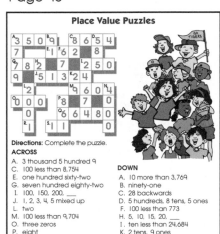

Directions: Complete the puzzle.

ACROSS
A. 3 thousand 5 hundred 9
C. 100 less than 8,754
E. one hundred sixty-two
G. seven hundred eighty-two
I. 100, 150, 200, ___
J. 1, 2, 3, 4, 5 mixed up
L. two
M. 100 less than 9,704
O. three zeros
P. eight
Q. 10,000 more than 56,480
R. one
S. 1 ten, 1 one

DOWN
A. 10 more than 3,769
B. ninety-one
C. 28 backwards
D. 5 hundreds, 8 tens, 5 ones
F. 100 less than 773
H. 5, 10, 15, 20, ___
I. ten less than 24,684
K. 2 tens, 9 ones
L. two thousand one
N. 1000, 2000, 3000, ___
P. eight hundreds, 6 tens, 1 one

Page 47

Write That Number

Directions: Write the numeral form for each number.

Example: three hundred forty-two = 342

1. six hundred fifty thousand, two hundred twenty-five __650,225__

2. nine hundred ninety-nine thousand, nine hundred ninety-nine __999,999__

3. one hundred six thousand, four hundred thirty-seven __106,437__

4. three hundred fifty-six thousand, two hundred two __356,202__

5. Write the number that is two more than 356,909. __356,911__

6. Write the number that is five less than 448,394. __448,389__

7. Write the number that is ten more than 285,634. __285,644__

8. Write the number that is ten less than 395,025. __395,015__

Directions: Write the following numbers in word form.

9. 3,208 __three thousand, two hundred, eight__

10. 13,656 __thirteen thousand, six hundred fifty-six__

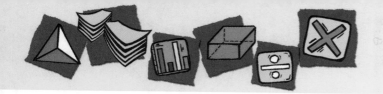

Page 51

Place Value

The place value of a digit, or numeral, is shown by where it is in the number. For example, in the number 1,234, 1 has the place value of thousands, 2 is hundreds, 3 is tens, and 4 is ones.

Hundred Thousands	Ten Thousands	Thousands	Hundreds	Tens	Ones
9	4	3	8	5	2

943,852

Directions: Match the numbers in Column A with the words in Column B.

A	B
62,453	two hundred thousand
7,641	three thousand
486,113	four hundred thousand
11,277	eight hundreds
813,463	seven tens
594,483	five ones
254,089	six hundreds
79,841	nine ten thousands
27,115	five tens

Page 52

Place Value

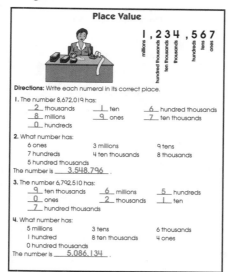

1,234,567

millions / hundred thousands / ten thousands / thousands / hundreds / tens / ones

Directions: Write each numeral in its correct place.

1. The number 8,672,019 has:
   - _2_ thousands
   - _1_ ten
   - _6_ hundred thousands
   - _8_ millions
   - _9_ ones
   - _7_ ten thousands
   - _0_ hundreds

2. What number has:
   - 6 ones
   - 3 millions
   - 9 tens
   - 7 hundreds
   - 4 ten thousands
   - 8 thousands
   - 5 hundred thousands

   The number is _3,548,796_.

3. The number 6,792,510 has:
   - _9_ ten thousands
   - _6_ millions
   - _5_ hundreds
   - _0_ ones
   - _2_ thousands
   - _1_ ten
   - _7_ hundred thousands

4. What number has:
   - 5 millions
   - 3 tens
   - 6 thousands
   - 1 hundred
   - 8 ten thousands
   - 4 ones
   - 0 hundred thousands

   The number is _5,086,134_.

Page 53

Rounding: The Nearest Ten

Directions: If the ones number is 5 or greater, "round up" to the nearest 10. If the ones number is 4 or less, the tens number stays the same and the ones number becomes a zero.

Examples: 15 round up to 20   23 round down to 20   47 round up to 50

7 _10_	58 _60_
12 _10_	81 _80_
33 _30_	94 _90_
27 _30_	44 _40_
73 _70_	88 _90_
25 _30_	66 _70_
39 _40_	70 _70_

Page 54

Rounding: The Nearest Hundred

Directions: If the tens number is 5 or greater, "round up" to the nearest hundred. If the tens number is 4 or less, the hundreds number remains the same.

Remember... Look at the number directly to the right of the place you are rounding to.

Examples: 230 round down to 200   470 round up to 500   150 round up to 200   732 round down to 700

456 _500_	120 _100_
340 _300_	923 _900_
867 _900_	550 _600_
686 _700_	231 _200_
770 _800_	492 _500_

Page 55

Estimate by Rounding Numbers

Directions: Estimate by rounding numbers to different place values. Use these rules.

Example: Round 283 to the nearest hundred.

- Find the digit in the place to be rounded. (2)83
- Now, look at the digit to its right. 2(8)3
- If the digit to the right is less than 5, the digit being rounded remains the same.
- If the digit to the right is 5 or more, the digit being rounded is increased by 1. 2(8)3
- Digits to the right of the place to be rounded become 0s. Digits to the left remain the same. Rounds to 300

Examples: Round 4,385 . . .

to the nearest thousand	to the nearest hundred	to the nearest ten
4,385	4,385	4,385
3 is less than 5.	8 is more than 5.	5 = 5.
The 4 stays the same.	The 3 is rounded up to 4.	The 8 is rounded up to 9.
4,000	4,400	4,390

Directions: Complete the table.

NUMBERS TO BE ROUNDED	ROUND TO THE NEAREST THOUSAND	NEAREST HUNDRED	NEAREST TEN
2,725	3,000	2,700	2,730
10,942	11,000	10,900	10,940
6,816	7,000	6,800	6,810
2,309	2,000	2,300	2,310
7,237	7,000	7,200	7,240
959	1,000	1,000	960

Page 56

Round, Round, Round You Go

Directions: Round numbers according to each set of directions.

Round each number to the nearest ten.
45 _50_   72 _70_   61 _60_   255 _260_
27 _30_   184 _180_   43 _40_   97 _100_

Round each number to the nearest hundred.
562 _600_   1,246 _1,200_   761 _800_   4,593 _4,600_
347 _300_   859 _900_   238 _200_   76 _100_

Round each number to the nearest thousand.
6,543 _7,000_   83,246 _83,000_   3,741 _4,000_   66,357 _66,000_
7,219 _7,000_   9,814 _10,000_   2,166 _2,000_   8,344 _8,000_

Round each number to the nearest ten thousand.
32,467 _30,000_   871,362 _870,000_   334,212 _330,000_
57,891 _60,000_   45,621 _50,000_   79,356 _80,000_

Round each number to the nearest hundred thousand.
116,349 _100,000_   946,477 _900,000_   732,166 _700,000_
762,887 _800,000_   365,851 _400,000_   225,631 _200,000_

Round each number to the nearest million.
2,765,437 _3,000,000_   7,762,997 _8,000,000_
1,469,876 _1,000,000_   5,564,783 _6,000,000_
14,537,123 _15,000,000_   4,117,655 _4,000,000_

Page 57

Big City

Directions: What city is home to the CN Tower? Follow the directions below to find out.

1. If 31,842 rounded to the nearest thousand is 31,000, put an **A** above number 2.
2. If 62 rounded to the nearest ten is 60, put an **O** above number 2 .
3. If 4,234 rounded to the nearest hundred is 4,200, put an **O** above number 7.
4. If 3,291 rounded to the nearest thousand is 3,000, put an **R** above number 3.
5. If 5,599 rounded to the nearest thousand is 6,000, put an **O** above number 4.
6. If 1,549 rounded to the nearest hundred is 1,500, put an **T** above number 6.
7. If 885 rounded to the nearest hundred is 800, put a **W** above number 2.
8. If 74 rounded to the nearest ten is 80, put an **R** above number 6.
9. If 248 rounded to the nearest hundred is 300, put an **R** above number 4.
10. If 615 rounded to the nearest ten is 620, put a **T** above number 1.
11. If 6,817 rounded to the nearest thousand is 7,000, put a **N** above number 5.

T O R O N T O
1 2 3 4 5 6 7

Page 58

Front-End Estimation

Front-end estimation is useful when you don't need to know the exact amount, but a close answer will do.

When we use front-end estimation, we use only the first number, and then add the numbers together to get the estimate.

Example:

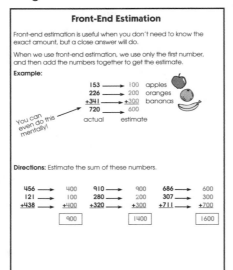

153 →	100	apples
226 →	200	oranges
+341 →	+300	bananas
720	600	
actual	estimate	

You can even do this mentally!

Directions: Estimate the sum of these numbers.

456 → 400   910 → 900   686 → 600
121 → 100   280 → 200   307 → 300
+438 → +400   +320 → +300   +711 → +700

900   **1400**   **1600**

Page 59

Addition

Add the ones. Rename 13 as 10 + 3.

54 + 9

4 + 9 = 13 or 10 + 3

54 + 9 = 3

Add the tens.

54 + 9 = 63

Directions: Add.

1.	27 +5 = 32	35 +8 = 43	87 +4 = 91	38 +9 = 47	42 +8 = 50	46 +5 = 51
2.	45 +9 = 54	27 +7 = 34	7 +38 = 45	20 +65 = 85	24 +9 = 33	8 +38 = 46
3.	27 +3 = 30	45 +6 = 51	8 +36 = 44	9 +29 = 38	6 +58 = 64	42 +9 = 51
4.	76 +7 = 83	3 +47 = 50	4 +26 = 30	27 +4 = 31	5 +18 = 23	9 +19 = 28
5.	6 +15 = 21	41 +9 = 50	52 +8 = 60	65 +9 = 74	7 +38 = 45	6 +16 = 22
6.	9 +28 = 37	36 +7 = 43	59 +2 = 61	7 +36 = 43	4 +47 = 51	9 +38 = 47

Page 60

Addition

Add the ones. Rename 15 as 10 + 5.

48 + 27

8 + 7 = 15 or 10 + 5

48 + 27 = 5

Add the tens.

48 + 27 = 75

Directions: Add.

1.	37 +25 = 62	48 +37 = 85	26 +54 = 80	35 +29 = 64	54 +18 = 72	62 +29 = 91
2.	29 +28 = 57	38 +37 = 75	47 +25 = 72	63 +27 = 90	79 +19 = 98	64 +17 = 81
3.	58 +26 = 84	45 +18 = 63	27 +57 = 84	44 +29 = 73	36 +36 = 72	77 +17 = 94
4.	49 +48 = 97	26 +37 = 63	73 +19 = 92	18 +28 = 46	15 +47 = 62	29 +27 = 56
5.	18 +55 = 73	28 +24 = 52	38 +37 = 75	48 +43 = 91	58 +16 = 74	68 +28 = 96
6.	26 +66 = 92	19 +54 = 73	57 +29 = 86	45 +36 = 81	52 +18 = 70	33 +29 = 62

Page 61

Addition: Regrouping

Addition means putting together or adding two or more numbers to find the sum. For example, 3 + 5 = 8. To regroup is to use ten ones to form one ten, ten tens to form one 100, and so on.

Directions: Add using regrouping.

Example:

Add the ones.

88 + 21 = 9

Add the tens with regrouping.

88 + 21 = 109

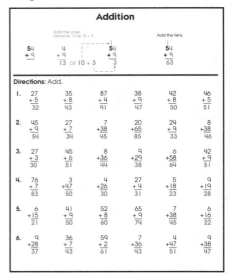

37 +72 = 109	56 +67 = 123	51 +88 = 139	37 +55 = 92	70 +68 = 138
93 +54 = 147	47 +82 = 129	81 +77 = 158	23 +92 = 115	36 +71 = 107

92 + 13 = **105**   73 + 83 = **156**   54 + 61 = **115**

The Blues scored 63 points. The Reds scored 44 points. How many points were scored in all?   **107**

Page 62

Addition: Regrouping

Directions: Study the example. Add using regrouping.

Examples:

Add the ones. Regroup.

1
156 +267 = 3

Add the tens. Regroup.

1 1
156 +267 = 23

Add the hundreds.

1
156 +267 = 423

29 46 +12 = 87	81 78 +33 = 192	52 67 +23 = 142	49 37 +19 = 105	162 +349 = 511
273 +198 = 471	655 +297 = 952	783 +148 = 931	385 +169 = 554	428 +122 = 550

Sally went bowling. She had scores of 115, 129, and 103. What was her total score for three games?   **347**

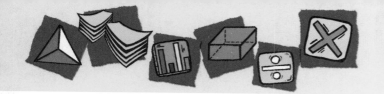

Page 63

Addition: Regrouping

Directions: Add using regrouping. Then use the code to discover the name of a jungle animal.

348 +752 = 1,100	642 +277 = 919	386 +787 = 1,173	184 +875 = 1,059	578 +874 = 1,452
653 +768 = 1,421	653 +359 = 1,012	946 +239 = 1,185	393 +257 = 650	199 +843 = 1,042
721 +679 = 1,400				

TALL GIRAFFE

1012	1173	1059	1421	919	650	1452	1042	1100	1400	1185
R	L	L	I	A	F	G	F	T	E	A

Page 64

Addition: Regrouping

Directions: Study the example. Add using regrouping.

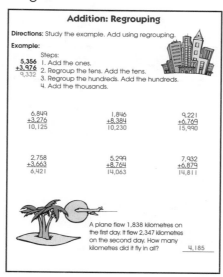

Example:

5,356
+3,976
9,332

Steps:
1. Add the ones.
2. Regroup the tens. Add the tens.
3. Regroup the hundreds. Add the hundreds.
4. Add the thousands.

6,849 +3,276 = 10,125	1,846 +8,384 = 10,230	9,221 +6,769 = 15,990
2,758 +3,663 = 6,421	5,299 +8,764 = 14,063	7,932 +6,879 = 14,811

A plane flew 1,838 kilometres on the first day. It flew 2,347 kilometres on the second day. How many kilometres did it fly in all? 4,185

Page 65

Addition: Mental Math

Directions: Try to do these addition problems in your head without using paper and pencil.

7 +4 = 11	6 +3 = 9	8 +1 = 9	10 +2 = 12	2 +9 = 11	6 +6 = 12
10 +20 = 30	40 +20 = 60	80 +100 = 180	60 +30 = 90	50 +70 = 120	100 +40 = 140
350 +150 = 500	300 +500 = 800	400 +800 = 1,200	450 +10 = 460	680 +100 = 780	900 +70 = 970
1,000 +200 = 1,200	4,000 400 +30 = 4,430	300 200 500 +80 = 580	8,000 500 +60 = 8,560	9,800 +150 = 9,950	7,000 300 +30 = 7,330

Page 66

Mushrooming Addition

Directions: Follow the arrows to add.

Example:
52 + 28 = 80
28 + 91 = 119
119 + 80 = ?

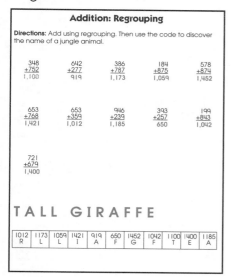

Page 67

Fishy Addition

Directions: Add.

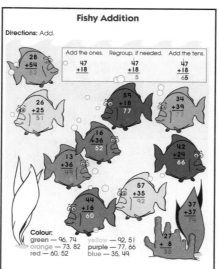

Add the ones.	Regroup, if needed.	Add the tens.
47 +18	47 +18 = 5	47 +18 = 65

28 +54 = 82
26 +25 = 51
59 +18 = 77
34 +39 = 73
16 +36 = 52
13 +36 = 49
42 +24 = 66
44 +16 = 60
57 +35 = 92
37 +37 = 74
27 +8 = 35

Colour:
green — 96, 74
orange — 73, 82
red — 60, 52
yellow — 92, 51
purple — 77, 66
blue — 35, 49

Page 68

Make the Windows Shine!

Directions: Add.

476 +319 = 795	248 +629 = 877	327 +544 = 871	
572 +318 = 890	815 +177 = 992	527 +144 = 671	
429 +343 = 772	462 +319 = 781	462 +529 = 991	648 +238 = 886
756 +127 = 883	563 +208 = 771	646 +248 = 894	924 +66 = 990
628 +259 = 887	526 +347 = 873	927 +46 = 973	765 +218 = 983

Page 69

Addition Ace

Directions: Add. Colour the ribbon according to the code below.

138 +49 = 187	327 +513 = 840	834 +128 = 962	108 +146 = 254	
			506 +91 = 597	249 +128 = 377

If the sum is in the:
- 100s - green
- 200s - yellow
- 300s - red
- 400s - blue
- 500s - purple
- 600s - orange
- 700s - pink
- 800s - gold
- 900s - silver

367 +424 = 791	724 +39 = 763	704 +283 = 987	691 +205 = 896	265 +319 = 584
432 +249 = 681	528 +349 = 877	924 +56 = 980	306 +248 = 554	226 +165 = 391
	826 +164 = 990	328 +145 = 473	426 +261 = 687	747 +143 = 890

Page 70

Space Shuttle Addition

Add the ones.	Regroup.	Add the tens and regroup.	Add the hundreds.
362 +439 = 1	362 +439 = 1	362 +439 = 01	362 +439 = 801

Directions: Add.

371 +439 = 810	629 +184 = 813	146 +587 = 733	264 +483 = 747	438 +290 = 728
347 +328 = 675	362 +459 = 821	528 +391 = 919	382 +249 = 631	327 +649 = 976
283 +346 = 629	409 +292 = 701		465 +193 = 658	566 +283 = 849
			283 +519 = 802	423 +392 = 815
			625 +246 = 871	498 +123 = 621

Page 71

Underwater Addition

Directions: Add.

446 +489 = 935	476 +527 = 1,003	509 +375 = 884	251 +368 = 619
	708 +507 = 1,215	438 +419 = 857	334 +278 = 612
464 +456 = 920	589 +322 = 911	288 +377 = 665	811 +386 = 1,197	609 +475 = 1,084
	531 +249 = 780	810 +428 = 1,238		
831 +438 = 1,269	445 +476 = 921	211 +396 = 607	230 +284 = 514	319 +287 = 606
	714 +185 = 899	767 +246 = 1,013	911 +427 = 1,338	

Page 72

Let's Climb to the Top!

Directions: Add.

328 +449 = 777	246 +492 = 738	462 +781 = 1,243	621 +489 = 1,110	429 +636 = 1,065
	409 +736 = 1,145	921 +87 = 1,008	562 +614 = 1,176	824 +597 = 1,421
	982 +220 = 1,202	207 +913 = 1,120		826 +95 = 921
	547 +782 = 1,329	284 +493 = 777		506 +214 = 720
200 +489 = 689	684 +519 = 1,203	425 +594 = 1,019	536 +184 = 720	623 +192 = 815

Page 73

Picnic Problems

Directions: Help the ant find a path to the picnic. Solve the problems. Shade the box if an answer has a 9 in it.

836 +90 = 926	536 +248 = 784	952 +8 = 960	362 +47 = 409	486 +293 = 779	368 +529 = 897
789 526 +214 = 1,529	2,846 +6,478 = 9,324	932 +365 = 1,297	374 +299 = 673	835 +552 = 1,387	956 874 +65 = 1,895
4,768 +2,894 = 7,662	38 456 +3,894 = 4,388	4,507 +2,743 = 7,250	404 +289 = 693	1,843 +6,752 = 8,595	4,367 +3,574 = 7,941
639 +77 = 716	587 342 +679 = 1,608	5,379 1,865 +2,348 = 9,592	450 +145 = 595	594 +278 = 872	459 +367 = 826
29 875 +2,341 = 3,245	387 29 +5,614 = 6,030	462 379 +248 = 1,089			

Page 74

Grand Prix Addition

Directions: Solve each problem. Beginning at 7,000, run through this racetrack to find the path the race car took. When you reach 7,023, you're ready to exit and gas up for the next race.

3,536 +3,482 = 7,018	1,792 +5,225 = 7,017	3,838 +3,178 = 7,016	3,767 +3,248 = 7,015	1,874 +5,140 = 7,014	4,809 +2,204 = 7,013
3,561 +3,458 = 7,019	4,162 +2,858 = 7,020	3,771 +4,213 = 7,984	4,123 +2,887 = 7,010	5,879 +1,132 = 7,011	1,725 +5,287 = 7,012
3,544 +3,478 = 7,022	1,273 +5,748 = 7,021	2,435 +5,214 = 7,649	4,853 +2,156 = 7,009	3,589 +3,419 = 7,008	5,218 +1,789 = 7,007
5,997 +1,026 = 7,023	5,289 +1,713 = 7,002	3,698 +3,305 = 7,003	4,756 +2,248 = 7,004	4,248 +2,757 = 7,005	4,658 +2,348 = 7,006
4,853 +2,147 = 7,000	2,216 +4,785 = 7,001	1,157 +6,412 = 7,569	3,720 +3,698 = 7,418	3,612 +3,552 = 7,164	1,687 +5,662 = 7,349

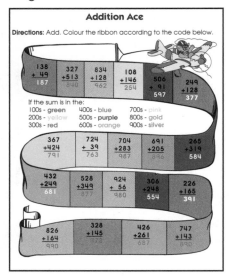
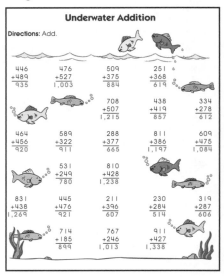

Page 75

Gearing Up

Add the ones. Regroup.	Add the tens. Regroup.	Add the hundreds. Regroup.	Add the thousands. Regroup.
7,465 +4,978 3	7,465 +4,978 43	7,465 +4,978 443	7,465 +4,978 12,443

Directions: Solve the problems. Colour each answer that has a
3—blue, 4—red and 5—yellow.

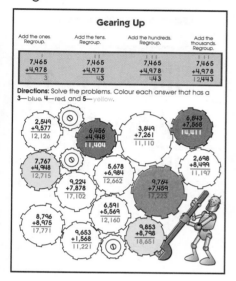

2,549
+9,577
12,126

6,456
+4,948
11,404

3,849
+7,261
11,110

6,843
+7,568
14,411

7,767
+4,948
12,715

5,678
+6,984
12,662

2,698
+8,499
11,197

9,224
+7,878
17,102

9,764
+7,459
17,223

8,796
+8,975
17,771

6,591
+5,569
12,160

9,653
+1,568
11,221

9,853
+8,798
18,651

Page 76

Bubble Math

Directions: Add to solve the problems.

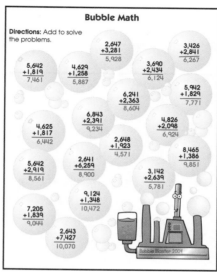

5,642 +1,819 = 7,461
4,629 +1,258 = 5,887
2,647 +3,281 = 5,928
3,426 +2,841 = 6,267
3,690 +2,434 = 6,124
6,241 +2,363 = 8,604
5,942 +1,829 = 7,771
4,625 +1,817 = 6,442
6,843 +2,391 = 9,234
4,826 +2,098 = 6,924
5,642 +2,919 = 8,561
2,641 +6,259 = 8,900
2,648 +1,923 = 4,571
8,465 +1,386 = 9,851
3,142 +2,639 = 5,781
9,124 +1,348 = 10,472
7,205 +1,839 = 9,044
2,643 +7,427 = 10,070

Page 77

Cotton Pickin' Math

Directions: Solve the problems.

7,215 62 141 +2,015 9,433	4,621 35 1,318 + 9 5,983	6,117 24 315 +2,136 8,592	2,481 2,514 2 + 43 5,040	3,204 182 23 + 5 3,414
8,143 60 235 +1,423 9,861	35 242 6 +1,203 1,486	7,006 242 31 + 31 7,288	521 3,134 64 + 243 3,962	496 8,172 83 + 199 8,950
6,201 325 41 +2,136 8,703	5,242 342 8 + 51 5,643	4,162 328 41 + 503 5,034	6,425 41 324 + 3 6,793	
4,205 81 3 + 414 4,703	2,516 310 82 + 4 2,911	5,426 310 512 + 4 6,252		

Page 78

Problem Solving

Directions: Solve each problem.

Work Space:

1. Last year there were 44 monkeys on an island. There are 8 more monkeys this year. How many monkeys are on the island now?

   There were __44__ monkeys last year.
   There are __8__ more monkeys this year.
   There are __52__ monkeys on the island now.

2. There were 72 children and 9 adults in our group at the zoo. How many people were in our group?

   __72__ children were in our group.
   __9__ adults were in our group.
   __81__ people were in our group.

3. One group of monkeys was fed 6 kilograms of fruit. Another group was fed 19 kilograms. How much fruit was that in all?

   That was __25__ kilograms of fruit in all.

4. The children drank 68 cartons of milk. There were 8 cartons left. How many cartons of milk were there to start with?

   There were __76__ cartons of milk to start with.

Page 79

Problem Solving

Directions: Solve each problem.

Work Space:

1. January has 31 days. February has 29 days this year. How many days are in the two months?

   There are __31__ days in January.
   There are __29__ days in February this year.
   There are __60__ days in January and February.

2. Jeff weighs 46 kilograms. His father is 36 kilograms heavier. How much does Jeff's father weigh?

   Jeff weighs __46__ kilograms.
   His father is __36__ kilograms heavier.
   His father weighs __82__ kilograms.

3. Lauren had 29 points. She earned 13 more. How many points did she have then?

   Lauren had __29__ points.
   She earned __13__ more.
   She had __42__ points then.

4. Adam gained 18 kilograms in the last two years. Two years ago, he weighed 59 kilograms. How much does he weigh today?

   Adam weighs __77__ kilograms today.

Page 80

Palindrome Sums

A **number palindrome** is similar to a word palindrome in that it reads the same backward or forward.

Examples:
75,457
1,689,861

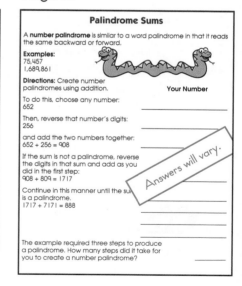

Directions: Create number palindromes using addition.

Your Number

To do this, choose any number:
652

Then, reverse that number's digits:
256

and add the two numbers together:
652 + 256 = 908

If the sum is not a palindrome, reverse the digits in that sum and add as you did in the first step:
908 + 809 = 1717

Continue in this manner until the sum is a palindrome.
1717 + 7171 = 888

Answers will vary.

The example required three steps to produce a palindrome. How many steps did it take for you to create a number palindrome?

Page 81

Subtraction

	To subtract the ones, rename 63 as "5 tens and 13 ones."	Subtract the ones.	Subtract the tens.
63 - 9	5 13 63 - 9	5 13 63 - 9 4	5 13 63 - 9 54

Directions: Subtract.

1. 53   27   46   54   32   65
   - 8   - 9   - 9   - 5   - 6   - 7
   ---- ---- ---- ---- ---- ----
    45   18   37   49   26   58

2. 28   48   35   44   67   92
   - 9   - 9   - 6   - 7   - 8   - 9
   ---- ---- ---- ---- ---- ----
    19   39   29   37   59   83

3. 52   62   61   73   50   42
   - 6   - 4   - 6   - 5   - 9   - 5
   ---- ---- ---- ---- ---- ----
    46   58   55   68   41   37

4. 96   73   80   42   63   51
   - 8   - 6   - 7   - 3   - 4   - 9
   ---- ---- ---- ---- ---- ----
    88   67   73   39   59   42

5. 94   88   33   27   46   64
   - 8   - 9   - 4   - 9   - 8   - 7
   ---- ---- ---- ---- ---- ----
    86   79   29   18   38   57

6. 23   76   40   41   53   25
   - 9   - 8   - 4   - 6   - 7   - 7
   ---- ---- ---- ---- ---- ----
    14   68   36   35   46   18

Page 82

Subtraction

	To subtract the ones, rename 92 as "8 tens and 12 ones."	Subtract the ones.	Subtract the tens.
92 - 38	8 12 92 - 38	8 12 92 - 38 4	8 12 92 - 38 54

Directions: Subtract.

1. 35   27   54   63   84   28
   - 17 - 19 - 37 - 26 - 59 - 19
   ---- ---- ---- ---- ---- ----
    18   8   17   37   25   9

2. 42   56   41   53   86   92
   - 24 - 39 - 27 - 15 - 78 - 26
   ---- ---- ---- ---- ---- ----
    18   17   14   38   8   66

3. 43   37   26   55   43   28
   - 15 - 29 - 19 - 36 - 27 - 19
   ---- ---- ---- ---- ---- ----
    28   8   7   19   16   9

4. 54   35   22   56   38   31
   - 26 - 18 - 15 - 29 - 19 - 18
   ---- ---- ---- ---- ---- ----
    28   17   7   27   19   13

5. 83   94   65   73   80   92
   - 25 - 16 - 39 - 17 - 28 - 35
   ---- ---- ---- ---- ---- ----
    58   78   26   56   52   57

6. 35   90   56   41   50   61
   - 26 - 55 - 27 - 16 - 38 - 15
   ---- ---- ---- ---- ---- ----
     9   35   29   25   12   46

Page 83

Subtracting Two-Digit Numbers

With Regrouping

Step 1: Decide whether to regroup. In the ones column, 3 is less than 9 so, regroup 4 tens 3 ones to 3 tens 13 ones.

4 3
- 1 9

Step 2: Subtract the ones.

4 3
- 1 9
4

Step 3: Subtract the tens.

3
4 3
- 1 9
2 4

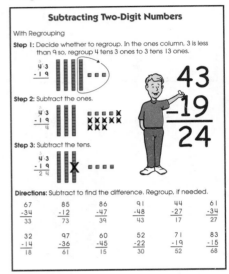

43
-19
24

Directions: Subtract to find the difference. Regroup, if needed.

 67   85   86   91   44   61
- 34 - 12 - 47 - 48 - 27 - 34
---- ---- ---- ---- ---- ----
 33   73   39   43   17   27

 32   97   60   52   71   83
- 14 - 36 - 45 - 22 - 19 - 15
---- ---- ---- ---- ---- ----
 18   61   15   30   52   68

Page 84

Subtraction: Regrouping

Subtraction means "taking away" or subtracting one number from another to find the difference. For example, 10 - 3 = 7. To regroup is to use one ten to form ten ones, one 100 to form ten tens, and so on.

Directions: Study the example. Subtract using regrouping.

Example:
  32 =   2 tens + 12 ones
- 13 =   1 ten   +   3 ones
  19 =   1 ten   +   9 ones

 33   86   92   71
- 28 - 59 - 37 - 48
---- ---- ---- ----
  5   27   55   23

 63   45   31   55
- 47 - 18 - 22 - 39
---- ---- ---- ----
 16   27   9   16

82 - 69 = __13__   73 - 36 = __37__

The Yankees won 85 games. The Cubs won 69 games. How many more games did the Yankees win? __16__

Page 85

Subtraction: Regrouping

Directions: Regrouping for subtraction is the opposite of regrouping for addition. Study the example. Subtract using regrouping. Then use the code to colour the flowers.

Example:
  647
- 453
  194

Steps:
1. Subtract ones.
2. Subtact tens. Five tens cannot be subtracted from 4 tens.
3. Regroup tens by regrouping 6 hundreds (5 hundreds + 10 tens).
4. Add the 10 tens to the four tens.
5. Subtract 5 tens from 14 tens.
6. Subtract the hundreds.

If the answer has: 1 one, colour it red; 8 ones, colour it pink; 5 ones, colour it yellow.

 428   368   943   528   726
- 397 - 173 - 652 - 270 - 331
----   ----   ----   ----   ----
  31   195   291   258   395

 549   749   637
- 361 - 568 - 242
----   ----   ----
 188   181   395

Page 86

Subtraction: Regrouping

Directions: Study the example. Follow the steps. Subtract using regrouping.

Example:
  634
- 455
  179

Steps:
1. Subtract ones. You cannot subtract 5 ones from 4 ones.
2. Regroup ones by regrouping 3 tens to 2 tens + 10 ones.
3. Subtract 5 ones from 14 ones.
4. Regroup tens by regrouping hundreds (5 hundreds + 10 tens).
5. Subtract 5 tens from 12 tens.
6. Subtract hundreds.

 635   553   832   944
- 169 - 174 - 563 - 578
----   ----   ----   ----
 466   379   269   366

 423   941   733   266
- 268 - 872 - 498 - 197
----   ----   ----   ----
 155   69   235   69

 387   594   960   887
- 198 - 385 - 759 - 598
----   ----   ----   ----
 189   209   201   289

Sue goes to school 185 days a year. Yoko goes to school 313 days a year. How many more days of school does Yoko attend each year? __128__

Page 87

Subtraction: Regrouping

Directions: Study the example. Follow the steps. Subtract using regrouping. If you have to regroup to subtract ones and there are no tens, you must regroup twice.

Example:

300
- 182
118

Steps:
1. Subtract ones. You cannot subtract 2 ones from 0 ones.
2. Regroup. No tens. Regroup hundreds (2 hundreds + 10 tens).
3. Regroup tens (9 tens + 10 ones).
4. Subtract 2 ones from ten ones.
5. Subtract 8 tens from 9 tens.
6. Subtract 1 hundred from 2 hundreds.

602 - 423 = 179	306 - 128 = 178	600 - 263 = 337	807 - 499 = 308	703 - 328 = 375
800 - 557 = 243	206 - 137 = 69	400 - 224 = 176	508 - 379 = 129	909 - 769 = 140
207 - 138 = 69	604 - 397 = 207	308 - 199 = 109	700 - 531 = 169	900 - 278 = 622

Page 88

Subtraction: Regrouping

Directions: Subtract. Regroup when necessary. The first one is done for you.

| 7,354 - 5,295 = 2,059 | 4,214 - 3,185 = 1,029 | 8,437 - 5,338 = 3,099 | 6,837 - 4,318 = 2,519 |
| 5,735 - 3,826 = 1,909 | 1,036 - 947 = 89 | 6,735 - 6,646 = 89 | 3,841 - 1,953 = 1,888 |

Columbus discovered America in 1492. Jacques Cartier discovered Canada in 1534. How many years difference was there between these two dates?

1534 - 1492 = 42 years

Page 89

Subtraction: Mental Math

Directions: Try to do these subtraction problems in your head without using paper and pencil.

9 - 3 = 6	12 - 6 = 6	7 - 6 = 1	5 - 1 = 4	15 - 5 = 10	2 - 0 = 2
40 - 20 = 20	90 - 80 = 10	100 - 50 = 50	20 - 20 = 0	60 - 10 = 50	70 - 40 = 30
450 - 250 = 200	500 - 300 = 200	250 - 20 = 230	690 - 100 = 590	320 - 20 = 300	900 - 600 = 300
1,000 - 400 = 600	8,000 - 500 = 7,500	7,000 - 900 = 6,100	4,000 - 2,000 = 2,000	9,500 - 4,000 = 5,500	5,000 - 2,000 = 3,000

Page 90

Hats, Hats, Hats

Directions: Subtract to find the difference. If the bottom number is larger than the top number in a column, you will need to regroup from the column to the left.

Example:

736 - 629 = 107

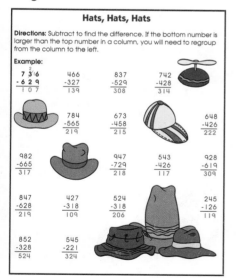

466 - 327 = 139	837 - 529 = 308	742 - 428 = 314
784 - 565 = 219	673 - 458 = 215	648 - 426 = 222
982 - 665 = 317	947 - 729 = 218	543 - 426 = 117	928 - 619 = 309
847 - 628 = 219	427 - 318 = 109	524 - 318 = 206	245 - 126 = 119
852 - 328 = 524	545 - 221 = 324		

Page 91

Soaring to the Stars

Directions: Connect the dots in order and form two stars. Begin one star with the subtraction problem whose difference is 100 and end with the problem whose difference is 109. Begin the other star with 110 and end with 120. Then, colour the pictures.

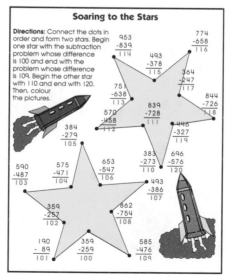

953 - 839 = 114	774 - 658 = 116
493 - 378 = 115	364 - 247 = 117
751 - 638 = 113	844 - 726 = 118
570 - 458 = 112	839 - 728 = 111
384 - 279 = 105	446 - 327 = 119
590 - 487 = 103	575 - 471 = 104	653 - 547 = 106	383 - 273 = 110	696 - 576 = 120
359 - 257 = 102	493 - 386 = 107	862 - 754 = 108
190 - 89 = 101	359 - 259 = 100	585 - 476 = 109

Page 92

Dino-Code

How is a T-Rex like an explosion?

Directions: To find out, solve the following problems and write the matching letter above each answer on the blanks.

He's . . . F U L L O F
195 185 92 92 171 195

D I N O – M I G H T !
265 74 183 171 93 74 45 181 191

Remember to regroup when the bottom number is larger than the top number in a column.

F = 348 - 153 = 195	L = 765 - 673 = 92	G = 427 - 382 = 45
T = 637 - 446 = 191	H = 878 - 697 = 181	U = 548 - 363 = 185
O = 824 - 653 = 171	N = 439 - 256 = 183	I = 447 - 373 = 74
M = 568 - 475 = 93	D = 748 - 483 = 265	

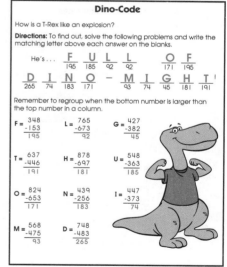

Page 93

Paint by Number

Directions: Solve each problem. Colour each shape according to the key below.

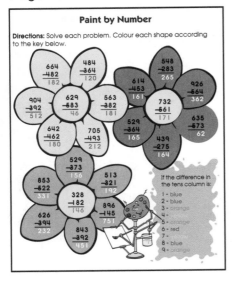

664 −482 = 182	484 −364 = 120	548 −283 = 265
904 −392 = 512	629 −583 = 46	563 −382 = 181	614 −453 = 161	732 −561 = 171	926 −564 = 362
642 −462 = 180	705 −493 = 212	529 −364 = 165	635 −573 = 62
529 −373 = 156	439 −275 = 164
853 −622 = 331	328 −182 = 146	513 −321 = 192
626 −394 = 232	843 −392 = 451	896 −145 = 751

If the difference in the tens column is:
1 – blue
2 – blue
3 – orange
4 –
5 – orange
6 – red
7 –
8 – blue
9 – orange

Page 94

Sailing Through Subtraction

Directions: Subtract, regrouping when needed.

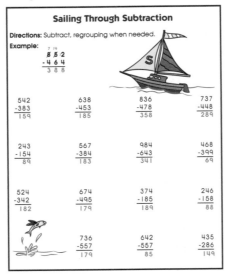

Example:
```
  7 14
  8 5 2
 - 4 6 4
  3 8 8
```

542 −383 = 159	638 −453 = 185	836 −478 = 358	737 −448 = 289
243 −154 = 89	567 −384 = 183	984 −643 = 341	468 −399 = 69
524 −342 = 182	674 −495 = 179	374 −185 = 189	246 −158 = 88
	736 −557 = 179	642 −557 = 85	435 −286 = 149

Page 95

Gobble, Gobble

Directions: Solve each problem. Colour the picture according to the key below. If the answer has a **3** in it, colour it orange. **4**—red, **5**—purple, **6**—brown, **7**—yellow, **8**—blue, and **9**—green. Remember to regroup when needed.

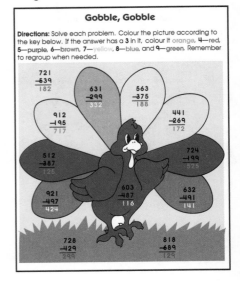

721 −539 = 182	631 −299 = 332	563 −375 = 188
912 −195 = 717		441 −269 = 172
512 −387 = 125		724 −199 = 525
921 −497 = 424	603 −487 = 116	632 −491 = 141
728 −429 = 299		818 −689 = 129

Page 96

Round and Round She Goes

When regrouping with zeros, follow these steps:

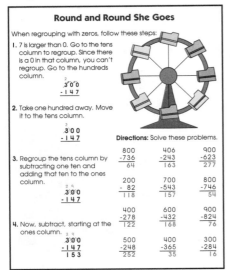

1. 7 is larger than 0. Go to the tens column to regroup. Since there is a 0 in that column, you can't regroup. Go to the hundreds column.
```
    2
  3 0 0
 - 1 4 7
```

2. Take one hundred away. Move it to the tens column.
```
    2
  3 0 0
 - 1 4 7
```

3. Regroup the tens column by subtracting one ten and adding that ten to the ones column.
```
    2 9
  3 0 0
 - 1 4 7
```

4. Now, subtract, starting at the ones column.
```
    2 9
  3 0 0
 - 1 4 7
  1 5 3
```

Directions: Solve these problems.

800 −736 = 64	406 −243 = 163	900 −623 = 277
200 − 82 = 118	700 −543 = 157	800 −746 = 54
400 −278 = 122	600 −432 = 168	900 −824 = 76
500 −248 = 252	400 −365 = 35	300 −284 = 16

Page 97

Jungle Math

Directions: Solve these problems.

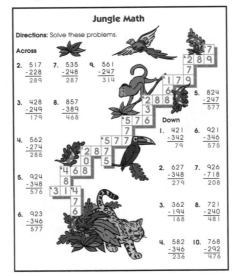

Across

2. 517 −228 = 289
3. 428 −249 = 179
4. 562 −274 = 288
5. 924 −348 = 576
6. 923 −346 = 577
7. 535 −248 = 287
8. 857 −389 = 468
9. 561 −247 = 314
5. 824 −247 = 577

Down

1. 421 −342 = 79
2. 627 −348 = 279
3. 362 −194 = 168
4. 582 −346 = 236
6. 921 −346 = 575
7. 926 −718 = 208
8. 721 −240 = 481
10. 768 −292 = 476

Page 98

Timely Zeros

Directions: Subtract.

300 −189 = 111	803 −324 = 479	504 −362 = 142		
900 −648 = 252	800 −724 = 76	702 −561 = 141		
200 −149 = 51	600 −476 = 124	500 −362 = 138	807 −298 = 509	406 −328 = 78
300 −243 = 57	600 −421 = 179	700 −348 = 352	308 −189 = 119	500 −384 = 116
	302 −195 = 107	600 −247 = 353	400 −108 = 292	
		205 −148 = 57	308 −189 = 119	

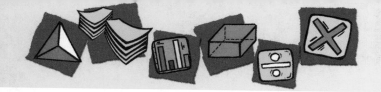

Page 99

Subtraction Maze

Directions: Solve the problems. Remember to regroup when needed.

4,172 −1,536 **2,636**	6,723 −2,586 **4,137**	547 −259 **288**	834 −463 **371**	562 −325 **237**	7,146 −3,498 **3,648**
9,427 −6,648 **2,779**	8,149 −5,372 **2,777**	5,389 −1,652 **3,737**	421 −275 **146**	7,456 −3,724 **3,732**	818 −639 **179**
772 −586 **186**	6,529 −4,538 **1,991**	5,379 −2,835 **2,544**	6,275 −3,761 **2,514**	5,612 −1,505 **4,107**	8,355 −5,366 **2,989**

Directions: Shade in the answers from above to find the path.

	2,514	288	186	3,732	2,989
	2,779	156	1,901	2,414	4,137
3,748	3,337	2,777	371	179	1,991
3,048	3,737	146	2,717 →		
679	237	374	4,107		
886	2,636	2,544	3,648	KITTY	

Page 100

High Class Math

Directions: Solve these problems.

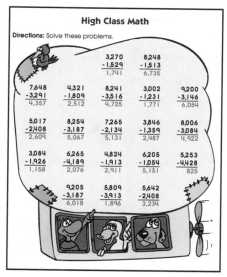

	3,270 −1,529 **1,741**	8,248 −1,513 **6,735**	

7,648 −3,291 **4,357**	4,321 −1,809 **2,512**	8,241 −3,516 **4,725**	3,002 −1,231 **1,771**	9,200 −3,146 **6,054**
5,017 −2,408 **2,609**	8,254 −3,187 **5,067**	7,265 −2,134 **5,131**	3,846 −1,359 **2,487**	8,006 −3,084 **4,922**
3,084 −1,926 **1,158**	6,265 −4,189 **2,076**	4,824 −1,913 **2,911**	6,205 −1,054 **5,151**	5,253 −4,428 **825**
	9,205 −3,187 **6,018**	5,809 −3,913 **1,896**	5,642 −2,408 **3,234**	

Page 101

Kite Craze!

Directions: Subtract.

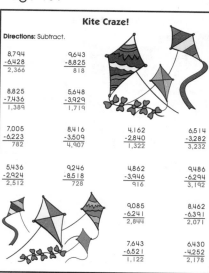

8,794 −6,428 **2,366**	9,643 −8,825 **818**		
8,825 −7,436 **1,389**	5,648 −3,929 **1,719**		
7,005 −6,223 **782**	8,416 −3,509 **4,907**	4,162 −2,840 **1,322**	6,514 −3,282 **3,232**
5,436 −2,924 **2,512**	9,246 −8,518 **728**	4,862 −3,946 **916**	9,486 −6,294 **3,192**
		9,085 −6,241 **2,844**	8,462 −6,391 **2,071**
		7,643 −6,521 **1,122**	6,430 −4,252 **2,178**

Page 102

Subtraction on Stage!

Directions: Subtract.

5,648 −2,425 **3,223**	2,148 − 825 **1,323**		
7,641 −5,246 **2,395**	7,648 −3,289 **4,359**	5,408 −1,291 **4,117**	8,209 −4,182 **4,027**
8,419 −2,182 **6,237**	6,249 −1,526 **4,723**	6,428 −4,159 **2,269**	4,287 −2,492 **1,795**
7,645 −2,826 **4,819**	2,016 −1,021 **995**	8,247 −6,459 **1,788**	9,047 −6,152 **2,895**
			5,231 −1,642 **3,589**
			7,689 −2,845 **4,844**

Page 103

Subtraction Search

Directions: Solve each problem. Find the answer in the chart and circle it. The answers may go in any direction.

6,003 −2,737 **3,266**	5,040 −3,338 **1,702**	9,000 −5,725 **3,275**
7,200 −4,356 **2,844**	3,406 −1,298 **2,108**	5,602 −3,138 **2,464**
7,006 −5,429 **1,577**	3,006 −2,798 **208**	3,605 −2,718 **887**
5,904 −3,917 **1,987**	5,039 −1,954 **3,085**	8,704 −2,496 **6,208**
4,081 −3,594 **487**	6,508 − 399 **6,109**	5,039 −2,467 **2,572**	9,006 − 575 **8,431**	5,001 −2,351 **2,650**
	8,002 −5,686 **2,316**	6,058 −2,175 **3,883**	9,504 −7,368 **2,136**	7,290 −1,801 **5,489**

2	1	6	3	2	7	5
6	3	3	2	1	0	8
2	1	6	3	3	4	
0	2	2	6	5	0	9
8	5	4	2	0	8	7
8	9	0	6	1	5	6
3	2	8	4	2	1	
8	3	4	8	8	5	0
8	1	9	8	7	2	9
3	4	5	8	5	6	7
8	1	3	7	0	4	2
9	3	2	1	7	0	2

Page 104

Problem Solving

Directions: Solve each problem.

Work Space:

1. There were 48 words on a spelling test. Sarah missed 9 of them. How many words did she spell correctly?

   There were __48__ words on the test.
   Sarah missed __9__ words.
   She spelled __39__ words correctly

2. Ryan earned 91 points. Mike earned 5 points less than Ryan. How many points did Mike earn?

   Ryan earned __91__ points.
   Mike earned __5__ points less than Ryan.
   Mike earned __86__ points.

3. Sheila lost 7 of the 45 games she played. How many games did she win?

   She won __38__ games.

4. Travis had 50 tickets to sell. He sold some and had 6 left. How many tickets did he sell?

   Travis sold __44__ tickets.

5. Angela's great-grandfather is 82 years old. How old was he 4 years ago?

   Four years ago, he was __78__ years old.

1.
2.
3.
4.
5.

Page 105

Problem Solving

Directions: Solve each problem.

Work Space:

1. Joseph weighs 43 pounds. Zach weighs 12 pounds less than Joseph. How much does Zach weigh?

   Joseph weighs __43__ kilograms.
   Zach weighs __12__ kilograms less than Joseph.
   Zach weighs __31__ kilograms.

2. There are 73 children in the gym. Forty-five of them are boys. How many girls are in the gym?

   There are __73__ children in the gym.
   There are __45__ boys in the gym.
   There are __28__ girls in the gym.

3. A store has 84 bicycles. They have 45 girls' bicycles. How many boys' bicycles do they have?

   __39__ bicycles are boys' bicycles.

4. It takes 50 points to win a prize. Paige has 38 points. How many more points does Paige need to win a prize?

   Paige needs __12__ points.

Page 106

Addition and Subtraction

Directions: Add.

1.
   53 +6 = 59
   24 +2 = 26
   2 +35 = 37
   8 +81 = 89
   64 +3 = 67
   25 +2 = 27

2.
   36 +5 = 41
   54 +8 = 62
   8 +39 = 47
   2 +59 = 61
   48 +8 = 56
   26 +7 = 33

3.
   42 +33 = 75
   72 +14 = 86
   54 +23 = 77
   61 +28 = 89
   19 +40 = 59
   26 +52 = 78

4.
   54 +27 = 81
   35 +36 = 71
   59 +38 = 97
   54 +19 = 73
   27 +48 = 75
   39 +39 = 78

Directions: Subtract.

5.
   37 -3 = 34
   29 -4 = 25
   54 -4 = 50
   87 -2 = 85
   56 -5 = 51
   89 -6 = 83

6.
   47 -9 = 38
   72 -5 = 67
   45 -7 = 38
   55 -9 = 46
   40 -5 = 35
   34 -7 = 27

7.
   54 -12 = 42
   42 -30 = 12
   75 -64 = 11
   46 -23 = 23
   93 -81 = 12
   89 -41 = 48

8.
   73 -25 = 48
   85 -49 = 36
   92 -24 = 68
   64 -56 = 8
   77 -48 = 29
   88 -38 = 50

Page 107

Addition and Subtraction

To check 34 + 19 = 53, subtract 19 from ____.
34 +19 = 53, -19 = 34   These should be the same.

To check 53 - 19 = 34, add ____ to 34.
53 -19 = 34, +19 = 53   These should be the same.

Directions: Add. Check each answer.

1.
   54 +7 = 61
   46 +9 = 55
   63 +18 = 81
   58 +27 = 85
   21 +49 = 70
   45 +46 = 91

2.
   26 +38 = 64
   37 +19 = 56
   41 +9 = 50
   58 +18 = 76
   67 +27 = 94
   35 +38 = 73

Directions: Subtract. Check each answer.

3.
   62 -8 = 54
   48 -9 = 39
   35 -16 = 19
   96 -29 = 67
   52 -14 = 38
   43 -5 = 38

4.
   36 -18 = 18
   57 -8 = 49
   67 -19 = 48
   52 -17 = 35
   51 -23 = 28
   60 -46 = 14

Page 108

Problem Solving

Directions: Answer each question.

Work Space:

1. This morning, the temperature was 23° degrees. This afternoon, it was 31° degrees. How many degrees did it go up?

   Are you to add or subtract? __Subtract__
   How many degrees did the temperature go up? __8__

2. There were 45 people at a meeting. After 28 of them left, how many people were still at the meeting?

   Are you to add or subtract? __Subtract__
   How many people were still at the meeting? __17__

3. Renée drove 67 kilometres in the morning and 24 kilometres in the afternoon. How far did she drive?

   Are you to add or subtract? __Add__
   How far did she drive? __91__

4. A clown has 26 orange and 28 blue balloons. How many balloons is that?

   Are you to add or subtract? __Add__
   How many orange and blue balloons are there? __54__

Page 109

Problem Solving

Directions: Answer each question.

Work Space:

1. Nicholas is on a trip of 170 kilometres. So far, he has gone 90 kilometres. How many kilometres must he go?

   Are you to add or subtract? __Subtract__
   How many more kilometres must he go? __80__

2. A school has 20 men teachers. It has 30 women teachers. How many teachers are in the school?

   Are you to add or subtract? __Add__
   How many teachers are in the school? __50__

3. Logan weighs 31 kilograms. His older brother weighs 91 kilograms. How many more kilograms does his older brother weigh?

   Are you to add or subtract? __Subtract__
   How many more kilograms does his older brother weigh? __30__

4. Jessica has 110 pennies. Emily has 90 pennies. Jessica has how many more pennies than Emily?

   Jessica has __20__ more pennies than Emily.

Page 110

Addition and Subtraction

Directions: Add.

1.
   5 +6 = 11
   50 +60 = 110
   7 +7 = 14
   70 +80 = 150
   90 +80 = 170
   70 +70 = 140

2.
   53 +95 = 148
   44 +74 = 118
   82 +96 = 178
   67 +70 = 137
   55 +52 = 107
   73 +86 = 159

3.
   63 +78 = 141
   82 +89 = 171
   97 +27 = 124
   56 +75 = 131
   88 +88 = 176
   97 +44 = 141

4.
   26 +53 = 79
   66 +25 = 91
   74 +65 = 139
   39 +87 = 126
   82 +17 = 99
   76 +72 = 148

Directions: Subtract.

5.
   16 -7 = 9
   160 -70 = 90
   15 -9 = 6
   150 -90 = 60
   140 -60 = 80
   170 -80 = 90

6.
   136 -53 = 83
   165 -74 = 91
   154 -90 = 64
   186 -93 = 93
   179 -82 = 97
   147 -67 = 80

7.
   146 -97 = 49
   158 -69 = 89
   172 -85 = 87
   163 -77 = 86
   125 -58 = 67
   116 -39 = 77

8.
   176 -53 = 123
   184 -35 = 149
   154 -72 = 82
   153 -74 = 79
   146 -32 = 114
   107 -s 40 = 67

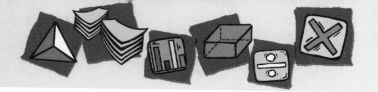

Page 111

Skipping Through the Tens

Directions: Skip count by tens. Begin with the number on the first line. Write each number that follows.

0, _10_, _20_, _30_, _40_, _50_, _60_, _70_, _80_, _90_, **100**

3, _13_, _23_, _33_, _43_, **53**, _63_, _73_, _83_, _93_, **103**

1, _11_, _21_, _31_, _41_, _51_, _61_, _71_, _81_, _91_, **101**

8, _18_, _28_, _38_, _48_, _58_, **68**, _78_, _88_, _98_, **108**

6, _16_, _26_, _36_, _46_, _56_, _66_, _76_, _86_, _96_, **106**

4, _14_, _24_, _34_, _44_, _54_, _64_, _74_, _84_, _94_, **104**

2, _12_, _22_, _32_, _42_, _52_, _62_, _72_, _82_, **92**, **102**

5, _15_, _25_, _35_, **45**, _55_, _65_, _75_, _85_, _95_, **105**

7, _17_, _27_, _37_, _47_, _57_, _67_, **77**, _87_, _97_, **107**

9, _19_, _29_, _39_, _49_, _59_, _69_, _79_, _89_, _99_, **109**

What is ten more than . . . ?

26 _36_   29 _39_

44 _54_   77 _87_

53 _63_   91 _101_

24 _34_   49 _59_

66 _76_   35 _45_

54 _64_   82 _92_

Page 112

Counting to 100

Directions: Skip count to 100.

By twos:

2	4	**6**	**8**	10	12	14	**16**	18	20	**22**	24	26	28
30	32	34	36	38	40	42	**44**	46	48	50	52	54	**56**
58	60	62	64	**66**	68	70	72	74	76	**78**	80	82	84
86	88	90	92	**94**	96	**98**	**100**						

By threes:

3	6	**9**	12	15	18	**21**	24	27	30	33	36	**39**	42
45	48	51	**54**	**57**	60	63	66	69	72	**75**	78	81	84
87	**90**	93	96	**99**	**102**								

By fours:

4	**8**	12	16	20	24	28	32	36	**40**	44	48	52	56
60	64	68	72	76	80	**84**	**88**	92	96	**100**			

On another sheet of paper, count by fives to 100. Then, count by sixes.

Page 113

Count the Legs!

Directions: Multiplication is a quick way to add. For example, count the legs of the horses below. They each have 4 legs. You could add 4 + 4 + 4. But it is quicker to say that there are 3 groups of 4 legs. In multiplication, that is 3 x 4.

Multiply to find the number of legs. Write each problem twice.

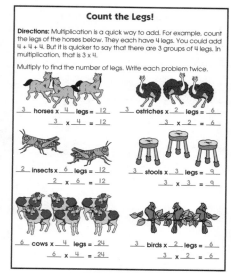

_3_ horses x _4_ legs = _12_   _3_ ostriches x _2_ legs = _6_

_3_ x _4_ = _12_   _3_ x _2_ = _6_

_2_ insects x _6_ legs = _12_   _3_ stools x _3_ legs = _9_

_2_ x _6_ = _12_   _3_ x _3_ = _9_

_6_ cows x _4_ legs = _24_   _3_ birds x _2_ legs = _6_

_6_ x _4_ = _24_   _3_ x _2_ = _6_

Page 114

Multiplication

Multiplication is a short way to find the sum of adding the same number a certain amount of times. For example, we write 7 x 4 = 28 instead of 7 + 7 + 7 + 7 = 28.

Directions: Study the example. Multiply.

Example:

There are two groups of seashells.
There are 3 seashells in each group.
How many seashells are there in all?   2 x 3 = 6

4 + 4 = _8_   3 + 3 + 3 = _9_
2 x 4 = _8_   3 x 3 = _9_

2 x3 6	3 x5 15	4 x3 12	6 x2 12	7 x3 21
5 x2 10	6 x3 18	4 x2 8	7 x2 14	8 x3 24
5 x5 25	9 x4 36	8 x5 40	6 x6 36	9 x3 27

Page 115

Multiplication

2 x 3 is read "two times three."   2 x 3 means 3 + 3.
3 x 2 is read "three times two."   3 x 2 means 2 + 2+ 2.
4 x 5 is read "four times five."   4 x 5 means 5 + 5 + 5 + 5.

3 x 6 is read "three times six."   3 x 6 means _____

2 x 7 is read "two times seven."   2 x 7 means _____

Directions: Complete the following as shown.

1. 3 x 2 is read _three times two_

2. 3 x 4 is read _three times four_

3. 5 x 2 is read _five times two_

4. 4 x 8 is read _four times eight_

5. 4 x 7 is read _four times seven_

Directions: Complete the following as shown.

6. 2 x 4 means _4 + 4_   4 x 2 means _2 + 2 + 2 + 2_

7. 3 x 5 means _5 + 5 + 5_   5 x 3 means _3 + 3 + 3 + 3 + 3_

8. 3 x 7 means _7 + 7 + 7_   7 x 3 means _3 + 3 + 3_

9. 4 x 6 means _6 + 6 + 6 + 6_   6 x 4 means _4 + 4 + 4 + 4 + 4 + 4_

10. 2 x 8 means _8 + 8_   8 x 2 means _2 + 2 + 2 + 2 + 2 + 2 + 2 + 2_

11. 3 x 9 means _9 + 9 + 9_   9 x 3 means _3 + 3 + 3 + 3 + 3 + 3 + 3 + 3 + 3_

Page 116

Multiplication

3 x 4 means 4 + 4 + 4.   4 x 3 means 3 + 3 + 3 + 3.

4
4
4
x3
12   4
+4
+4
12   4
4
4
x3
12   3
3
3
+3
12

Directions: Add or multiply.

1.	8 +8 16	8 x2 16	4 +4 8	4 x2 8	5 +5 10	5 x2 10
2.	6 +6 12	6 x2 12	7 +7 14	7 x2 14	2 +2 4	2 x2 4
3.	9 +9 18	9 x2 18	3 +3 6	3 x2 6	1 +1 2	1 x2 2
4.	2 +2 6	3 x3 6	3 3 9	3 x3 9	4 4 +4 12	4 x3 12
5.	5 5 +5 15	5 x3 15	6 6 18	6 x3 18	7 7 +7 21	7 x3 21
6.	8 8 +8 24	8 x3 24	9 9 +9 27	9 x3 27	1 +1 3	1 x3 3

Page 117

Multiplication: Zero and One

Any number multiplied by zero equals zero. One mutiplied by any number equals that number. Study the example. Multiply.

Example:

How many full sails are there in all?

2 boats x 1 sail on each boat = **2** sails

How many full sails are there now?

2 boats x **0** sails = **0** sails

Directions: Multiply.

1	2	3	4	0	7
×5	×1	×0	×1	×6	×0
5	**2**	**0**	**4**	**0**	**0**

9	8	3	4	7	6
×1	×0	×1	×0	×1	×1
9	**0**	**3**	**0**	**7**	**6**

Page 118

Multiplication

Directions: Multiply.

3	4	3
×5	×6	×8
15	**24**	**24**

5	4	5
×5	×8	×4
25	**32**	**20**

6	3	2	7	9
×7	×9	×8	×6	×4
42	**27**	**16**	**42**	**36**

6	5	7	5	8
×8	×6	×7	×3	×9
48	**30**	**49**	**15**	**72**

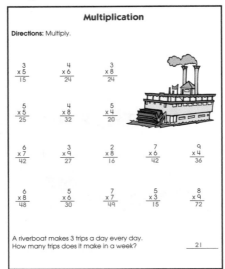

A riverboat makes 3 trips a day every day. How many trips does it make in a week? **21**

Page 119

Multiplication

1	2	0	0		0	1	2	1
×0	×0	×3	×4		×1	×1	×1	×3
0	**0**	**0**	**0**		**0**	**1**	**2**	**3**

Directions: Multiply.

#						
1.	0 ×2 = **0**	9 ×1 = **9**	1 ×7 = **7**	6 ×0 = **0**	1 ×5 = **5**	0 ×7 = **0**
2.	4 ×0 = **0**	8 ×1 = **8**	1 ×4 = **4**	0 ×9 = **0**	7 ×0 = **0**	6 ×1 = **6**
3.	5 ×0 = **0**	0 ×3 = **0**	5 ×1 = **5**	6 ×1 = **6**	1 ×1 = **1**	8 ×0 = **0**
4.	0 ×7 = **0**	0 ×4 = **0**	3 ×0 = **0**	0 ×0 = **0**	7 ×1 = **7**	1 ×5 = **5**
5.	0 ×7 = **0**	1 ×9 = **9**	1 ×6 = **6**	0 ×5 = **0**	1 ×0 = **0**	2 ×1 = **2**
6.	1 ×4 = **4**	1 ×1 = **1**	4 ×0 = **0**	8 ×1 = **8**	0 ×6 = **0**	2 ×3 = **6**
7.	0 ×9 = **0**	6 ×1 = **6**	0 ×2 = **0**	1 ×1 = **1**	0 ×0 = **0**	3 ×1 = **3**
8.	1 ×2 = **2**	6 ×0 = **0**	7 ×0 = **0**	1 ×3 = **3**	4 ×1 = **4**	0 ×0 = **0**

Page 120

Fact Snacks

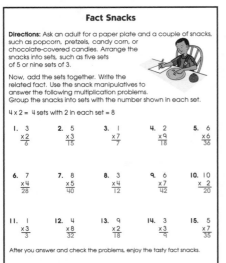

Directions: Ask an adult for a paper plate and a couple of snacks, such as popcorn, pretzels, candy corn, or chocolate-covered candies. Arrange the snacks into sets, such as five sets of 5 or nine sets of 3.

Now, add the sets together. Write the related fact. Use the snack manipulatives to answer the following multiplication problems. Group the snacks into sets with the number shown in each set.

4 x 2 = 4 sets with 2 in each set = 8

1. 3 ×2 = **6**	2. 5 ×3 = **15**	3. 1 ×7 = **7**	4. 2 ×9 = **18**	5. 6 ×6 = **36**
6. 7 ×4 = **28**	7. 8 ×5 = **40**	8. 3 ×4 = **12**	9. 6 ×7 = **42**	10. 10 ×2 = **20**
11. 1 ×3 = **3**	12. 4 ×8 = **32**	13. 9 ×2 = **18**	14. 3 ×3 = **9**	15. 5 ×7 = **35**

After you answer and check the problems, enjoy the tasty fact snacks.

Page 121

Multiplying

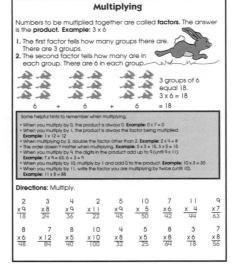

Numbers to be multiplied together are called **factors.** The answer is the **product. Example:** 3 x 6

1. The first factor tells how many groups there are. There are 3 groups.
2. The second factor tells how many are in each group. There are 6 in each group.

3 groups of 6 equal 18.
3 x 6 = 18

6 + 6 + 6 = 18

Some helpful hints to remember when multiplying:

- When you multiply by 0, the product is always 0. **Example:** 0 x 7 = 0
- When you multiply by 1, the product is always the factor being multiplied. **Example:** 1 x 12 = 12
- When multiplying by 2, double the factor other than 2. **Example:** 2 x 4 = 8
- The order doesn't matter when multiplying. 5 x 3 = 15, 3 x 5 = 15
- When you multiply by 9, the digits in the product add up to 9 (until 9 x 11). **Example:** 7 x 9 = 63, 6 + 3 = 9
- When you multiply by 10, multiply by 1 and add 0 to the product. **Example:** 10 x 3 = 30
- When you multiply by 11, write the factor you are multiplying by twice (until 10). **Example:** 11 x 8 = 88

Directions: Multiply.

2	3	4	2	5	10	7	11	9
×9	×8	×9	×11	×9	×5	×6	×4	×7
18	**24**	**36**	**22**	**45**	**50**	**42**	**44**	**63**

8	7	8	10	4	5	8	3	7
×6	×12	×5	×10	×8	×5	×8	×6	×8
48	**84**	**40**	**100**	**32**	**25**	**64**	**18**	**56**

Page 122

Factor Fun

When you change the order of the factors, you have the same product.

Directions: Multiply.

7	3	6	5	2	3
×3	×7	×5	×6	×3	×2
21	**21**	**30**	**30**	**6**	**6**

4	6	2	9	8	4
×6	×4	×9	×2	×4	×8
24	**24**	**18**	**18**	**32**	**32**

7	2	3	6	9	4
×2	×7	×6	×3	×4	×9
14	**14**	**18**	**18**	**36**	**36**

8	3	5	2	9	3
×3	×8	×2	×5	×3	×9
24	**24**	**10**	**10**	**27**	**27**

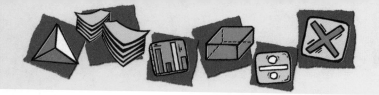

Page 123

Racing to the Finish

Directions: Multiply.

5 ×3 = 15	2 ×8 = 16	4 ×6 = 24	9 ×3 = 27	7 ×5 = 35	3 ×9 = 27
4 ×2 = 8	6 ×2 = 12	4 ×4 = 16	0 ×6 = 0	3 ×2 = 6	7 ×2 = 14
6 ×5 = 30	3 ×4 = 12	8 ×3 = 24	4 ×5 = 20	5 ×2 = 10	7 ×4 = 28
6 ×3 = 18	4 ×8 = 32	2 ×2 = 4	8 ×5 = 40	3 ×7 = 21	5 ×5 = 25
5 ×9 = 45	9 ×2 = 18	4 ×6 = 24	9 ×4 = 36		

Page 124

Climbing Granite Boulders!

Directions: Multiply.

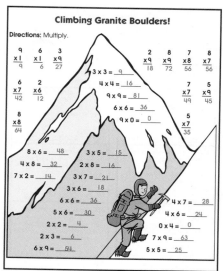

9 ×1 = 9   6 ×1 = 6   3 ×9 = 27   2 ×9 = 18   8 ×9 = 72   7 ×8 = 56   8 ×7 = 56

6 ×7 = 42   6 ×2 = 12   7 ×7 = 49   5 ×9 = 45

8 ×8 = 64   5 ×7 = 35

3 x 3 = 9
4 x 4 = 16
9 x 9 = 81
6 x 6 = 36
9 x 0 = 0

8 x 6 = 48   3 x 5 = 15
4 x 8 = 32   2 x 8 = 16
7 x 2 = 14   3 x 7 = 21
3 x 6 = 18
6 x 6 = 36   4 x 7 = 28
5 x 6 = 30   4 x 6 = 24
2 x 2 = 4   0 x 4 = 0
2 x 3 = 6   7 x 9 = 63
6 x 9 = 54   5 x 5 = 25

Page 125

Multiplication

Directions: Time yourself as you multiply. How quickly can you complete this page?

3 ×2 = 6	8 ×7 = 56	1 ×0 = 0	1 ×6 = 6	3 ×4 = 12	0 ×4 = 0
4 ×1 = 4	4 ×4 = 16	2 ×5 = 10	9 ×3 = 27	9 ×9 = 81	5 ×3 = 15
0 ×8 = 0	2 ×6 = 12	9 ×6 = 54	8 ×5 = 40	7 ×3 = 21	4 ×2 = 8
3 ×5 = 15	2 ×0 = 0	4 ×6 = 24	1 ×3 = 3	0 ×0 = 0	3 ×3 = 9

Page 126

Multiplication Table

Directions: Complete the multiplication table. Use it to practise your multiplication facts.

X	0	1	2	3	4	5	6	7	8	9	10
0	0	0	0	0	0	0	0	0	0	0	0
1	0	1	2	3	4	5	6	7	8	9	10
2	0	2	4	6	8	10	12	14	16	18	20
3	0	3	6	9	12	15	18	21	24	27	30
4	0	4	8	12	16	20	24	28	32	36	40
5	0	5	10	15	20	25	30	35	40	45	50
6	0	6	12	18	24	30	36	42	48	54	60
7	0	7	14	21	28	35	42	49	56	63	70
8	0	8	16	24	32	40	48	56	64	72	80
9	0	9	18	27	36	45	54	63	72	81	90
10	0	10	20	30	40	50	60	70	80	90	100

Page 127

Multiplication

Factors are the numbers multiplied together in a multiplication problem. The answer is called the product. If you change the order of the factors, the product stays the same.

Example:

There are 4 groups of fish.
There are 3 fish in each group.
How many fish are there in all?
4   x   3   = 12
factor x factor = product

Directions: Draw 3 groups of 4 fish.

3 x 4 = 12

Compare your drawing and answer with the example. What did you notice?

Directions: Fill in the missing numbers. Multiply.

5 x 4 = 20   3 x 6 = 18   4 x 2 = 8
4 x 5 = 20   6 x 3 = 18   2 x 4 = 8

3 ×7 = 21	7 ×3 = 21	2 ×9 = 18	9 ×2 = 18	8 ×4 = 32	4 ×8 = 32
5 ×2 = 10	2 ×5 = 10	6 ×3 = 18	3 ×6 = 18	5 ×6 = 30	6 ×5 = 30

Page 128

Double Trouble

Directions: Solve each multiplication problem. Below each answer, write the letter from the code that matches the answer. Read the coded question and write the answer in the space provided.

1	4	9	16	25	36	49	64	81	100	121	144
E	G	H	I	N	O	S	T	U	W	X	Y

10 ×10 = 100 (W)   3 ×3 = 3... 9 (H)   6 ×6 = 36 (O)   4 ×4 = 16 (I)   7 ×7 = 49 (S)

W H O   I S

7 ×7 = 49 (S)   4 ×4 = 16 (I)   8 ×8 = 64 (T)   8 ×8 = 64 (T)   4 ×4 = 16 (I)   5 ×5 = 25 (N)   2 ×2 = 4 (G)

S I T T I N G

5 ×5 = 25 (N)   1 ×1 = 1 (E)   11 ×11 = 121 (X)   8 ×8 = 64 (T)   8 ×8 = 64 (T)   6 ×6 = 36 (O)   12 ×12 = 144 (Y)   6 ×6 = 36 (O)   9 ×9 = 81 (U)

N E X T   T O   Y O U?

Answer:  Answers will vary.

Page 133

Crossword Number Fun

Directions: Write the word form of each product in the puzzle.

Across

3. 9 x 4 = __36__
8. 10 x 5 = __50__
9. 2 x 9 = __18__
10. 3 x 12 = __36__
12. 7 x 11 = __77__
14. 4 x 10 = __40__
15. 6 x 5 = __30__
16. 0 x 7 = __0__

Down

1. 7 x 8 = __56__
2. 6 x 1 = __6__
4. 2 x 5 = __10__
5. 11 x 3 = __33__
6. 5 x 1 = __5__
7. 5 x 4 = __20__
11. 12 x 8 = __96__
13. 3 x 8 = __24__

Page 134

Wacky Waldo's Snow Show

Wacky Waldo's Snow Show is an exciting and fantastic sight. Waldo has trained whales and bears to skate together on the ice. There is a hockey game between a team of sharks and a pack of wolves. Elephants ride sleds down steep hills. Horses and buffaloes ski swiftly down mountains.

Directions: Write each problem and its answer.

1. Wacky Waldo has 4 ice-skating whales. He has 4 times as many bears who ice skate. How many bears can ice skate?

   __4__ x __4__ = __16__

2. Waldo's Snow Show has 4 shows on Thursday, but it has 6 times as many on Saturday. How many shows are there on Saturday?

   __4__ x __6__ = __24__

3. The Sharks' hockey team has 3 great white sharks. It has 6 times as many tiger sharks. How many tiger sharks does it have?

   __3__ x __6__ = __18__

4. The Wolves' hockey team has 4 grey wolves. It has 8 times as many red wolves. How many red wolves does it have?

   __4__ x __8__ = __32__

5. Waldo taught 6 buffaloes to ski. He was able to teach 5 times as many horses to ski. How many horses did he teach?

   __6__ x __5__ = __30__

6. Buff, a skiing buffalo, took 7 nasty spills when he was learning to ski. His friend Harry Horse fell down 8 times as often. How many times did Harry fall?

   __7__ x __8__ = __56__

Page 135

Problem Solving

Directions: Solve each problem.

Work Space:

1. Ashley wants to buy 5 erasers. They cost 9 cents each. How much will she have to pay?

   Ashley wants to buy __5__ erasers.
   One eraser costs __9__ cents.
   Ashley will have to pay __45__ cents.

2. There are 5 rows of mailboxes. There are 7 mailboxes in each row. How many mailboxes are there in all?

   There are __7__ mailboxes in each row.
   There are __5__ rows of mailboxes.
   There are __35__ mailboxes in all.

3. Milton, the pet monkey, eats 4 meals every day. How many meals does he eat in a week?

   There are __7__ days in a week.
   Milton eats __4__ meals every day.
   Milton eats __28__ meals in a week.

4. In a baseball game each team gets 3 outs per inning. How many outs does each team get in a 5-inning game?

   There are __5__ innings in the game.
   Each team gets __3__ outs per inning.
   The team gets __15__ outs in the 5-inning game.

Page 136

Problem Solving

Directions: Solve each problem.

Work Space:

1. Neal has 6 books. Each book weighs 1 kilogram. What is the weight of all the books?

   Neal has __6__ books.
   Each book weighs __1__ kilogram.
   The six books weigh __6__ kilograms.

2. A basketball game has 4 time periods. Kate's team is to play 8 games. How many periods will her team play?

   Kate's team is to play __8__ games.
   Each game has __4__ time periods.
   Kate's team will play __32__ time periods in all.

3. Meagan works 8 hours every day. How many hours does she work in 5 days?

   She works __40__ hours in 5 days.

4. Shane can ride his bicycle 5 kilometres in an hour. At that speed how far could he ride in 2 hours?

   Shane could ride __10__ kilometres in 2 hours.

5. Calvin bought 5 bags of balloons. Each bag had 6 balloons. How many balloons did he buy?

   Calvin bought __30__ balloons in all.

Page 137

Problem Solving

Directions: Solve each problem.

Work Space:

1. There are 6 rows of cactus plants. Each row has 4 plants. How many cactus plants are there in all?

   There are __6__ rows of cactus plants.
   There are __4__ cactus plants in each row.
   There are __24__ cactus plants in all.

2. There are 8 marigold plants in each row. There are 6 rows. How many marigold plants are there?

   There are __8__ marigold plants in each row.
   There are __6__ rows of marigold plants.
   There are __48__ marigold plants in all.

3. There are 6 rosebushes in each row. There are 9 rows. How many rosebushes are there?

   There are __6__ rosebushes in each row.
   There are __9__ rows of rosebushes.
   There are __54__ rosebushes in all.

Page 138

Problem Solving

Directions: Solve each problem.

Work Space:

1. In Tori's building there are 7 floors. There are 9 apartments on each floor. How many apartments are in the building?

   There are __7__ floors in this building.
   There are __9__ apartments on each floor.
   There are __63__ apartments in this building.

2. The science club meets 4 times each month. The club meets for 7 months. How many meetings will the science club have?

   The science club meets __4__ times each month.
   The club meets for __7__ months.
   The club will have __28__ meetings in all.

3. Each bag of corn weighs 8 kilograms. There are 7 bags. How much do the bags weigh in all?

   Each bag weighs __8__ kilograms.
   There are __7__ bags.
   The bags weigh __56__ kilograms in all.

4. There are 7 days in a week. How many days are there in 5 weeks?

   There are __35__ days in 5 weeks.

Page 139

Problem Solving

Directions: Solve each problem.

Work Space:

1. There are 8 chairs around each table. There are 9 tables. How many chairs are around all the tables?

   There are __8__ chairs around each table.
   There are __9__ tables.
   There are __72__ chairs around all the tables.

2. Workers are eating lunch at 9 tables. Each table has 9 workers. How many workers are eating lunch?

   There are __9__ tables.
   __9__ workers are at each table.
   __81__ workers are eating lunch.

3. The workers drink 9 litres of milk each day. They are at work 5 days a week. How many litres of milk do they drink in 5 days?

   They drink __45__ litres of milk in 5 days.

4. A bowling league bowls 4 times each month. How many times will the league bowl in 9 months?

   The bowling league will bowl __36__ times.

5. A regular baseball game is 9 innings long. How many innings are in 7 regular games?

   There are __63__ innings in 7 regular games.

1.

2.

3.

4.

5.

Page 140

Problem Solving

Directions: Solve each problem.

Work Space:

1. Some students formed 5 teams. There were 8 students on each team. How many students were there?

   There were __5__ teams.
   There were __8__ students on each team.
   There were __40__ students in all.

2. The waiter put 9 napkins on each table. There were 9 tables. How many napkins did the waiter use?

   The waiter put __9__ napkins on each table.
   There were __9__ tables.
   The waiter used __81__ napkins in all.

3. Dr. Mede rides her bicycle 6 kilometres every day. How far would she ride in 9 days?

   Dr. Mede rides __6__ kilometres every day.
   She rides for each of __9__ days.
   She would ride __54__ kilometres in all.

4. Mr. Brown works 7 hours each day. How many hours will he work in 6 days?

   Mr. Brown will work __42__ hours in 6 days.

5. There are 8 hot dogs in each package. How many hot dogs are there in 9 packages?

   There are __72__ hot dogs in 9 packages.

1.

2.

3.

4.

5.

Page 141

Backward Multiplication

Division problems are like multiplication problems—just turned around. As you solve 8 ÷ 4, think, "How many groups of 4 make 8?" or "What number 'times' 4 is eight?"

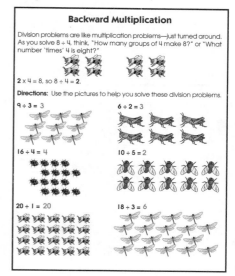

2 x 4 = 8, so 8 ÷ 4 = 2.

Directions: Use the pictures to help you solve these division problems.

9 ÷ 3 = 3

6 ÷ 2 = 3

16 ÷ 4 = 4

10 ÷ 5 = 2

20 ÷ 1 = 20

18 ÷ 3 = 6

Page 142

What Exactly Is Division?

In division, you begin with an amount of something (the dividend), separate it into small groups (the divisor), then find out how many groups are created (the quotient).

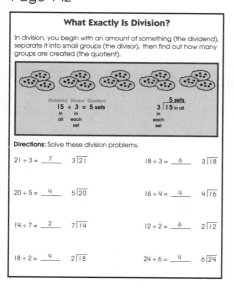

Dividend Divisor Quotient
15 ÷ 3 = 5 sets
in all / in each set

5 sets
3) 15 in all / in each set

Directions: Solve these division problems.

21 ÷ 3 = __7__   3)21

18 ÷ 3 = __6__   3)18

20 ÷ 5 = __4__   5)20

16 ÷ 4 = __4__   4)16

14 ÷ 7 = __2__   7)14

12 ÷ 2 = __6__   2)12

18 ÷ 2 = __9__   2)18

24 ÷ 6 = __4__   6)24

Page 143

Division

Division is a way to find out how many times one number is contained in another number. For example, 28 ÷ 4 = 7 means that there are seven groups of four in 28.

Directions: Study the example. Divide.

Example:

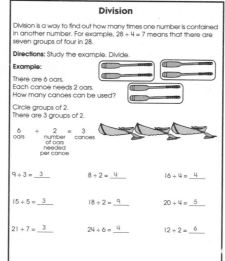

There are 6 oars.
Each canoe needs 2 oars.
How many canoes can be used?

Circle groups of 2.
There are 3 groups of 2.

6 oars ÷ 2 number of oars needed per canoe = 3 canoes

9 ÷ 3 = __3__   8 ÷ 2 = __4__   16 ÷ 4 = __4__

15 ÷ 5 = __3__   18 ÷ 2 = __9__   20 ÷ 4 = __5__

21 ÷ 7 = __3__   24 ÷ 6 = __4__   12 ÷ 2 = __6__

Page 144

Division

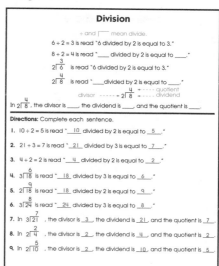

÷ and ⟍ mean divide.

6 ÷ 2 = 3 is read "6 divided by 2 is equal to 3."

8 ÷ 2 = 4 is read "___ divided by 2 is equal to ___."

2)6 (3) is read "6 divided by 2 is equal to 3."

2)8 (4) is read "___ divided by 2 is equal to ___."

divisor → 2)8 ← quotient / dividend

In 2)8, the divisor is ___, the dividend is ___, and the quotient is ___.

Directions: Complete each sentence.

1. 10 ÷ 2 = 5 is read "__10__ divided by 2 is equal to __5__."

2. 21 ÷ 3 = 7 is read "__21__ divided by 3 is equal to __7__."

3. 4 ÷ 2 = 2 is read "__4__ divided by 2 is equal to __2__."

4. 3)18 (6) is read "__18__ divided by 3 is equal to __6__."

5. 2)18 (9) is read "__18__ divided by 2 is equal to __9__."

6. 3)24 (8) is read "__24__ divided by 3 is equal to __8__."

7. In 3)21 (7), the divisor is __3__, the dividend is __21__, and the quotient is __7__.

8. In 2)4 (2), the divisor is __2__, the dividend is __4__, and the quotient is __2__.

9. In 2)10 (5), the divisor is __2__, the dividend is __10__, and the quotient is __5__.

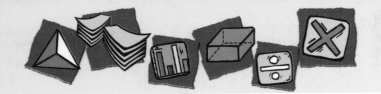

Page 145

Division

6 ✕'s in all
2 ✕'s in each group.
How many groups?   ✕ ✕
                        ✕ ✕
6 ÷ 2 = __3__   ✕ ✕

There are __3__ groups

6 ✕'s in all
3 groups of ✕'s
How many ✕'s in each group?

6 ÷ 3 = _____

There are _____ ✕'s in each group

Directions: Complete the following.

1. 10 ★'s in all.
   2 ★'s in each group.
   How many groups?
   10 ÷ 2 = __5__
   There are __5__ groups.

   10 ★'s in all.
   5 groups of ★'s.
   How many ★'s in each group?
   10 ÷ 5 = __2__
   There are __2__ ★'s in each group.

2. 8 ■'s in all.
   2 ■'s in each group.
   How many groups?
   8 ÷ 2 = __4__
   There are __4__ groups.

   8 ■'s in all.
   4 groups of ■'s.
   How many ■'s in each group?
   8 ÷ 4 = __2__
   There are __2__ ■'s in each group.

3. 4 ◯'s in all.
   2 ◯'s in each group.
   How many groups?
   4 ÷ 2 = __2__
   There are __2__ groups.

   4 ◯'s in all.
   2 groups of ◯'s.
   How many ◯'s in each group?
   4 ÷ 2 = __2__
   There are __2__ ◯'s in each group.

Page 146

Division

Directions: Divide. Draw a line from the boat to the sail with the correct answer.

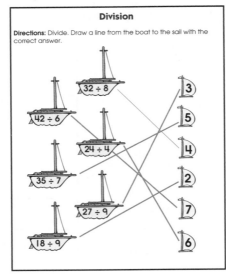

32 ÷ 8 → 4
42 ÷ 6 → 7
24 ÷ 4 → 6
35 ÷ 7 → 5
27 ÷ 9 → 3
18 ÷ 9 → 2

Page 147

Division

Division is a way to find out how many times one number is contained in another number. The ÷ sign means "divided by." Another way to divide is to use ⌐. The **dividend** is the larger number that is divided by the smaller number, or **divisor**. The answer of a division problem is called the **quotient**.

Directions: Study the example. Divide.

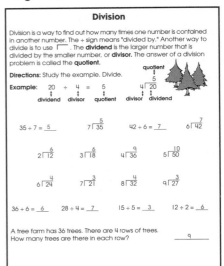

Example:
20 ÷ 4 = 5
dividend divisor quotient

     quotient
      5
4 ⟌ 20
divisor dividend

35 ÷ 7 = __5__   7 ⟌ 35 = 5   42 ÷ 6 = __7__   6 ⟌ 42 = 7

2 ⟌ 12 = 6   3 ⟌ 18 = 6   4 ⟌ 36 = 9   5 ⟌ 50 = 10

6 ⟌ 24 = 4   7 ⟌ 21 = 3   8 ⟌ 32 = 4   9 ⟌ 27 = 3

36 ÷ 6 = __6__   28 ÷ 4 = __7__   15 ÷ 5 = __3__   12 ÷ 2 = __6__

A tree farm has 36 trees. There are 4 rows of trees.
How many trees are there in each row?   __9__

Page 148

Division: Zero and One

Directions: Study the rules of division and the examples. Divide, then write the number of the rule you used to solve each problem.

Examples:

Rule 1: 1 ⟌ 5 = 5   Any number divided by 1 is that number.

Rule 2: 5 ⟌ 5 = 1   Any number except 0 divided by itself is 1.

Rule 3: 7 ⟌ 0 = 0   Zero divided by any number is zero.

Rule 4: 0 ⟌ 7   You cannot divide by zero.

1 ⟌ 6 = 6   Rule __1__   4 ÷ 1 = __4__   Rule __1__

7 ⟌ 7 = 1   Rule __2__   9 ÷ 9 = __1__   Rule __2__

9 ⟌ 0 = 0   Rule __3__   7 ÷ 1 = __7__   Rule __1__

1 ⟌ 4 = 4   Rule __1__   6 ÷ 0 = __not possible__   Rule __4__

ZERO ONE

Page 149

Blastoff!

Directions: Divide.

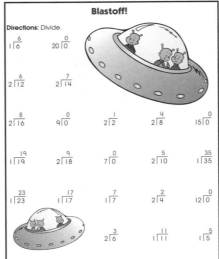

1 ⟌ 6 = 6   20 ⟌ 0 = 0

2 ⟌ 12 = 6   2 ⟌ 14 = 7

2 ⟌ 16 = 8   9 ⟌ 0 = 0   2 ⟌ 2 = 1   2 ⟌ 8 = 4   15 ⟌ 0 = 0

1 ⟌ 19 = 19   2 ⟌ 18 = 9   7 ⟌ 0 = 0   2 ⟌ 10 = 5   1 ⟌ 35 = 35

1 ⟌ 23 = 23   1 ⟌ 17 = 17   1 ⟌ 7 = 7   2 ⟌ 4 = 2   12 ⟌ 0 = 0

2 ⟌ 6 = 3   1 ⟌ 11 = 11   1 ⟌ 5 = 5

Page 150

Carrier Math Messengers

Directions: Divide.

3 ⟌ 12 = 4   8 ⟌ 48 = 6   2 ⟌ 18 = 9

5 ⟌ 25 = 5   9 ⟌ 72 = 8   4 ⟌ 24 = 6   9 ⟌ 72 = 8

6 ⟌ 42 = 7   8 ⟌ 40 = 5   2 ⟌ 4 = 2   7 ⟌ 56 = 8   9 ⟌ 63 = 7

9 ⟌ 45 = 5   7 ⟌ 7 = 1   3 ⟌ 15 = 5   2 ⟌ 8 = 4   7 ⟌ 63 = 9

3 ⟌ 24 = 8   5 ⟌ 30 = 6   9 ⟌ 54 = 6

8 ⟌ 48 = 6

9 ⟌ 81 = 9   7 ⟌ 28 = 4   4 ⟌ 32 = 8

Page 151

Lizzy the Lizard Bags Her Bugs

Directions: Lizzy the Lizard separates her bugs into separate bags so that her lunch is ready for the week. Help her decide how to divide the bugs.

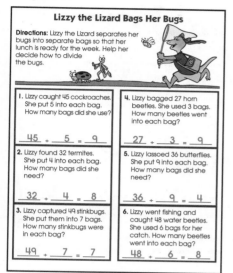

1. Lizzy caught 45 cockroaches. She put 5 into each bag. How many bags did she use?

   $\underline{45} \div \underline{5} = \underline{9}$

2. Lizzy found 32 termites. She put 4 into each bag. How many bags did she need?

   $\underline{32} \div \underline{4} = \underline{8}$

3. Lizzy captured 49 stinkbugs. She put them into 7 bags. How many stinkbugs were in each bag?

   $\underline{49} \div \underline{7} = \underline{7}$

4. Lizzy bagged 27 horn beetles. She used 3 bags. How many beetles went into each bag?

   $\underline{27} \div \underline{3} = \underline{9}$

5. Lizzy lassoed 36 butterflies. She put 9 into each bag. How many bags did she need?

   $\underline{36} \div \underline{9} = \underline{4}$

6. Lizzy went fishing and caught 48 water beetles. She used 6 bags for her catch. How many beetles went into each bag?

   $\underline{48} \div \underline{6} = \underline{8}$

Page 152

Problem Solving

Directions: Solve each problem.

Work Space:

1. Twenty-four people are at work. They work in 3 departments. The same number of people work in each department. How many people work in each department?

   There are __24__ people.
   They work in __3__ departments.
   There are __8__ people in each department.

2. Dan put 8 books into 2 stacks. Each stack had the same number of books. How many books were in each stack?

   There were __8__ books in all.
   They were put into __2__ stacks.
   There were __4__ books in each stack.

3. Janice put 16 litres of water into 2 jars. She put the same number of litres into each jar. How many litres of water did she put into each jar?

   Janice put __16__ litres of water into jars.
   She used __2__ jars.
   Janice put __8__ litres of water into each jar.

4. Kim has 27 apples. She wants to put the same number of apples in each of 3 boxes. How many apples should she put in each box?

   She should put __9__ apples in each box.

Page 153

Problem Solving

Directions: Solve each problem.

Work Space:

1. A loaf of bread has 24 slices. Mrs. Spencer uses 4 slices each day. How long will a loaf of bread last her?

   A loaf of bread has __24__ slices.
   Mrs. Spencer uses __4__ slices a day.
   The loaf of bread will last __6__ days.

2. A football team played 28 quarters. There are 4 quarters in a game. How many games did they play?

   The football team played __28__ quarters.
   There are __4__ quarters in each game.
   The football team played __7__ games.

3. A basketball game is 32 minutes long. The game is separated into 4 periods. Each period has the same number of minutes. How long is each period?

   A basketball game is __32__ minutes long.
   The game is separated into __4__ period.
   Each period is __8__ minutes long.

4. Emma worked 25 problems. She worked 5 problems on each sheet of paper. How many sheets of paper did she use?

   She used __5__ sheets of paper.

Page 154

Problem Solving

Directions: Solve each problem.

Work Space:

1. Dana bought 16 rolls. The rolls came in 2 packs. The same number of rolls were in each pack. How many rolls were in each pack?

   Dana bought __16__ rolls.
   These rolls filled __2__ packs.
   There were __8__ rolls in each pack.

2. There are 9 families in an apartment building. There are 3 families on each floor. How many floors are in the building?

   There are __9__ families in the building.
   There are __3__ families on each floor.
   There are __3__ floors in the building.

3. Arlene put 36 oranges in bags. She put 4 oranges in each bag. How many bags did she fill?

   Arlene put __36__ oranges in bags.
   She put __4__ oranges in each bag.
   Arlene filled __9__ bags with oranges.

4. Marcos read 35 pages of science in 5 days. He read the same number of pages each day. How many pages did he read each day?

   Marcos read __7__ pages each day.

Page 155

Fractions

A **fraction** is a number that names part of a whole, such as $\frac{1}{2}$ or $\frac{1}{3}$.

Directions: Write the fraction that tells what part of each figure is colored. The first one is done for you.

Example:

2 parts shaded
5 parts in the whole figure

$\frac{2}{5}$

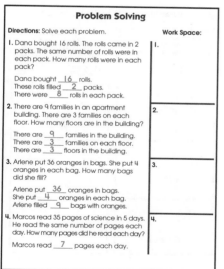

$\frac{1}{3}$ $\frac{1}{2}$ $\frac{3}{4}$

$\frac{5}{9}$ $\frac{2}{4}$ $\frac{3}{6}$

$\frac{1}{4}$ $\frac{4}{8}$ $\frac{3}{6}$

Page 156

Fractions: Equivalent

Fractions that name the same part of a whole are equivalent fractions.

Example:

$\frac{1}{2} = \frac{2}{4}$

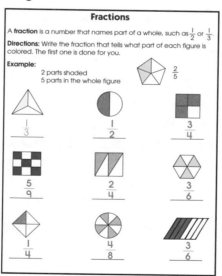

Directions: Fill in the numbers to complete the equivalent fractions.

$\frac{1}{4} = \frac{2}{8}$ $\frac{2}{3} = \frac{4}{6}$

$\frac{1}{6} = \frac{2}{12}$ $\frac{2}{3} = \frac{4}{6}$

$\frac{1}{3} = \frac{4}{12}$ $\frac{1}{5} = \frac{3}{15}$ $\frac{1}{4} = \frac{2}{8}$

$\frac{1}{2} = \frac{3}{6}$ $\frac{2}{3} = \frac{6}{9}$ $\frac{2}{6} = \frac{6}{18}$

Page 157

Fractions: Division

A fraction is a number that names part of an object. It can also name part of a group.

Directions: Study the example. Divide by the bottom number of the fraction to find the answers.

Example:
There are 6 cheerleaders.
$\frac{1}{2}$ of the cheerleaders are boys.
How many cheerleaders are boys?

6 cheerleaders ÷ 2 groups = 3 boys

$\frac{1}{2}$ of 6 = 3 $\frac{1}{2}$ of 8 = 4

$\frac{1}{2}$ of 10 = 5 $\frac{1}{3}$ of 9 = 3 $\frac{1}{5}$ of 10 = 2

$\frac{1}{4}$ of 12 = 3 $\frac{1}{8}$ of 32 = 4 $\frac{1}{3}$ of 27 = 9

$\frac{1}{5}$ of 30 = 6 $\frac{1}{2}$ of 14 = 7 $\frac{1}{9}$ of 18 = 2

$\frac{1}{6}$ of 24 = 4 $\frac{1}{3}$ of 18 = 6 $\frac{1}{10}$ of 50 = 5

Page 158

Fractions: Comparing

Directions: Circle the fraction in each pair that is larger.

Example:

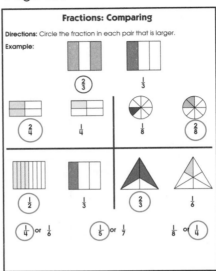

Page 159

Graham Cracker Denominator

Directions: Find a cracker. If possible, use one that has four pieces. Break your crackers into as many or as few pieces as desired but make each piece the same size.

With fractions, the number of pieces into which an object is broken is how the bottom number, the **denominator**, obtains its numerical value. Remember that you started with one cracker that is in pieces now. Write the number of pieces as a denominator.

☐ ← numerator

denominator → ☐

To determine the top number, the numerator, eat part of the cracker. In the diagram at the right, cross out the part you ate. This is the numerator.

Write two fractions—a fraction to show what is left and a fraction to show what was eaten.

numerator ☐ of the cracker is left.   numerator ☐ of the cracker is gone.
denominator ☐   denominator ☐

Eat another piece of the cracker... you ate in the diagram. Now, w...

numerator ☐ ...ator ☐ of the cracker is gone.
denominator ☐ ...denominator ☐

Eat another pie... cracker. Cross out the part you ate in the diagra... ow, write how much is left.

numerator ☐ of the cracker is left.   numerator ☐ of the cracker is gone.
denominator ☐   denominator ☐

Which part changes, the (numerator) or the denominator?

Answers will vary.

Page 160

Fraction Fun

4 gloves are shaded. 9 gloves in all.

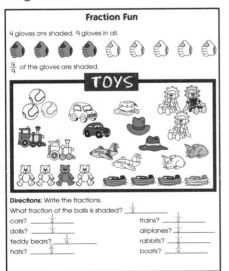

$\frac{4}{9}$ of the gloves are shaded.

TOYS

Directions: Write the fractions.

What fraction of the balls is shaded? $\frac{1}{3}$

cars? $\frac{2}{?}$ trains? $\frac{1}{?}$
dolls? $\frac{2}{?}$ airplanes? $\frac{2}{?}$
teddy bears? $\frac{4}{?}$ rabbits? $\frac{2}{?}$
hats? $\frac{3}{?}$ boats? $\frac{4}{?}$

Page 161

Button Collection

Directions: Collect sets of buttons and put them in a box or container. Count the number of buttons in each box or container. Create a response sheet like the one on the bottom of this page. You can choose how to group each of your objects. Those become the categories you write at the top of the response sheet.

Remember: A fraction has two numbers with a horizontal line drawn between them. The bottom number is called the **denominator**. The denominator tells how many equal parts or total pieces are in the whole. The top number is called the **numerator**. The numerator tells how many parts of the whole there are. $\frac{2}{5}$

Example: $\frac{2}{5}$ ← the part of the total buttons with 2 holes / ← total number of buttons in the set

What is the fraction of buttons in this set with 2 holes?

Response Sheet

Box #	# of buttons in box	Buttons with 2 holes	Buttons with 4 holes	White buttons	Gold buttons	Black buttons	Brown buttons

Answers will vary.

Page 162

The Mystery of the Missing Sweets

Directions: Some mysterious person is sneaking away with pieces of desserts from Sam Sillicook's Diner. Help him figure out how much is missing.

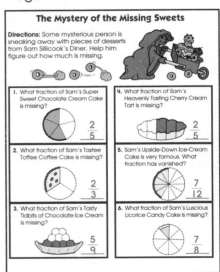

1. What fraction of Sam's Super Sweet Chocolate Cream Cake is missing? $\frac{2}{5}$

2. What fraction of Sam's Tastee Toffee Coffee Cake is missing? $\frac{2}{3}$

3. What fraction of Sam's Tasty Tidbits of Chocolate Ice Cream is missing? $\frac{5}{9}$

4. What fraction of Sam's Heavenly Tasting Cherry Cream Tart is missing? $\frac{2}{5}$

5. Sam's Upside-Down Ice-Cream Cake is very famous. What fraction has vanished? $\frac{7}{12}$

6. What fraction of Sam's Luscious Licorice Candy Cake is missing? $\frac{7}{8}$

Page 163

Star Gazing

To find $\frac{1}{2}$ of the stars, divide by 2.

Example:
$\frac{1}{2}$ of 10 = 5

Directions: Solve the problems.

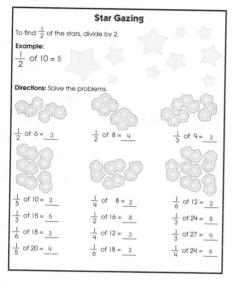

$\frac{1}{2}$ of 6 = 3 $\frac{1}{2}$ of 8 = 4 $\frac{1}{3}$ of 9 = 3

$\frac{1}{5}$ of 10 = 2 $\frac{1}{4}$ of 8 = 2 $\frac{1}{6}$ of 12 = 2

$\frac{1}{3}$ of 15 = 5 $\frac{1}{2}$ of 16 = 8 $\frac{1}{3}$ of 24 = 8

$\frac{1}{6}$ of 18 = 3 $\frac{1}{4}$ of 12 = 3 $\frac{1}{3}$ of 27 = 9

$\frac{1}{5}$ of 20 = 4 $\frac{1}{6}$ of 18 = 3 $\frac{1}{4}$ of 24 = 6

Page 164

What Fraction Am I?

Directions: Identify the fraction for each shaded section.

Example: There are 5 sections on this figure. 2 sections are shaded. $\frac{2}{5}$ of the sections are shaded. 3 sections are not shaded. $\frac{3}{5}$ of the sections are not shaded.

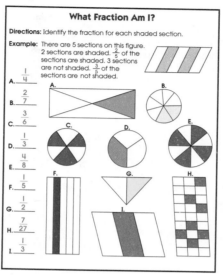

A. $\frac{1}{4}$
B. $\frac{2}{7}$
C. $\frac{3}{6}$
D. $\frac{1}{3}$
E. $\frac{4}{8}$
F. $\frac{1}{5}$
G. $\frac{1}{2}$
H. $\frac{7}{27}$
I. $\frac{1}{3}$

Page 167

The Parts Equal the Whole

The one long Fraction Bar on page 165 is a whole. Each bar thereafter is broken up into equal parts.

Directions: Name what part of the whole each bar is. Write its fraction on it.

Colour the whole bar yellow, the halves blue, the thirds green, the fourths red, and the sixths orange. Then, cut the bars apart carefully on the lines. Store the pieces in an envelope.

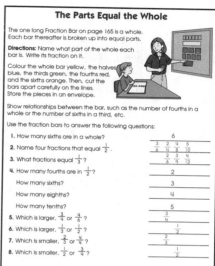

Show relationships between the bar, such as the number of fourths in a whole or the number of sixths in a third, etc.

Use the fraction bars to answer the following questions:

1. How many sixths are in a whole? — 6
2. Name four fractions that equal $\frac{1}{2}$. — $\frac{3}{6}$ $\frac{2}{4}$ $\frac{4}{8}$ $\frac{5}{10}$
3. What fractions equal $\frac{1}{3}$? — $\frac{2}{6}$ $\frac{3}{9}$ $\frac{4}{12}$
4. How many fourths are in $\frac{1}{2}$? — 2
   How many sixths? — 3
   How many eighths? — 4
   How many tenths? — 5
5. Which is larger, $\frac{3}{4}$ or $\frac{4}{6}$? — $\frac{3}{4}$
6. Which is larger, $\frac{1}{3}$ or $\frac{1}{2}$? — $\frac{1}{2}$
7. Which is smaller, $\frac{2}{3}$ or $\frac{4}{6}$? — $\frac{2}{3}$
8. Which is smaller, $\frac{1}{2}$ or $\frac{3}{4}$? — $\frac{1}{2}$

Page 168

Doing Decimals

Just as a fraction stands for part of a whole number, a **decimal** also shows part of a whole number. And with decimals, the number is always broken into ten or a power of ten (hundred, thousand, etc.) parts. These place values are named tenths, hundredths, thousandths, etc.

A **decimal point** is a dot placed between the ones place and the tenths place.

0.2 is read as "two tenths."   0.4 is four tenths.

Directions: Write the answer as a decimal for the shaded parts.

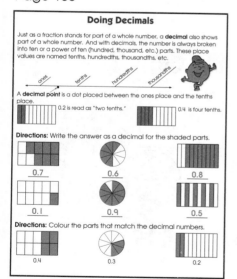

0.7   0.6   0.8

0.1   0.9   0.5

Directions: Colour the parts that match the decimal numbers.

0.4   0.3   0.2

Page 169

Decimals

A decimal is a number with one or more numbers to the right of a decimal point. A decimal point is a dot placed between the ones place and the tens place of a number, such as 2.5.

Example:
$\frac{3}{10}$ can be written as .3.   They are both read as three-tenths.

Directions: Write the answer as a decimal for the shaded parts.

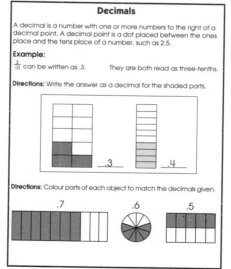

.3   .4

Directions: Colour parts of each object to match the decimals given.

.7   .6   .5

Page 170

Decimals

A decimal is a number with one or more numbers to the right of a decimal point, such as 6.5 or 2.25. **Equivalent** means numbers that are equal.

Directions: Draw a line between the equivalent numbers.

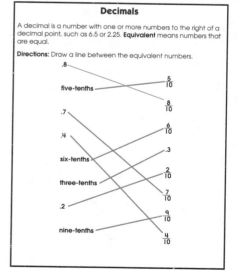

.8 $\frac{5}{10}$
five-tenths $\frac{8}{10}$
.7 $\frac{6}{10}$
.4   .3
six-tenths $\frac{2}{10}$
three-tenths $\frac{7}{10}$
.2 $\frac{9}{10}$
nine-tenths $\frac{4}{10}$

Page 171

Decimals Greater Than 1

Directions: Write the decimal for the part that is shaded.

Example: $2\frac{4}{10}$

Write: 2.4   Read: two and four-tenths

$1\frac{2}{10} = \underline{1.2}$ $3\frac{6}{10} = \underline{3.6}$

$2\frac{3}{10} = \underline{2.3}$ $2\frac{7}{10} = \underline{2.7}$

Directions: Write each number as a decimal.

four and two-tenths = $\underline{4.2}$ seven and one-tenth = $\underline{7.1}$

$3\frac{4}{10} = \underline{3.4}$ $6\frac{9}{10} = \underline{6.9}$ $8\frac{3}{10} = \underline{8.3}$ $7\frac{5}{10} = \underline{7.5}$

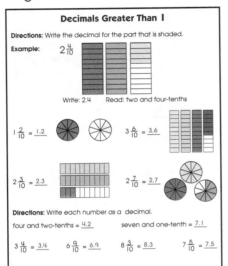

Page 172

Decimals: Addition and Subtraction

Decimals are added and subtracted in the same way as other numbers. Simply carry down the decimal point to your answer.

Directions: Add or subtract.

Examples:

$\begin{array}{r} 1.3 \\ +\ 2.8 \\ \hline 4.1 \end{array}$ $\begin{array}{r} 4.5 \\ -\ 2.2 \\ \hline 2.3 \end{array}$

$\begin{array}{r} 1.3 \\ +\ 2.2 \\ \hline 3.5 \end{array}$ $\begin{array}{r} 4.6 \\ -\ 3.4 \\ \hline 1.2 \end{array}$ $\begin{array}{r} 5.1 \\ +\ 8.8 \\ \hline 13.9 \end{array}$ $\begin{array}{r} 6.7 \\ -\ 4.3 \\ \hline 2.4 \end{array}$

$\begin{array}{r} 7.9 \\ -\ 3.7 \\ \hline 4.2 \end{array}$ $\begin{array}{r} 6.4 \\ +\ 8.7 \\ \hline 15.1 \end{array}$ $\begin{array}{r} 11.4 \\ -\ 9.5 \\ \hline 1.9 \end{array}$ $\begin{array}{r} 0.5 \\ +\ 3.6 \\ \hline 4.1 \end{array}$

$9.3 + 1.2 = \underline{10.5}$ $2.5 - 0.7 = \underline{1.8}$ $1.2 + 5.0 = \underline{6.2}$

Bob jogs around the school every day. The distance for one time around is 0.7 of a kilometre. If he jogs around the school two times, how many kilometres does he jog each day? 1.4

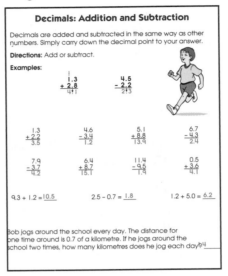

Page 173

Decimal Divisions

Decimals are often used with whole numbers.

Examples: 2.8   3.5

Directions: Write the decimal for each picture.

1.2   5.7   2.4

Directions: Shade in the picture to show the decimal number.

1.9   3.5   0.4   4.1

When reading decimals with whole numbers, say "point" or "and" for the decimal point.

Directions: Write the word names for each decimal from above.

1.9 _one point nine_   one and nine tenths or

0.4 _four tenths or point four_

3.5 _three point five_   three and five tenths or

4.1 _point one_   four and one tenth or four

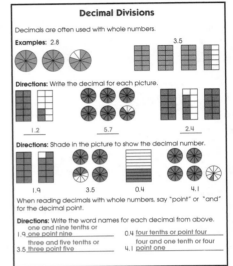

Page 174

How Hot Are You?

Directions: Write the number for each word name. Cross off the number in the cloud. The number that is left is your body temperature. Hint: Remember to add a zero to hold any place value not given.

1. six and eight tenths — 6.8
2. four and nine tenths — 4.9
3. thirteen and seven tenths — 13.7
4. twenty-one and one tenth — 21.1
5. five and fifteen hundredths — 5.15
6. nine and sixty-two hundredths — 9.62
7. fifteen and four hundredths — 15.04
8. fifty-seven and eighty-two hundredths — 57.82
9. three and seven tenths — 3.7
10. sixty and forty-three hundredths — 60.43
11. ninety and seven hundredths — 90.07
12. fourteen and two hundredths — 14.02
13. five and seven hundredths — 5.07
14. ten and one tenth — 10.1
15. thirty and twenty hundredths — 30.20

Your body temperature is: 31.0

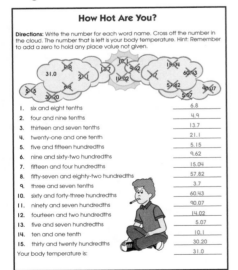

Page 175

Get the Point

When you add or subtract decimals, remember to include the decimal point.

Add. $\begin{array}{r} 3.6 \\ +\ 3.3 \\ \hline 6.9 \end{array}$ Subtract. $\begin{array}{r} 6.8 \\ -\ 2.6 \\ \hline 4.2 \end{array}$

Directions: Solve these problems.

$\begin{array}{r} 4.2 \\ +\ 5.2 \\ \hline 9.4 \end{array}$ $\begin{array}{r} 6.4 \\ +\ 1.4 \\ \hline 7.8 \end{array}$ $\begin{array}{r} 3.1 \\ +\ 7.8 \\ \hline 10.9 \end{array}$ $\begin{array}{r} 4.7 \\ +\ 3.2 \\ \hline 7.9 \end{array}$ $\begin{array}{r} 4.9 \\ +\ 2.0 \\ \hline 6.9 \end{array}$ $\begin{array}{r} 4.27 \\ +\ 5.52 \\ \hline 9.79 \end{array}$

$\begin{array}{r} 5.9 \\ -\ 3.2 \\ \hline 2.7 \end{array}$ $\begin{array}{r} 6.7 \\ -\ 5.6 \\ \hline 1.1 \end{array}$ $\begin{array}{r} 7.8 \\ -\ 2.5 \\ \hline 5.3 \end{array}$ $\begin{array}{r} 5.8 \\ -\ 3.3 \\ \hline 2.5 \end{array}$ $\begin{array}{r} 3.9 \\ -\ 1.5 \\ \hline 2.4 \end{array}$ $\begin{array}{r} 4.86 \\ -\ 1.76 \\ \hline 3.10 \end{array}$

$\begin{array}{r} 0.23 \\ +\ 0.25 \\ \hline 0.48 \end{array}$ $\begin{array}{r} 0.43 \\ +\ 0.16 \\ \hline 0.59 \end{array}$ $\begin{array}{r} 0.26 \\ +\ 0.42 \\ \hline 0.68 \end{array}$ $\begin{array}{r} 0.64 \\ +\ 0.15 \\ \hline 0.79 \end{array}$ $\begin{array}{r} 0.68 \\ +\ 0.31 \\ \hline 0.99 \end{array}$ $\begin{array}{r} 6.73 \\ +\ 1.15 \\ \hline 7.88 \end{array}$

$\begin{array}{r} 0.87 \\ -\ 0.42 \\ \hline 0.45 \end{array}$ $\begin{array}{r} 0.98 \\ -\ 0.35 \\ \hline 0.63 \end{array}$ $\begin{array}{r} 0.79 \\ -\ 0.15 \\ \hline 0.64 \end{array}$ $\begin{array}{r} 0.87 \\ -\ 0.67 \\ \hline 0.20 \end{array}$ $\begin{array}{r} 0.83 \\ -\ 0.12 \\ \hline 0.71 \end{array}$ $\begin{array}{r} 5.86 \\ -\ 3.83 \\ \hline 2.03 \end{array}$

$\begin{array}{r} 3.13 \\ +\ 2.26 \\ \hline 5.39 \end{array}$ $\begin{array}{r} 4.72 \\ +\ 1.15 \\ \hline 5.87 \end{array}$ $\begin{array}{r} 6.87 \\ +\ 2.11 \\ \hline 8.98 \end{array}$ $\begin{array}{r} 4.98 \\ -\ 2.32 \\ \hline 2.66 \end{array}$ $\begin{array}{r} 5.97 \\ -\ 2.54 \\ \hline 3.43 \end{array}$ $\begin{array}{r} 6.98 \\ -\ 1.45 \\ \hline 5.53 \end{array}$

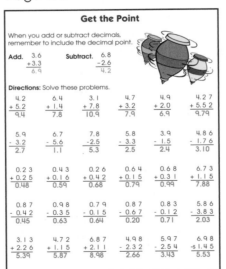

Page 176

Geometry

Geometry is the branch of mathematics that has to do with points, lines, and shapes.

cube   rectangular prism   cone   cylinder   sphere

Directions: Use the code to colour the picture.

Colour:
cubes — blue
rectangular prisms — red
cones — green
cylinders — yellow
spheres — orange

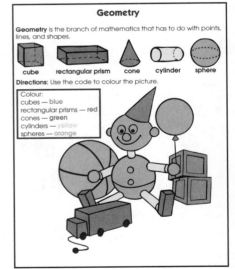

Page 177

Geometric Coloring

Directions: Colour the geometric shapes in the box below.

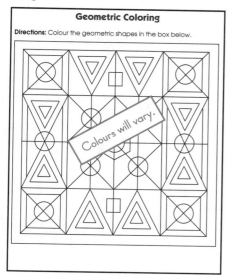

Colours will vary.

Page 178

Geometry Match-Ups

A **polygon** is a closed shape with straight sides.

Directions: Cut out each polygon on the next page. To make them more durable, glue them onto cardboard or oaktag. Use the shapes to fill out the table below. (Keep the shapes for other activities as well.)

Game: Play this game with a partner. Put the shapes in a bag or cover them with a sheet of paper. Player One pulls out a shape and tells how many sides and angles it has. Without showing the shape, he/she puts the polygon back. Player Two should name the shape. Then, Player Two puts his/her hand in the bag and, without looking, tries to find the polygon from the description. Then, switch roles. Continue the game until all the polygons have been identified.

When you finish playing, complete the chart below.

Drawing of the shape (or polygon)	Shape name	Number of sides	Number of angles (or corners)
△	triangle	3	3
☐	square	4	4
⬠	pentagon	5	5
▭	rectangle	4	4
⬡	hexagon	6	6

Page 181

Geometry: Lines, Segments, Rays, Angles

Geometry is the branch of mathematics that has to do with points, lines, and shapes.

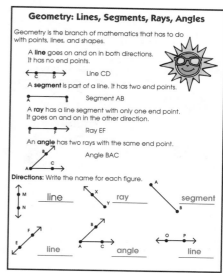

A **line** goes on and on in both directions. It has no end points.

←→ C   D   Line CD

A **segment** is part of a line. It has two end points.

A ●———● B   Segment AB

A **ray** has a line segment with only one end point. It goes on and on in the other direction.

Ray EF

An **angle** has two rays with the same end point.

Angle BAC

Directions: Write the name for each figure.

line   ray   segment

line   angle   line

Page 182

Look At the World From a Different Angle

Lines come together in many different ways. The point where two lines meet is called an **angle**. You may have to look at the things around you in a different way to find these angles.

Use the table below to record your observations from around the house. Look for objects that illustrate each category on the chart. Draw a sketch of each object and label it. Find as many objects for each category as possible.

 acute

 perpendicular

Directions: Look around the house and find one object that illustrates all five geometric categories. Sketch the object and label the various types of angles, lines, or shapes that it has.

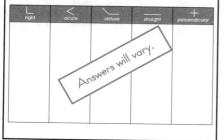

∟ right	< acute	⟋ obtuse	— straight	+ perpendicular

Answers will vary.

Page 187

Geometry: Perimeter

The **perimeter** is the distance around an object. Find the perimeter by adding the lengths of all the sides.

Directions: Find the perimeter for each object (m = metre).

10 m   36 m   11 m

14 m   26 m

8 m   17 m   10 m

Page 188

Perimeter Problems

The perimeter is the distance around the outside of a shape. Find the perimeters for the figures below by adding the lengths of all the sides.

Examples:

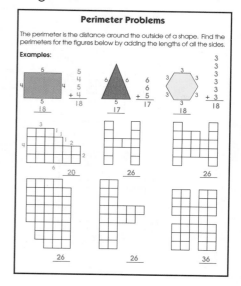

20   26   26

26   26   36

Page 189

Map Skills: Scale

A **map scale** shows how far one place is from another. This map scale shows that 1 centimetre on this page equals 1 kilometre at the real location.

Directions: Use a ruler and the map scale to find out how far it is from Ann's house to other places. Round to the nearest centimetre.

Map Scale:
1 cm = 1 km

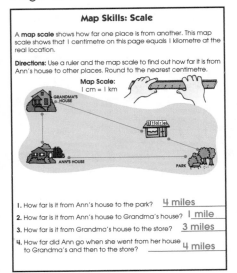

1. How far is it from Ann's house to the park? __4 miles__
2. How far is it from Ann's house to Grandma's house? __1 mile__
3. How far is it from Grandma's house to the store? __3 miles__
4. How far did Ann go when she went from her house to Grandma's and then to the store? __4 miles__

Page 190

Map Skills: Scale

Directions: Use a ruler and the map scale to measure the map and answer the questions. Round to the nearest metre.

Map Scale
1 cm = 10 m

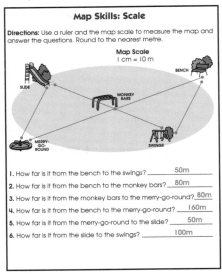

1. How far is it from the bench to the swings? __50m__
2. How far is it from the bench to the monkey bars? __80m__
3. How far is it from the monkey bars to the merry-go-round? __80m__
4. How far is it from the bench to the merry-go-round? __160m__
5. How far is it from the merry-go-round to the slide? __50m__
6. How far is it from the slide to the swings? __100m__

Page 191

Coordinates

Directions: Locate the points on the grid and colour in each box.
What animal did you form? __Answers will vary.__

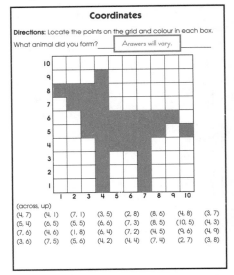

(across, up)

(4, 7)	(4, 1)	(7, 1)	(3, 5)	(2, 8)	(8, 6)	(4, 8)	(3, 7)
(5, 4)	(6, 5)	(5, 5)	(6, 6)	(7, 3)	(8, 5)	(10, 5)	(4, 3)
(7, 6)	(4, 6)	(1, 8)	(6, 4)	(7, 2)	(4, 5)	(9, 6)	(4, 9)
(3, 6)	(7, 5)	(5, 6)	(4, 2)	(4, 4)	(7, 4)	(2, 7)	(3, 8)

Page 192

Gliding Graphics

Directions: Draw the lines as directed from point to point for each graph.

Draw a line from:

- F,7 to D,1
- B,1 to A,8
- D,1 to I,6
- A,8 to D,11
- I,6 to N,8
- D,11 to F,9
- N,8 to M,3
- F,9 to F,7
- M,3 to F,1
- F,7 to I,9
- F,1 to G,4
- I,9 to I,6
- G,4 to E,4
- I,6 to F,7
- E,4 to B,1

Draw a line from:

- J, ⬛ to N,◣
- N,◣ to U,◣
- U,◣ to Z,⬛
- Z,⬛ to X,✥
- X,✥ to U,◣
- U,◣ to S,◙
- S,◙ to N,◣
- N,◣ to N,◙
- N,◙ to J,◙
- J,⬛ to L,||||
- L,|||| to Y,||||
- Y,|||| to Z,||||
- Z,|||| to L,⬛
- L,⬛ to J,⬛

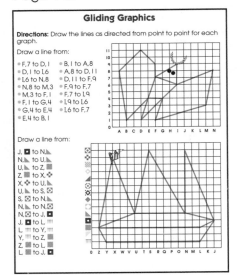

Page 193

Graphs

A **graph** is a drawing that shows information about numbers.

Directions: Colour the picture. Then tell how many there are of each object by completing the graph.

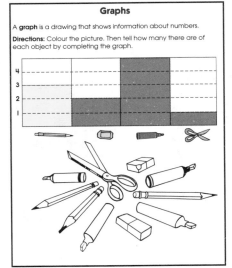

Page 194

Graphs

Directions: Answer the questions about the graph.

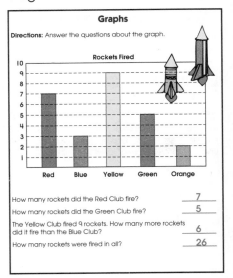

How many rockets did the Red Club fire? __7__

How many rockets did the Green Club fire? __5__

The Yellow Club fired 9 rockets. How many more rockets did it fire than the Blue Club? __6__

How many rockets were fired in all? __26__

Page 195

Flower Graph

A **pictograph** is a graph using pictures to give information. Cut out the flowers and glue them onto the pictograph. Each picture stands for 2 flowers.

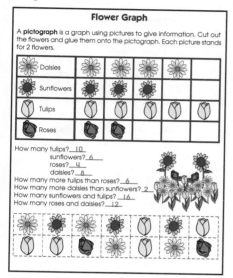

Daisies				
Sunflowers				
Tulips				
Roses				

How many tulips? _10_
sunflowers? _6_
roses? _4_
daisies? _8_
How many more tulips than roses? _6_
How many more daisies than sunflowers? _2_
How many sunflowers and tulips? _16_
How many roses and daisies? _12_

Page 197

Frog Bubbles

Directions: Complete the line graph to show how many bubbles each frog blew.

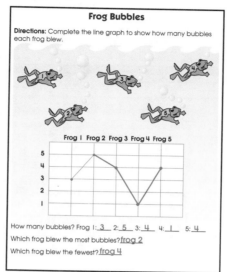

Frog 1 Frog 2 Frog 3 Frog 4 Frog 5

How many bubbles? Frog 1: _3_ 2: _5_ 3: _4_ 4: _1_ 5: _4_

Which frog blew the most bubbles? _frog 2_

Which frog blew the fewest? _frog 4_

Page 198

Potato Face

Directions: Read the line graphs to draw the potato faces.

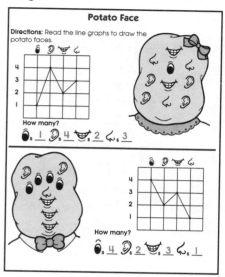

How many?
_1_ _4_ _2_ _3_

How many?
_4_ _2_ _3_ _1_

Page 199

Vote for Me!

Middletown School had an election to choose the new members of the Student Council. Grace, Bernie, Laurie, Sherry, and Sam all ran for the office of president. On the chart below are the five students' names with the number of the votes each received.

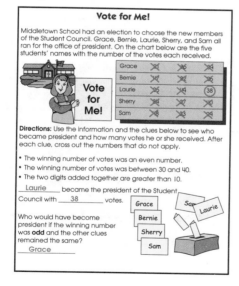

Grace	21	26	49
Bernie	17	22	11
Laurie	35	44	(38)
Sherry	39	13	49
Sam	48	23	44

Directions: Use the information and the clues below to see who became president and how many votes he or she received. After each clue, cross out the numbers that do not apply.

- The winning number of votes was an even number.
- The winning number of votes was between 30 and 40.
- The two digits added together are greater than 10.

Laurie became the president of the Student Council with _38_ votes.

Who would have become president if the winning number was **odd** and the other clues remained the same?

Grace

Page 200

School Statistics

Directions: Read each graph and follow the directions.

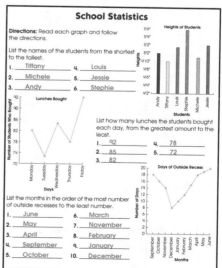

List the names of the students from the shortest to the tallest.

1. _Tiffany_   4. _Louis_
2. _Michele_   5. _Jessie_
3. _Andy_   6. _Stephie_

List how many lunches the students bought each day, from the greatest amount to the least.

1. _92_   4. _78_
2. _85_   5. _72_
3. _82_

List the months in the order of the most number of outside recesses to the least number.

1. _June_   6. _March_
2. _May_   7. _November_
3. _April_   8. _February_
4. _September_   9. _January_
5. _October_   10. _December_

Page 201

Candy Sales

Every year the students at Lincoln Elementary sell candy as a fund-raising project. These are the results of the sales for this year.

Grade Level	Number of Sales
Kindergarten	40
First	70
Second	50
Third	80
Fourth	85
Fifth	75

Directions: Colour the bar graph to show the number of sales made at each grade level.

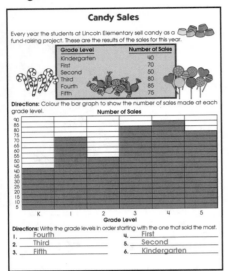

Directions: Write the grade levels in order starting with the one that sold the most.

1. Fourth
2. Third
3. Fifth
4. First
5. Second
6. Kindergarten

Page 202

Hot Lunch Favourites

The cooks in the cafeteria asked each third- and fourth-grade class to rate the hot lunches. They wanted to know which food the children liked the best.

The table shows how the students rated the lunches.
Key: Each ⚝ equals 2 students.

Food	Number of students who liked it best
hamburgers	⚝⚝⚝⚝⚝⚝
hot dogs	⚝⚝⚝⚝⚝⚝⚝
tacos	⚝⚝⚝⚝
chili	
soup and sandwiches	⚝
spaghetti	⚝⚝
fried chicken	⚝⚝⚝⚝
fish sticks	⚝⚝⚝

Directions: Colour the bar graph to show the information on the table. Remember that each ⚝ equals 2 people. The first one is done for you.

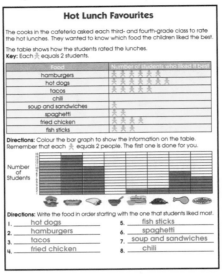

Directions: Write the food in order starting with the one that students liked most.

1. hot dogs
2. hamburgers
3. tacos
4. fried chicken
5. fish sticks
6. spaghetti
7. soup and sandwiches
8. chili

Page 203

Measurement: Ounce and Pound

Ounces and **pounds** are measurements of weight in the standard measurement system. The ounce is used to measure the weight of very light objects. The pound is used to measure the weight of heavier objects. 16 ounces = 1 pound.

Example:

8 ounces   15 pounds

Directions: Decide if you would use ounces or pounds to measure the weight of each object. Circle your answer.

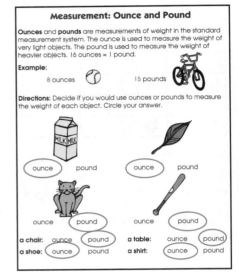

(ounce)   pound   (ounce)   pound

ounce   (pound)   ounce   (pound)

a chair: ounce (pound)   a table: ounce (pound)

a shoe: (ounce) pound   a shirt: (ounce) pound

Page 204

Measurement: Centimetre

A **centimetre** is a unit of length in the metric system. There are 2.54 centimeters in an inch.

Directions: Use a centimetre ruler to measure each object to the nearest half of a centimetre. Write **cm** to stand for centimetre.

Example:

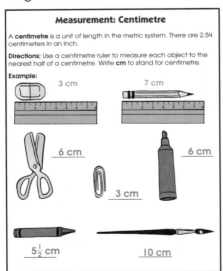

3 cm   7 cm

6 cm   6 cm

3 cm

5½ cm   10 cm

Page 205

Measurement: Inches

An **inch** is a unit of length in the standard measurement system.

Directions: Use a ruler to measure each object to the nearest $\frac{1}{4}$ inch. Write **in.** to stand for inch.

Example:

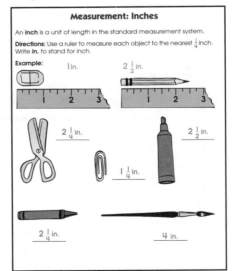

1 in.   2½ in.

2¼ in.   2½ in.

1¼ in.

2¼ in.   4 in.

Page 206

Measurement: Metre and Kilometre

Metres and **kilometers** are units of length in the metric system. A meter is equal to 39.37 inches. A kilometer is equal to about $\frac{5}{8}$ of a mile.

Directions: Decide whether you would use metres or kilometres to measure each object.

1 metre = 100 centimetres
1 kilometre = 1,000 metres

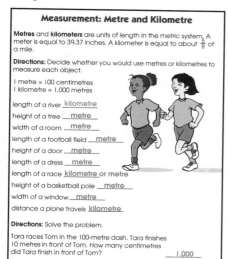

length of a river __kilometre__

height of a tree __metre__

width of a room __metre__

length of a football field __metre__

height of a door __metre__

length of a dress __metre__

length of a race __kilometre__ or metre

height of a basketball pole __metre__

width of a window __metre__

distance a plane travels __kilometre__

Directions: Solve the problem.

Tara races Tom in the 100-metre dash. Tara finishes 10 metres in front of Tom. How many centimetres did Tara finish in front of Tom?

__1,000__

Page 207

Measurement: Foot, Yard, Mile

Directions: Decide whether you would use foot, yard, or mile to measure each object.

1 foot = 12 inches
1 yard = 36 inches or 3 feet
1 mile = 1,760 yards

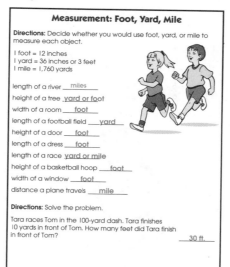

length of a river __miles__

height of a tree __yard or foot__

width of a room __foot__

length of a football field __yard__

height of a door __foot__

length of a dress __foot__

length of a race __yard or mile__

height of a basketball hoop __foot__

width of a window __foot__

distance a plane travels __mile__

Directions: Solve the problem.

Tara races Tom in the 100-yard dash. Tara finishes 10 yards in front of Tom. How many feet did Tara finish in front of Tom?

__30 ft.__

Page 208

How Does Your Home Measure Up?

Directions: Take a "measuring journey" through your house. To begin, brainstorm a list of various destinations around your house. Then, list five objects found in each room and write them on the left-hand side of a sheet of paper.

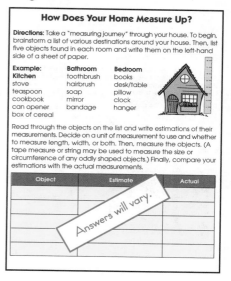

Example: Kitchen	Bathroom	Bedroom
stove	toothbrush	books
teaspoon	hairbrush	desk/table
cookbook	soap	pillow
can opener	mirror	clock
box of cereal	bandage	hanger

Read through the objects on the list and write estimations of their measurements. Decide on a unit of measurement to use and whether to measure length, width, or both. Then, measure the objects. (A tape measure or string may be used to measure the size or circumference of any oddly shaped objects.) Finally, compare your estimations with the actual measurements.

Object	Estimate	Actual

Answers will vary.

Page 209

Growing String Beans

Bar Graph

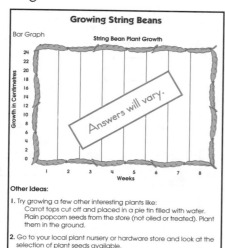

String Bean Plant Growth

Answers will vary.

(Growth in Centimetres: 0, 2, 4, 6, 8, 10, 12, 14, 16, 18, 20, 22, 24)

(Weeks: 1, 2, 3, 4, 5, 6, 7, 8)

Other Ideas:

1. Try growing a few other interesting plants like:
   Carrot tops cut off and placed in a pie tin filled with water.
   Plain popcorn seeds from the store (not oiled or treated). Plant them in the ground.

2. Go to your local plant nursery or hardware store and look at the selection of plant seeds available.

3. Plant a young tree in your yard and measure its growth each year.

Page 211

Hand—Foot—Ruler

Directions:

1. Measure the span of your hand by stretching your thumb and little finger as far apart as possible. Lay your hand on a ruler to find out this length (span). Record the centimetres of the span on the record sheet below.

2. Measure the length of your pace by taking one step forward and holding it. Have someone put the edge of a yardstick next to the heel of your back foot and measure to the back of the heel on your forward foot. Record the pace distance in centimetres on the record sheet.

3. Using a ruler or yardstick, measure the distances listed on the record sheet. Record all findings in centimetres.

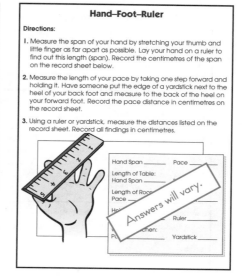

Hand Span _____ Pace _____
Length of Table:
Hand Span _____
Length of Room:
Pace _____
Ruler _____
Yardstick _____

Answers will vary.

Page 212

A Measurement of Our Own

Create your own new system of measurement. Brainstorm ideas on what and how you should base the new unit. For example, you may use the length of your finger, the length of a juice box, the length of your backpack, etc. as a base.

Next, create a ruler using your new unit of measurement. A foot is made of inches and a meter is made of centimeters. Break your standard unit into smaller units and add these to the ruler. When the ruler is complete, fill out the form below.

Directions: Answer the questions below.

1. What is the name of your unit of measurement?

2. What would your unit of measurement be best suited for measuring—long distances or microscopic organisms?

   Why?

3. Would you rather use your new unit ~~ment~~ versus the metric unit? _____ Wh~~y~~

4. Measure an object usin~~g~~
   What did it measur~~e~~
   If you were to t~~ell~~ ~~the~~ object you measured was that long, do ~~person~~ would be able to picture its length? _____ ~~why not?~~

5. Why do you think everyone in the entire country uses the exact same unit of measurement?

Answers will vary.

Page 215

Roman Numerals

Another way to write numbers is to use Roman numerals.

I	1	VII	7
II	2	VIII	8
III	3	IX	9
IV	4	X	10
V	5	XI	11
VI	6	XII	12

Directions: Fill in the Roman numerals on the watch.

What time is it on the watch?

___3___ o'clock

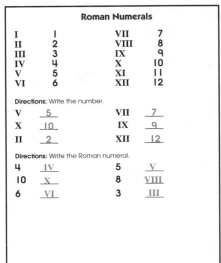

Page 216

Roman Numerals

I	1	VII	7
II	2	VIII	8
III	3	IX	9
IV	4	X	10
V	5	XI	11
VI	6	XII	12

Directions: Write the number.

V __5__   VII __7__

X __10__   IX __9__

II __2__   XII __12__

Directions: Write the Roman numeral.

4 __IV__   5 __V__

10 __X__   8 __VIII__

6 __VI__   3 __III__

Page 217

Roman Numerals

I means 1.	V means 5.	X means 10.
II means 1 + 1 or 2.		III means 1 + 1 + 1 or 3.
VI means 5 + 1 or 6.		IV means 5 – 1 or 4.
XXV means 10 + 10 + 5 or 25		IX means 10 – 1 or 9.

VII means 5 + 1 + __1__ or __7__ .   XXI means 10 + __10__ + 1 or __21__ .

XIV means __10__ + 4 or __14__ .   XIX means __10__ + 9 or __19__ .

Directions: Complete the following as shown.

1. XXIV = __24__   XX = __20__   XXII = __22__   VIII = __8__
2. IV = __4__   XXVI = __26__   XVII = __17__   XXXI = __31__
3. XXXVI = __36__   XXIX = __39__   XI = __11__   XXXIII = __33__
4. XVIII = __18__   IX = __19__   XXXIV = __34__   XIII = __13__
5. V = __5__   XXV = __25__   VI = __6__   XXI = __21__
6. XXXVIII = __38__ XXXV = __35__   XXVII = __27__   XVI = __16__
7. XXIII = __23__   XXXVII = __37__ XIV = __14__   XXXII = __32__

Directions: Write a Roman numeral for each of the following.

8. 3 = __III__   7 = __VII__   15 = __XV__
9. 19 = __XIX__   22 = __XXII__   28 = __XXVIII__
10. 30 = __XXX__   20 = __XX__   39 = __XXXIX__

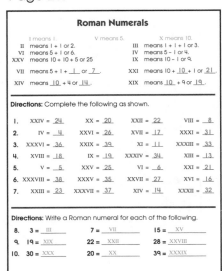

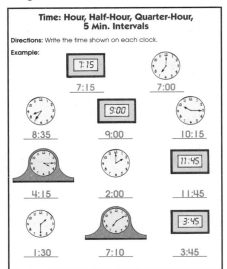

Page 218

Time: Hour, Half-Hour, Quarter-Hour, 5 Min. Intervals

Directions: Write the time shown on each clock.

Example:

7:15   7:15   7:00

8:35   9:00   10:15

4:15   2:00   11:45

1:30   7:10   3:45

Page 219

Time: A.M. and P.M.

In telling time, the hours between 12:00 midnight and 12:00 noon are A.M. hours. The hours between 12:00 noon and 12:00 midnight are P.M. hours.

Directions: Draw a line between the times that are the same.

Example:

7:30 in the morning — 7:30 A.M. / half-past seven A.M. / seven thirty in the morning

9:00 in the evening — 9:00 P.M. / nine o'clock at night

six o'clock in the evening — 8:00 A.M.
3:30 A.M. — six o'clock in the morning
4:15 P.M. — 6:00 P.M.
eight o'clock in the morning — eleven o'clock in the evening
quarter past five in the evening — three thirty in the morning
11:00 P.M. — four fifteen in the evening
6:00 A.M. — 5:15 P.M.

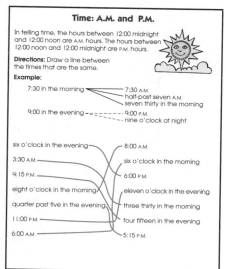

Page 220

Time: Minutes

A minute is a measurement of time. There are sixty seconds in a minute and sixty minutes in an hour.

Directions: Write the time shown on each clock.

Example:

Each mark is one minute. The hand is at mark number 6.

Write: 5:06
Read: six minutes after five.

7:08   6:03   4:11   5:15

5:38   1:33   2:47   11:53

12:01   9:22   3:18   8:37

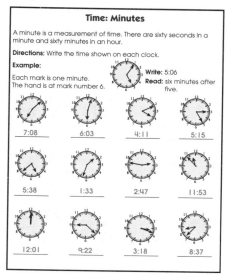

Page 221

Time on My Hands

Draw the hour and minute hands to show each time below.

Example:

3:35   10:05   4:55   8:10

12:50   9:20   7:25   1:15

11:45   3:30   6:40   12:55

2:00   5:35   3:15   10:50

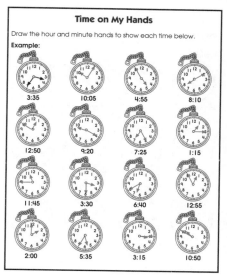

Page 222

Minute Men

Directions: Draw the hour and minute hands on these clocks.

Example:

4:42   9:03   6:51

1:24   7:33   10:11

3:58   12:01   2:49

4:17   5:36   8:23

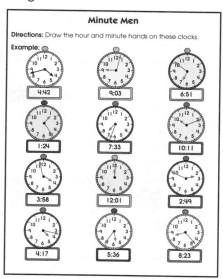

Page 223

Take Time for These

Directions: Write the time shown on these clocks.

Example:

6:47   1:29   11:51   3:42

7:02   8:26   2:34   12:31

9:12   5:17   4:04   10:59

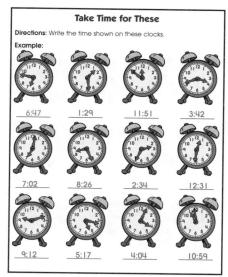

Page 224

Father Time Teasers

Directions: Write the times below.

Example:

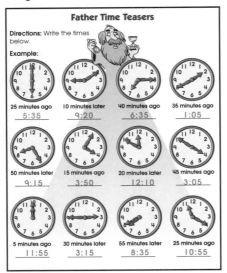

25 minutes ago	10 minutes later	40 minutes ago	35 minutes ago
5:35	9:20	6:35	1:05

50 minutes later	15 minutes later	20 minutes later	45 minutes ago
9:15	3:50	12:10	3:05

5 minutes ago	30 minutes later	55 minutes later	25 minutes ago
11:55	3:15	8:35	10:55

Page 225

Time "Tables"

Directions: Draw the hands on these clocks.

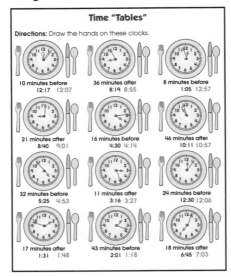

10 minutes before	36 minutes after	8 minutes before
12:17 12:07	8:19 8:55	1:05 12:57

21 minutes after	16 minutes before	46 minutes after
8:40 9:01	4:30 4:14	10:11 10:57

32 minutes before	11 minutes after	24 minutes before
5:25 4:53	3:16 3:27	12:30 12:06

17 minutes after	43 minutes before	18 minutes after
1:31 1:48	2:01 1:18	6:45 7:03

Page 226

Monkeying Around

Directions: Nat can t tell time. He needs your help to solve these problems.

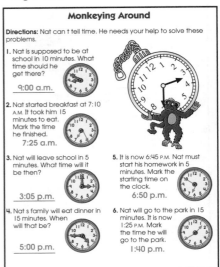

1. Nat is supposed to be at school in 10 minutes. What time should he get there?

   9:00 a.m.

2. Nat started breakfast at 7:10 A.M. It took him 15 minutes to eat. Mark the time he finished.

   7:25 a.m.

3. Nat will leave school in 5 minutes. What time will it be then?

   3:05 p.m.

4. Nat s family will eat dinner in 15 minutes. When will that be?

   5:00 p.m.

5. It is now 6:45 P.M. Nat must start his homework in 5 minutes. Mark the starting time on the clock.

   6:50 p.m.

6. Nat will go to the park in 15 minutes. It is now 1:25 P.M. Mark the time he will go to the park.

   1:40 p.m.

Page 227

Money: Coins and Dollars

penny = 1¢ or $.01

nickel = 5¢ or $.05

quarter = 25¢ or $.25

dime = 10¢ or $.10

dollar = 100¢ or $1.00

Directions: Write the amount for each group of money shown. Use a dollar sign and decimal point. The first one is done for you.

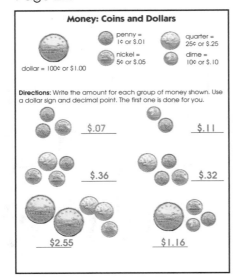

$.07

$.11

$.36

$.32

$2.55

$1.16

Page 228

Garage Sale

Directions: Use the fewest number of coins possible to equal the amount shown in each box. Write or draw the coins you would use in each box.

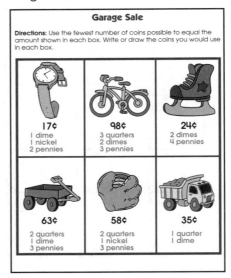

17¢	98¢	24¢
1 dime 1 nickel 2 pennies	3 quarters 2 dimes 3 pennies	2 dimes 4 pennies

63¢	58¢	35¢
2 quarters 1 dime 3 pennies	2 quarters 1 nickel 3 pennies	1 quarter 1 dime

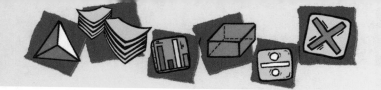

Page 229

Money

1 penny	1 nickel	1 dime	1 quarter	1 dollar
1 cent	5 cents	10 cents	25 cents	100 cents
1¢ or $0.01	5¢ or $0.05	10¢ or $0.10	25¢ or $0.25	$1.00

25 pennies have a value of __25__ cents or __1__ quarter.
5 pennies have a value of __5__ cents or __1__ nickel.
$2.57 means __2__ dollars and __57__ cents.
$3.45 means __3__ dollars and __45__ cents.

Directions: Complete the following.

1. 5 pennies have a value of __5__ cents or __1__ nickel.
2. 10 pennies have a value of __10__ cents or __1__ dime.
3. 20 pennies have a value of __20__ cents or __2__ dimes.
4. 15 pennies have a value of __15__ cents or __3__ nickels.
5. 20 pennies have a value of __20__ cents or __4__ nickels.

Directions: Complete the following as shown.

6. $14.05 means __14__ dollars and __5__ cents.
7. $12.07 means __12__ dollars and __7__ cents.
8. $8.14 means __8__ dollars and __14__ cents.
9. $0.65 means __0__ dollars and __65__ cents.
10. $10.01 means __10__ dollars and __01__ cents.

Page 230

Your Answer's Safe With Me

Directions: Find the right "combination" to open each safe. Draw the bills and coins needed to make each amount.

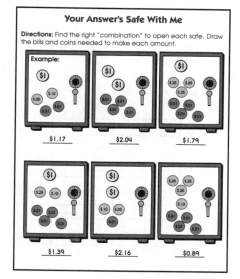

Example:

$1.17 $2.04 $1.79

$1.39 $2.16 $0.89

Page 231

Easy Street

Directions: What is each house worth? Count the money in each house on Easy Street. Write the amount on the line below it.

Example:

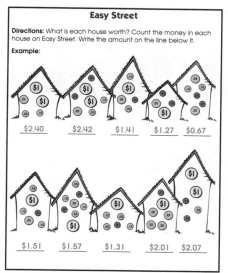

$2.40 $2.42 $1.41 $1.27 $0.67

$1.51 $1.57 $1.31 $2.01 $2.07

Page 232

A Collection of Coins

Directions: Write the number of coins needed to make the amount shown.

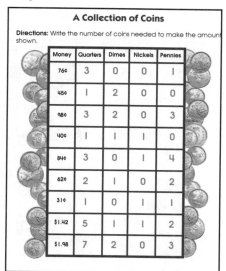

Money	Quarters	Dimes	Nickels	Pennies
76¢	3	0	0	1
45¢	1	2	0	0
98¢	3	2	0	3
40¢	1	1	1	0
84¢	3	0	1	4
62¢	2	1	0	2
31¢	1	0	1	1
$1.42	5	1	1	2
$1.98	7	2	0	3

Page 233

Monetary Message

Directions: What's the smartest thing to do with your money? To find out, solve the following problems and write the matching letter above the answer.

S A V E   I T   '
$42.71 $33.94 $50.42 $100.73 $45.70 $2.39

A N D   I T   W I L L
$33.94 $26.13 $88.02 $45.70 $2.39 $51.12 $45.70 $11.01 $11.01

A D D   U P !
$33.94 $88.02 $88.02 $55.76 $42.79

V = $42.13
+ 8.29
$50.42

A = $ 4.56
+ 29.38
$33.94

N = $ 4.65
+ 21.48
$26.13

S = $23.46
+ 19.25
$42.71

P = $ 9.31
+ 33.48
$42.79

L = $ 6.73
+ 4.28
$11.01

E = $81.49
+ 19.24
$100.73

T = $ .42
1.94
+ .03
$2.39

U = $50.84
+ 4.92
$55.76

I = $ 7.49
+ 38.21
$45.70

D = $ 3.04
+ 84.98
$88.02

W = $ 1.89
+ 49.23
$51.12

Page 234

Add 'Em Up!

Directions: Write the prices, then add. Regroup, when needed.

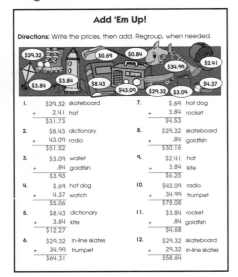

1.	$29.32 + 2.41 $31.73	skateboard hat	7.	$.69 + 3.84 $4.53	hot dog rocket
2.	$8.43 + 43.09 $51.52	dictionary radio	8.	$29.32 + .84 $30.16	skateboard goldfish
3.	$3.09 + .84 $3.93	wallet goldfish	9.	$2.41 + 3.84 $6.25	hat kite
4.	$.69 + 4.37 $5.06	hot dog watch	10.	$43.09 + 34.99 $78.08	radio trumpet
5.	$8.43 + 3.84 $12.27	dictionary kite	11.	$3.84 + .84 $4.68	rocket goldfish
6.	$29.32 + 34.99 $64.31	in-line skates trumpet	12.	$29.32 + 29.32 $58.64	skateboard in-line skates

Page 235

Making Change

When you do not have the exact change to buy something at a store, the clerk must give you change. The first amount of money is what you give the clerk. The second amount is what the item costs.

Directions: In the box, list the fewest number of coins and bills you will receive in change.

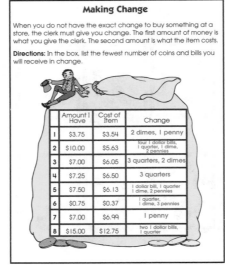

	Amount I Have	Cost of Item	Change
1	$3.75	$3.54	2 dimes, 1 penny
2	$10.00	$5.63	four 1 dollar bills, 1 quarter, 1 dime, 2 pennies
3	$7.00	$6.05	3 quarters, 2 dimes
4	$7.25	$6.50	3 quarters
5	$7.50	$6.13	1 dollar bill, 1 quarter, 1 dime, 2 pennies
6	$0.75	$0.37	1 quarter, 1 dime, 3 pennies
7	$7.00	$6.99	1 penny
8	$15.00	$12.75	two 1 dollar bills, 1 quarter

Page 236

Money: Counting Change

Directions: Subtract the money using decimals to show how much change a person would receive in each of the following.

Example:
Bill had 3 dollars.
He bought a baseball for $2.83.
How much change did he receive?

$3.00
− 2.83
$ .17

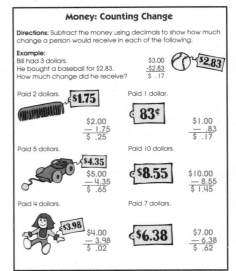

Paid 2 dollars.

$2.00
− 1.75
$ .25

Paid 1 dollar.

$1.00
− .83
$ .17

Paid 5 dollars.

$5.00
− 4.35
$ .65

Paid 10 dollars.

$10.00
− 8.55
$ 1.45

Paid 4 dollars.

$4.00
− 3.98
$ .02

Paid 7 dollars.

$7.00
− 6.38
$ .62

Page 237

Money: Five-Dollar Bill and Ten-Dollar Bill

Directions: Write the amount for each group of money shown. Use a dollar sign and decimal point. The first one is done for you.

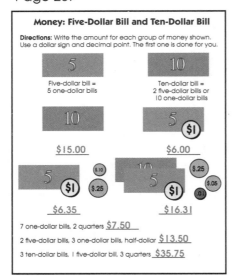

Five-dollar bill = 5 one-dollar bills

Ten-dollar bill = 2 five-dollar bills or 10 one-dollar bills

$15.00

$6.00

$6.35

$16.31

7 one-dollar bills, 2 quarters $7.50

2 five-dollar bills, 3 one-dollar bills, half-dollar $13.50

3 ten-dollar bills, 1 five-dollar bill, 3 quarters $35.75

Page 238

Money: Comparing

Directions: Compare the amount of money in the left column with the price of the object in the right column. Is the amount of money in the left column enough to purchase the object in the right column? Circle yes or no.

Example:

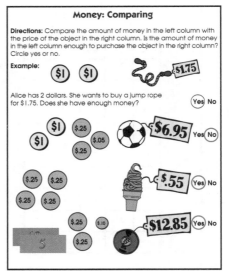

Alice has 2 dollars. She wants to buy a jump rope for $1.75. Does she have enough money?

Yes No

Yes No

Yes No

Yes No

Page 239

Money

| $9.05
+ 6.98
$16.03 | $12.00
0.45
+ 3.16
$15.61 | 45¢
+ 38¢
83¢ | $0.75
+ 0.38
$1.13 | $14.08
- 7.25
$6.83 | $13.00
- 6.05
$6.95 |

Add or subtract as usual.
Put a decimal point (.) and a $ or ¢ in the answer.
Be sure to line up the decimal points.

Directions: Add or subtract.

1.	$ 0.36 + 12.40 $12.76	$3.75 + 1.46 $5.21	$ 1.36 + 40.00 $41.36	37¢ + 68¢ 1.05¢	$4.35 + 0.07 $4.42
2.	$5.20 - 3.18 $2.02	$12.64 - 5.38 $7.26	$3.00 - 0.54 $2.46	88¢ - 76¢ 12¢	$24.42 - 1.08 $23.34
3.	$ 4.23 16.90 + 0.89 $22.02	$7.25 0.40 + 4.42 $12.07	$ 8.05 12.16 + 0.58 $20.79	47¢ 18¢ + 25¢ 90¢	$ 0.08 3.67 + 14.37 $18.12
4.	$15.40 - 3.62 $11.78	$5.70 - 2.08 $3.62	$11.30 - 0.86 $10.44	91¢ - 75¢ 16¢	$17.20 - 4.06 $13.14
5.	$27.00 - 13.45 $13.55	$65.21 + 3.80 $69.01	$0.12 + 1.88 $2.00	47¢ - 19¢ 28¢	$3.00 - 1.78 $1.22
6.	$16.49 + 28.98 $45.47	$40.60 - 7.56 $33.04	$5.00 - 2.72 $2.28	38¢ + 35¢ 73¢	$8.75 + 0.64 $9.39

Page 240

Match the Sale

Directions: Which item did each child purchase? Calculate the amount. Write each purchase price below.

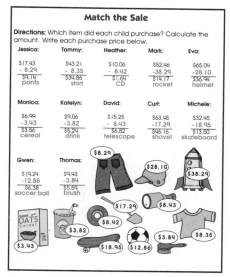

Jessica:	Tammy:	Heather:	Mark:	Eva:
$17.43 - 8.29 $9.14 pants	$43.21 - 8.35 $34.86 shirt	$10.06 - 8.42 $1.64 CD	$52.46 -38.29 $14.17 rocket	$65.04 -28.10 $36.94 helmet

Monica:	Katelyn:	David:	Curt:	Michele:
$6.99 - 3.43 $3.56 cereal	$9.06 - 3.82 $5.24 drink	$15.25 - 8.43 $6.82 telescope	$63.45 -17.29 $46.16 shovel	$32.45 -18.95 $13.50 skateboard

Gwen:	Thomas:
$19.24 -12.86 $6.38 soccer ball	$9.43 - 3.84 $5.59 brush

$8.29 $28.10 $38.29 $17.29 $8.43 $3.82 $8.42 $3.84 $8.35 $3.43 $18.95 $12.86

Page 241

Problem Solving

Directions: Solve each problem.

Work Space:

1. Caitlin's mother bought a dress for $22.98 and a blouse for $17.64. How much did these items cost altogether?

   They cost $40.62 altogether.

2. Find the total cost of a basketball at $18.69, a baseball at $8.05, and a football at $24.98.

   The total cost is $51.72.

3. Jeremy has $2.50. Landon has $1.75. Jeremy has how much more money than Landon?

   Jeremy has $0.75 more than Landon.

4. In problem **2**, how much more does the basketball cost than the baseball? How much more does the football cost than the basketball?

   The basketball costs $10.64 more than the baseball.

   The football costs $6.29 more than the basketball.

5. Alexandra saved $4.20 one week, $0.90 the next week, and $2.05 the third week. How much money did she save during these 3 weeks?

   Alexandra saved $7.15 in 3 weeks.

1.
2.
3.
4.
5.

Page 242

Spending Spree

Directions: Use the clues to figure out what each person bought. Then, subtract to find out how much change each had left.

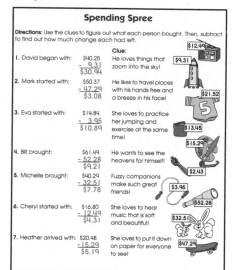

		Clue:
1. David began with:	$40.25 - 9.31 $30.94	He loves things that zoom into the sky!
2. Mark started with:	$50.37 - 47.29 $3.08	He likes to travel places with his hands free and a breeze in his face!
3. Eva started with:	$14.84 - 3.95 $10.89	She loves to practice her jumping and exercise at the same time!
4. Bill brought:	$61.49 - 52.28 $9.21	He wants to see the heavens for himself!
5. Michelle brought:	$40.29 - 32.51 $7.78	Fuzzy companions make such great friends!
6. Cheryl started with:	$16.80 - 12.49 $4.31	She loves to hear music that is soft and beautiful!
7. Heather arrived with:	$20.48 - 15.29 $5.19	She loves to put it down on paper for everyone to see!

$12.49 $9.31 $21.52 $13.45 $15.29 $2.43 $3.95 $52.28 $32.51 $47.29

Page 243

Foxy Felix's Shop

Directions: Solve these problems.

1. Mighty Man comics cost $0.13 at Foxy Felix's. You buy 4 of these comics. How much should you pay? $0.13 x 4 $ .52	4. Your sister decides to buy 2 CDs of the latest hit single by the Bird Brains. Each CD costs $0.89. How much will she pay? $0.89 x 2 = $1.78
2. Your best friend bought 9 marbles at Foxy Felix's. Each marble cost $0.19. How much money did he spend? $0.19 x 9 $1.71	5. Crazy stickers cost $0.21 each at Foxy Felix's. You buy 7 of them. How much should you pay? $0.21 x 7 $1.47
3. Baseball cards are $0.11 each at Foxy Felix's. How much will it cost you for 8 cards? $0.11 x 8 $ .88	6. Stinky Stickers have a skunk odour. Your best friend bought 7 Stinky Stickers, which cost $0.18 each. How much did he spend? $0.18 x 7 = $1.26

This page was
intentionally left blank.

Test Practice

Teaching Suggestions

Number Recognition

Have your child read the numbers on the license plates of other vehicles as you drive around town. This will not only reinforce number recognition, but letter recognition as well!

> ONTARIO
> ABCD-456

Safety Tip: Make sure your child knows his/her address. Have your child write his/her address (with your assistance) and keep it with him/her:

> My Child
> 12345 Oak Street
> Any City, Any Province AIA AIA

Help your child memorize his/her phone number as well. Practise writing it and dialing it on the phone.

Sequencing Numbers

Talk to your child about order and sequencing in everyday life. Make lists together.
Example: 1. Go to the bank.
           2. Go to the grocery store.

Have your child make a list of the things he/she will do today.

Put a puzzle together with your child. Talk about order and the way the pieces fit together to make the picture.

Teaching Suggestions

Counting

Have your child write his/her name. Count the number of letters in his/her name and the number of time each letter appears. Have your child do the same with your name and other family members' names.

Buy or make a calendar for your child to keep in his/her room. Have your child number the calendar. Put stickers on or draw pictures to mark special days. Have your child X each day.

Play the card game "War" with your child. Each player needs an equal number of cards. Each player places a card face down and turns them over at the same time. The player with the higher number gets to keep both cards.

Shapes

Encourage your child to look at the different shapes of traffic signs and road signs. What shapes does your child see?

Shapes are part of our everyday lives. What shapes does your child see in his/her home, yard, etc.? List the shapes and objects. Add more as you find them.

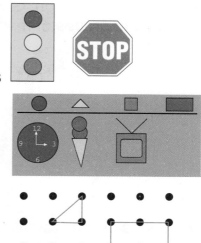

Play the "Dot" game with your child. Create your own "dot boards" and review other geometric shapes with your child.

Purchase or make a geoboard. To make a geoboard, pound 16 two-inch nails an equal distance apart in a one-inch thick piece of wood. Pull rubber bands over the nails to create various geometric shapes. Talk with your child about the shapes he/she has created.

Colours

Fill six clear plastic glasses half full with water. Have your child experiment with mixing drops of food colouring into each cup. Talk about the colors created, and how they were created. Help your child record his/her findings: red + yellow = orange. Have your child write the number problem on paper and read it to you.

Teaching Suggestions

Fractions

Let your child help you cut pie or pizza into equal slices.

Peel an orange. Separate the sections and talk about "fractions" as parts of a whole.

Pick clovers. Talk about equal parts as you pull off the petals.

Fold a piece of paper into four equal sections. Have your child shade three sections blue and one brown. Explain that $\frac{3}{4}$ of the Earth is water and $\frac{1}{4}$ is land.

Addition

Make your own "plus" sign. Glue two toothpicks or popsicle sticks together. Then, your child can create groups of manipulatives on either side of the "plus" sign to add.

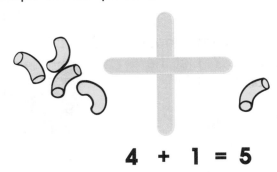

4 + 1 = 5

Use dry beans or other small manipulatives to practise counting. Have your child divide ten beans into two separate groups and combine them by adding.
For example:

Have your child write the number problem on paper and read it to you.

3 + 4 = 7

Look through magazines with your child. Encourage him/her to create addition problems from the pictures. For example: "One mommy plus two children equals three!"

Teaching Suggestions

Tens and Ones

Let your child practise "trading" with pennies, dimes and a dollar to reinforce the concept of ones, tens and hundreds. Roll a die and let your child take as many pennies from the "pot" as the die indicates. When he/she has ten pennies, he/she can trade them in for a dime. Continue playing and trading pennies for dimes. When your child gets ten dimes, he/she can trade them in for a dollar!

Rubber band or glue ten toothpicks together to represent "tens" and let your child practise counting by tens.

Money

Practise counting by fives with nickels and by tens with dimes.

Let your child label canned goods in your home with "prices." Your child will gain valuable practise counting and exchanging money by playing "store."

Give your child small amounts of money to purchase items when you go shopping. Encourage him/her to count his/her change after the transaction.

Encourage your child to create other combinations of money for the same amount. For example, ten cents can be made with one dime, with two nickels, with ten pennies and with one nickel and five pennies.

Measurement

Purchase a plastic or wooden ruler for your child, and let him/her measure various objects around the house. Record his/her findings and talk about length.

How to Help Your Child Prepare for Testing

Preparing All Year Round

Perhaps the most valuable way you can help your child prepare for tests is by providing enriching experiences. If a child is hungry, tired, or upset, this may result in a poor test score. Here are some tips on how you can help your child do his or her best on tests.

Read aloud with your child. Reading aloud helps develop vocabulary and fosters a positive attitude toward reading. Reading together is one of the most effective ways you can help your child succeed in school.

Share experiences. Baking cookies together, planting a garden, or making a map of your neighbourhood are examples of activities that help build skills that are measured on the tests such as sequencing and following directions.

Help your child know what to expect. Read and discuss with your child the test-taking tips in this book. Your child can prepare by working through a couple of strategies a day so that no practice session takes too long.

Help your child with his or her regular school assignments. Set up a quiet study area for homework. Supply this area with pencils, paper, markers, a calculator, a ruler, a dictionary, scissors, glue, and so on. Check your child's homework and offer to help if he or she gets stuck. But remember, it's your child's homework, not yours. If you help too much, your child will not benefit from the activity.

Keep in regular contact with your child's teacher. Attend parent-teacher conferences, school functions, PTA or PTO meetings, and school board meetings. This will help you get to know the educators in your district and the families of your child's classmates.

Learn to use computers as an educational resource. If you do not have a computer and Internet access at home, try your local library.

Remember—simply getting your child comfortable with testing procedures and helping him or her know what to expect can improve test scores!

Getting Ready for the Big Day

There are lots of things you can do on or immediately before test day to improve your child's chances of testing success. What's more, these strategies will help your child prepare him or herself for school tests, too, and promote general study skills that can last a lifetime.

Provide a good breakfast on test day.
Instead of sugar cereal, which provides immediate but not long-term energy, have your child eat a breakfast with protein or complex carbohydrates such as an egg, whole grain cereal or toast, or a banana-yogourt shake.

Promote a good night's sleep. A good night's sleep before the test is essential. Try not to overstress the importance of the test. This may cause your child to lose sleep because of anxiety. Doing some exercise after school and having a quiet evening routine will help your child sleep well the night before the test.

Assure your child that he or she is not expected to know all of the answers on the test. Help your child understand that you expect him or her to put forth a good effort—and that this is enough. Your child should not try to cram for these tests. Also avoid threats or bribes; these put undue pressure on children and may interfere with their best performance.

Keep the mood light and offer encouragement. To provide a break on test days, do something fun and special after school— take a walk around the neighbourhood, play a game, read a favourite book, or prepare a special snack together. These activities keep your child's mood light—even if the testing sessions have been difficult—and show how much you appreciate your child's effort.

Taking Tests

No matter what grade you're in, this is information you can use to prepare for tests. Here is what you'll find:

- Test-taking tips and strategies to use on test day and year-round.
- Important terms to know for Math.
- A checklist of skills to complete to help you understand what you need to know in Math.
- General study/homework tips.

By opening this book, you've already taken your first step towards test success. The rest is easy—all you have to do is get started!

What You Need to Know

There are many things you can do to increase your test success. Here's a list of tips to keep in mind when you take tests—and when you study for them, too.

Keep up with your school work.

One way you can succeed in school and on tests is by studying and doing your homework regularly. Studies show that

you remember only about one-fifth of what you memorize the night before a

test. That's one good reason not to try to learn it all at once! Keeping up with your work throughout the year will help you remember the material better. You also won't be as tired or nervous as if you try to learn everything at once.

Feel your best. One of the ways you can do your best on tests and in school is to make sure your body is ready. To do this, get a good night's sleep each night and eat

a healthy breakfast (not sugary cereal that will leave you tired by the middle of the morning). An egg or a milkshake with yogourt and fresh fruit will give you lasting energy. Also, wear comfortable clothes, maybe your lucky shirt or your favourite colour on test day. It can't hurt, and it may even keep you relaxed.

When you are taking the test, follow the directions. It is important to listen carefully to the directions your teacher gives and to read the written instructions carefully. Words like *not, none, rarely, never,* and *always* are very important in test directions and questions. You may want to circle words like these.

Look at each page carefully before you start answering. On math tests, look at the labels on graphs and charts. Think about what each graph or chart shows. Questions often will ask you to draw conclusions about the information.

Manage your time. *Time management* means using your time wisely on a test so that you can finish as much of it as possible and do your best. Look over the test or the parts that you are allowed to do at one time. Sometimes you may want to do the easier parts first. This way, if you

run out of time before you finish, you will have completed a good chunk of the work.

For tests that have a time limit, notice what time it is when the test begins and figure out when you need to stop. Check a few times as you work through the test to be sure you are making good progress and not spending too much time on any particular section.

You don't have to keep up with everyone else. You may notice other students in the class finishing before you do. Don't worry about this. Everyone works at a different pace. Just keep going, trying not to spend too long on any one question.

Fill in answer circles properly. Even if you know every answer on a test, you won't do well unless you fill in the circle next to the correct answer.

Fill in the entire circle, but don't spend too much time making it perfect. Make your mark dark, but not so dark that it goes through the paper! And be sure you only choose one answer for each question, even if you are not sure. If you choose two answers, both will be marked as wrong.

It's usually not a good idea to change your answers. Usually your first choice is the right one. Unless you realize that you misread the question, the directions, or some facts in a passage, it's usually safer to stay with your first answer. If you are pretty sure it's wrong, of course, go ahead and change it. Make sure you completely erase the first choice and neatly fill in your new choice.

Use context clues to figure out tough questions. If you come across a word or idea you don't understand, use context clues—the words in the sentences nearby— to help you figure out its meaning.

Sometimes it's good to guess. Should you guess when you don't know an answer on a test? That depends. If your teacher has made the test, usually you will score better if you answer as many questions as possible, even if you don't really know the answers.

Sometimes you should skip a question and come back to it. On many tests, you will score better if you answer more questions. This means that you should not spend too much time on any single question. Sometimes it gets tricky, though, keeping track of questions you skipped on your answer sheet.

If you want to skip a question because you don't know the answer, put a very light pencil mark next to the question in the test booklet. Try to choose an answer, even if you're not sure of it. Fill in the answer lightly on the answer sheet.

Check your work. First, scan your answer sheet. Make sure that you answered every question you could. Also, if you are using a bubble-type answer sheet, make sure that you filled in only one bubble for each question. Erase any extra marks on the page.

Finally—avoid test anxiety! If you get nervous about tests, don't worry. *Test anxiety* happens to lots of good students. Being a little nervous actually sharpens your mind. But if you get very nervous about tests, take a few minutes to relax the night before or the day of the test. One good way to relax is to get some exercise, even if you just have time to stretch, shake out your fingers, and wiggle your toes. If you can't move around, it helps just to take a few slow, deep breaths and picture yourself doing a great job!

Skills Checklists

Which math skills do you need more practise in? Use the following checklist to find out. Put a check mark next to each statement that is true for you. Then, use the unchecked statements to figure out which skills you need to review.

Keep in mind that if you are using these checklists in the middle of the school year, you may not have learned some skills yet. Talk to your teacher or a parent if you need help with a new skill.

Addition and Subtraction

☐ I know addition and subtraction facts to 18.

☐ I can regroup when adding or subtracting two- or three-digit numbers.

Multiplication and Division

☐ I practise my multiplication and division facts so I can do them quickly.

☐ I can multiply by one-digit numbers.

☐ I can regroup when multiplying with one-, two-, and three-digit numbers.

☐ I can divide by one-digit numbers with and without remainders.

Fractions and Decimals

☐ I can name parts of a whole (one-half, one-third, one-quarter).

☐ I can compare like and unlike fractions.

☐ I can read mixed numbers.

☐ I can read decimals to the tenths and hundredths places.

Geometry

For simple shapes, I can

☐ calculate perimeter and area.

☐ find lines of symmetry.

Measurement

I know my metric units of measure for

☐   length (centimetre, decimetre, metre, kilometre).

☐   mass (gram, kilogram).

☐   capacity (litre).

☐   I can solve simple problems with units of time, length, weight/mass, and capacity.

I know my standard units of measure for

☐   length (inch, foot, yard, mile).

☐   weight (ounce, pound).

☐   capacity (cup, pint, quart, gallon).

☐   time (seconds, minutes, hours).

Problem Solving

☐   When I do number problems, I read the directions carefully.

☐   When I do word problems, I read the problem carefully.

☐   I look for words that tell the operation I must use to solve the problem.

☐   I label my answer with units when necessary.

I use different strategies to solve different kinds of problems:

☐   I estimate.

☐   I make pictures, diagrams, and charts.

☐   I look for patterns.

Preparing All Year Round

Believe it or not, knowing how to study and manage your time is a skill you will use for the rest of your life. There are helpful strategies that you can use to be more successful in school. The following is a list of tips to keep in mind as you study for tests and school assignments.

Get organized. To make it easy to get your homework done, set up a place in which to do it each day. Choose a location where you can give the work your full attention. Find a corner of your room, the kitchen, or another quiet place where you won't be interrupted. Put all the tools you'll need in that area. Set aside a drawer or basket for school supplies. That way you won't have to go hunting each time you need a sharp pencil! Here are some things you may want to keep in your study corner for homework and school projects:

- pencils and pens
- pencil sharpener
- notebook paper
- tape
- glue
- scissors
- stapler
- crayons, markers, coloured pencils
- construction paper, printer paper
- dictionary

Schedule your assignments. The best way to keep track of homework and special projects is by planning and managing your time. Keep a schedule of homework assignments and other events to help you get organized. Make your own or make a copy of the Homework Log and Weekly Schedule provided on pages 300–301 of this book for each week you're in school.

Record your homework assignments on the log as completely as you can. Enter the book, page number, and exercise number of each assignment. Enter dates of tests as soon as you know them so that you can begin to study ahead of time. Study a section of the material each day. Then review all of it the day before the test.

Also make notes to help you remember special events and materials such as permission slips you need to return. List after-school activities so you can plan your homework and study time around them. Remember to record fun activities on your log, too. You don't want to forget that party you've been invited to or even just time you'd like to spend hanging out or studying with friends.

Do your homework right away. Set aside a special time every day after school to do your homework. You may want to take a break when you first get home, but give yourself plenty of time to do your homework, too. That way you won't get interrupted by dinner or get too tired to finish.

If you are bored or confused by an assignment and you really don't want to do it, promise yourself a little reward, perhaps a snack or 15 minutes of playing ball after you've really worked hard for 45 minutes or so. Then go back to work for a while if you need to, and take another break later.

Get help if you need it. If you need help, just ask. Call a friend or ask a family member for help. If these people can't help you, be sure to ask your teacher the next day about any work you didn't understand.

Use a computer. If you have one available, a computer can be a great tool for doing homework. Typing your homework on the computer lets you hand in neat papers, check your spelling easily, and look up the definitions of words you aren't sure about. If you have an Internet connection, you can also do research without leaving home.

Before you go online, talk with your family about ways to stay safe. Be sure never to give out personal information (your name, age, address, or phone number) without permission.

Practise, practise, practise! The best way to improve your skills in specific subject areas is through lots of practise. If you have trouble in a school subject such as math, science, social studies, language arts, or reading, doing some extra activities or projects can give you just the boost you need.

Homework Log
and Weekly Schedule

	Monday	Tuesday	Wednesday
MATH			
SOCIAL STUDIES			
SCIENCE			
READING			
LANGUAGE ARTS			
OTHER			

for the week of _____

Thursday	Friday	Saturday / Sunday	
			MATH
			SOCIAL STUDIES
			SCIENCE
			READING
			LANGUAGE ARTS
			OTHER

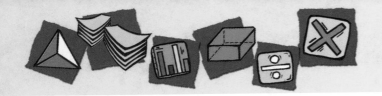

What's Ahead in This Book?

As you know, you will have to take many tests while in school. But there is no reason to be nervous about taking tests. You can prepare for them by doing your best in school all year. You can also learn about the types of questions you'll see on tests and helpful strategies for answering the questions. That's what this section is all about. It has been developed especially to help you and other third graders know what to expect—and what to do—on test day.

Next, you'll find a section on subject help for math. You'll discover traps to watch for and tricks you can use to make answering the questions easier. And there are plenty of practise questions provided to sharpen your skills even more.

Finally, you'll find two sections of questions. One is called Practice Test and the other is called Final Test. The questions are designed to look just like the ones you'll be given in school on a real math test. An answer key is at the back of the book so you can check your own answers. Once you check your answers, you can see in which areas you need more practise.

So good luck—test success is just around the corner!

Draw a Diagram

Many tests will ask you to solve math story problems. Sometimes these are also called word problems. Use the following strategies to help solve story problems quickly. Remember, though, not every strategy can be used with every story problem. You will have to choose the best strategy to use for each one.

Draw a Diagram

Sometimes it's helpful to draw a diagram to visualize the activity described in a story problem. Diagrams can help you understand a problem and figure out the correct answer.

EXAMPLE | **Cassie, Tony, Jose, and Ling are standing in line for lunch. Ling is in front of Tony, Jose is behind Tony, and Cassie is behind Ling but before Tony. Who is last in line?**

Ⓐ Cassie   Ⓑ Tony   Ⓒ Jose   Ⓓ Ling

- Draw several lines with a space for each child.

- Show each way Ling is in front of Tony.

- Using the grids you made, show Jose behind Tony.

There are 2 fewer grids because Jose *must* be behind Tony.

- Find the grid where Cassie would be after Ling and before Tony.
- The only line grid remaining has Jose last. The answer is C.

When you draw a diagram:
- ☑ Read the problem carefully.
- ☑ Determine what data you need to solve the problem.
- ☑ Determine how to draw a diagram to organize the data.
- ☑ Draw a diagram based on the data in the problem.
- ☑ Solve the problem.

Diagram Practise

Directions: Draw a diagram in the space provided to help you solve each problem. Then choose the correct answer.

1 Teri, Hank, Shawana, and Jimmy are the top finishers in a race. Teri finished before Hank, but after Shawana. Jimmy finished after Teri. Who won the race?

Ⓐ Shawana   Ⓒ Teri

Ⓑ Hank   Ⓓ Jimmy

2 In town, the restaurant is between the car wash and the grocery store. The grocery store is before the bank, but after the car wash. What is the order of the shops as you go down the street?

Ⓕ restaurant, bank, car wash, grocery

Ⓖ bank, car wash, restaurant, grocery

Ⓗ car wash, restaurant, grocery, bank

Ⓙ car wash, bank, restaurant, grocery

3 In our solar system Mercury is closest to the sun. Earth is between Venus and Mars. Venus is after Mercury, Jupiter is after Mars, but before Saturn. Uranus, Neptune, and Pluto are after Saturn. What is the fourth planet from the sun?

Ⓐ Earth   Ⓒ Saturn

Ⓑ Mars   Ⓙ Uranus

Trick Questions

Sometimes you're given trick questions on tests. These questions provide extra information that is not needed to solve the problem. You can deal with these questions by identifying the information required to solve the problem and setting aside the extra information that is unnecessary.

EXAMPLE **In the forest, 8 squirrels collected acorns from 9 trees. They collected 47 acorns from each tree. How many acorns did the squirrels collect in all?**

Ⓐ 376 acorns   Ⓒ 423 acorns

Ⓑ 705 acorns   Ⓓ 498 acorns

- To solve this problem, first determine what information you need to answer the question asked:
  How many acorns were collected?

- You need to know how many acorns from each tree the squirrels collected and the number of trees they collected them from. However, you do not need to know how many squirrels were collecting acorns to solve the problem.

  47 × 9 = 423 acorns

- You know the squirrels collected 423 acorns.
  The answer is **C**.

- The number of squirrels is extra information included in the problem to trick you. Be careful not to use this information to solve the problem.

  When you think you have extra information:
  ☐ Read the problem carefully.
  ☐ Determine what information you need to solve the problem.
  ☐ Check for extra information.
  ☐ Set the extra information aside so you don't use it by mistake.
  ☐ Solve the problem.

Trick Questions Practise

Directions: Solve these problems. If there is extra information, write it in the space provided. Choose the correct answer.

1 Cody played in 3 basketball games last week. In the first game he scored 17 points, in the second game he scored 22 points, and in the third game he scored 19 points. How many points did he score last week?

Extra information:_____

_____

(A) 48   (C) 58

(B) 61   (D) 51

2 Jason bought 48 apples, 36 oranges, and 24 bananas for the fruit stand at the school fair. All of the apples were sold. If only 4 people bought apples, and each person bought the same number of apples, how many apples did each person buy?

Extra information:_____

_____

(F) 12 apples

(G) 9 apples

(H) 27 apples

(J) 6 apples

3 A recipe needs $\frac{1}{3}$ cup of white sugar, $\frac{2}{3}$ cup of brown sugar, 2 eggs, and $\frac{1}{3}$ cup of flour. How many cups of dry ingredients does the recipe use?

Extra information:_____

_____

(A) $1\frac{1}{3}$ cups   (C) $3\frac{1}{3}$ cups

(B) $1\frac{2}{3}$ cups   (D) 1 cup

4 Every day for a week Colleen practised piano for 30 minutes. How long did she practise during the week?

Extra information:_____

_____

(F) 2 hours, 30 minutes

(G) 7 hours

(H) 1 hour, 30 minutes

(J) 3 hours, 30 minutes

Paper and Pencil

It often helps to work through problems using paper and pencil. By working out a problem this way you can see and check the work you have done. Using paper and pencil is helpful when you have a *multi*-step problem on a test. You can do the first part of the problem and then carry that work on to the second part of the problem.

EXAMPLE **Mr. Simms has four boxes. In each of the boxes there are 16 candles. Mr. Simms wants to use all of his candles and put an equal number on each of 8 tables. How many candles will be on each table?**

Ⓐ 64 candles   Ⓒ 32 candles

Ⓑ 8 candles   Ⓓ 56 candles

- There are two parts to the problem. First, you have to multiply to find out how many candles there are altogether. Then, you have to divide to find out how many will be on each table.

- Use paper and pencil to multiply 16 × 4. This is the complete number of candles.

$$\begin{array}{r} {}^2\,\,\,\, \\ 16 \\ \times\ 4 \\ \hline \textbf{64 candles} \end{array}$$

- Then, use paper and pencil again to take the answer from the first part of the problem and solve the second part of the problem.

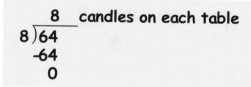

- You now know that there are 8 candles on each table. The answer is **B**.

When you use pencil and paper:
- ☐ Read the problem carefully.
- ☐ Write neatly so that you do not make errors.
- ☐ Solve the problem.

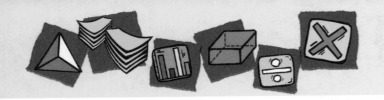

Paper and Pencil Practice

Directions: Solve these problems using paper and pencil.
Do your work in the space provided.

1 There are 8 classrooms at Tanglewood Elementary School that have 17 students in them. There are 7 classrooms that have 18 students in them. How many students are there in all 15 classrooms?

  Ⓐ 126 students   © 136 students

  Ⓑ 262 students   Ⓓ 321 students

2 At the county fair there are 2 dunking booths, 16 rides, 4 shows, 21 games, and 1 hall of mirrors. How many attractions are at the county fair altogether?

  Ⓕ 44 attractions   Ⓗ 43 attractions

  Ⓖ 23 attraction   Ⓙ 32 attractions

3 Taina had a rectangle made out of paper. She drew a line down the middle of the rectangle and then she drew a line diagonal through the rectangle. She then had 4 shapes drawn. What is one shape she made?

  Ⓐ Square   © Triangle

  Ⓑ Circle   Ⓓ Oval

4 Julie bought a model robot building kit for $135 and a model rocket building kit for $128. She started with $350. How much money does she have left?

  Ⓕ $215   Ⓗ $87

  Ⓖ $222   Ⓙ $78

Guess and Check

One way to solve word problems is to make a guess based on the information in the problem. Then you check it and revise your guess until you find the correct answer.

EXAMPLE   **You have 7 coins that complete $0.92. What combination of coins do you have?**

Ⓐ 2 quarters, 2 dimes, 1 nickel, 2 pennies

Ⓑ 3 quarters, 1 dime, 1 nickel, 2 pennies

Ⓒ 1 quarter, 3 dimes, 2 nickels, 1 penny

Ⓓ 2 quarters, 1 dime, 2 nickels, 3 pennies

- When you guess and check you need to try a set of numbers to see how close to $0.92 you can get.

    Guess: 2 quarters, 2 dimes, 1 nickel, 2 pennies

                $0.50 + 0.20 + 0.05 + 0.02 = $0.77

    Check: $0.77 < $0.92

- Since your number was small, you should try larger numbers.

    Guess: 3 quarters, 1 dime, 1 nickel, 2 pennies

                $0.75 + 0.10 + 0.05 + 0.02 = $ 0.92

    Check: $0.92 = 0.92

- Your guess is correct. The combination of 3 quarters, 1 dime, 1 nickel, and 2 pennies equals $0.92. The correct answer is **B**.

When you use guess and check:

    ☐ Read the problem carefully.

    ☐ Make a reasonable first guess.

    ☐ Revise your guess based on whether your answer was too high or low.

    ☐ Be sure your answer is reasonable based on the question.

Guess and Check Practice

Directions: Solve these problems using Guess and Check.

1 In Furry Friends Pet Store, one section of the store has parakeets and rabbits. There are 9 animals and 26 legs in that section of the store. How many 2 legged birds are there? How many 4 legged rabbits?

Ⓐ 5 parakeets, 4 rabbits

Ⓑ 4 parakeets, 3 rabbits

Ⓒ 2 parakeets, 5 rabbits

Ⓓ 6 parakeets, 1 rabbit

2 There are two numbers whose product is 81 and quotient is 9. What are the two numbers?

Ⓕ 9, 9

Ⓖ 3, 27

Ⓗ 7, 4

Ⓘ 4, 28

3 You have 4 coins that complete $0.37. What combination of coins do you have?

Ⓐ 2 quarters, 2 pennies

Ⓑ 1 quarter, 1 dime, 2 pennies

Ⓒ 2 dimes, 1 nickel, 1 penny

Ⓓ 1 quarter, 1 dime, 2 pennies

4 Jane plants 2 packets of seeds in the garden. She plants a complete of 26 seeds. Which 2 packets of seeds does she plant?

Ⓕ snapdragon and pansy

Ⓖ marigold and sunflower

Ⓗ sunflower and pansy

Ⓘ marigold and snapdragon

5 A shirt costs $10.99, pants cost $16.99, a sweater costs $14.99, and socks cost $4.99. What can Jim buy with $20.00?

Ⓐ sweater and shirt

Ⓑ pants and socks

Ⓒ sweater and socks

Ⓓ shirt and pants

Estimation

On multiple choice tests you can estimate the answer as a way to cross off some of the choices. This makes it easier for you to find the correct answer.

EXAMPLE

Jackson spent $44.53 on summer clothes for camp. How much change will he receive after giving the sales clerk $50.00?

  Ⓐ $4.57   Ⓒ $4.53

  Ⓑ $5.47   Ⓓ $5.43

- First, estimate the answer by rounding. You should round to the most precise place needed for the problem. In this case, round to the nearest dime.

  $44.53 rounds to $44.50

  $50.00 - $44.50 = 5.50

- You can cross off choices **A** and **C** since they have a 4 rather than a 5 in the dollars place.

- Find the exact answer by subtracting:

$$\begin{array}{r} \$50.00 \\ -\ 44.53 \\ \hline \$\ 5.47 \end{array}$$

- His change is $5.47. The correct answer is **B**.

When you estimate:
- ☐ Read the problem carefully.
- ☐ Round the numbers you need.
- ☐ Estimate the answer.
- ☐ Cross off any answers not close to your estimate.
- ☐ Find the exact answer.

Estimation Practice

Directions: Solve these problems using estimation.

1 Dominic and Lucy raced against each other. Dominic finished in 24.8 seconds. Lucy finished in 22.6 seconds. How much faster was Lucy?

Ⓐ 1.2 seconds

Ⓑ 2.2 seconds

Ⓒ 2.1 seconds

Ⓓ 3.2 seconds

2 4,093 + 589 =

Ⓕ 4,682

Ⓖ 4,873

Ⓗ 4,573

Ⓙ 4,684

3 567 − 344 =

Ⓐ 233

Ⓑ 323

Ⓒ 223

Ⓓ 342

4 There are 98 houses in Jan's neighbourhood. She delivers the newspaper to all but 75 of them. how many papers does she deliver?

Ⓕ 33

Ⓖ 23

Ⓗ 172

Ⓙ 13

5 On Saturday 564 people visited the zoo. On Sunday 678 people visited the zoo and on Monday 433 people visited the zoo. How many people in all visited the zoo?

Ⓐ 1,575

Ⓑ 1,721

Ⓒ 1,665

Ⓓ 1,675

Incomplete Information

One of the answer choices for some problems on tests may be "not enough information." In this case, you may not be given all of the information you need to solve the problem. If you determine that you cannot solve the problem with the information given, you fill in the "not enough information" choice.

EXAMPLE   **Rosa and Ruben went to see a movie with their parents. The movie started at 4:30. The tickets were $6.00. After the movie they went to dinner and arrived home at 8:00. How long was the movie?**

   Ⓐ 3 hours 30 minutes   Ⓒ 2 hours 30 minutes

   Ⓑ 3 hours   Ⓓ not enough information

- Read the problem to find out the question you need to answer.
  How long was the movie?

- Determine what information you have.
  When Rosa and Ruben went to the movie
  The cost of the tickets
  What time they arrived home after dinner

- You do not have enough information to answer the question since you do not know the start and end times of the movie.

- Reread the problem to verify that you do not have enough information to solve the problem.

- You do not have enough information. Your answer is **D**.

When you think you have incomplete information:
  ❑ Read the problem carefully.
  ❑ Determine what information you need to solve the problem.
  ❑ Check to see if you have all the information to solve the problem.
  ❑ Make sure the information you need to solve the problem is missing.

Incomplete Information Practice

Directions: Solve these problems.

1 Five children were having pizza for dinner. Michael had 2 slices, Colby had 1 slice, Stacey had 3 slices, and Jorge had 2 slices. How many slices did Mark have?

  Ⓐ 1 slice   Ⓒ 2 slices

  Ⓑ 3 slices   Ⓓ not enough information

2 Mr. Hoy planted 45 seeds in autumn. He planted 20 tomato seeds, 15 cucumber seeds, and the rest were for onions. How many seeds were for onions?

  Ⓕ 15 seeds   Ⓗ 10 seeds

  Ⓖ 12 seeds   Ⓙ not enough information

3 A hot air balloon stayed afloat for 25 minutes. The crew wanted to take a hot air balloon ride that lasted 40 minutes. How many tanks of gas would they need?

  Ⓐ 1 tank   Ⓒ 3 tanks

  Ⓑ 5 tanks   Ⓓ not enough information

4 Miss Cohen teaches piano lessons to 7 students every day. Each lesson lasts thirty minutes. How many minutes does Miss Cohen teach each day?

  Ⓕ 3 hours   Ⓗ 7 hours

  Ⓖ 3 hours 30 minutes   Ⓙ not enough information

5 There were 12 people in the public swimming pool. How many more people could be in the pool?

  Ⓐ 57 people   Ⓒ 45 people

  Ⓑ 33 people   Ⓓ not enough information

MAXIMUM CAPACITY 45 PEOPLE

Use a Calculator

You may be allowed to use a calculator with some tests. Using a calculator can save you time, especially when you need to compute multi-digit numbers. A calculator also allows you to quickly check your work.

EXAMPLE **The forest service in Red Park plants 322 new trees every year for 14 years. How many trees were planted in all over 14 years?**

   Ⓐ 5,609   Ⓒ 4,508

   Ⓑ 12,408   Ⓓ 4,216

• To solve the problem, you need to multiply a three-digit number by a two-digit number. It is quicker and easier to use your calculator, especially on a timed test.

$$
\begin{array}{r}
322 \\
\times\ 14 \\
\end{array}
$$

• They planted 4,508 trees. The answer is **C**.
• When you use a calculator you make a complex problem easier, but you must be sure to key in the correct numbers to find the correct answer.

When you use a calculator:
☐ Read the problem carefully.
☐ Be sure you key in the correct numbers.
☐ Solve the problem.

Calculator Practice

Directions: Solve these problems using a calculator.

1 Delcia earned $654.32 every week at her job. How much did Delcia earn in 12 weeks?

  Ⓐ $5,216.89   Ⓒ $7,851.84

  Ⓑ $7,345.81   Ⓓ $7,867.84

2 A FleetAir airplane holds 186 passengers. FleetAir flies 12 filled airplanes each day. How many people ride FleetAir each day?

  Ⓕ 2,232 people   Ⓗ   186 people

  Ⓖ 1,450 people   Ⓙ 1,203 people

3 At the first performance of a play there were 806 people in the audience. On the second night there were 943 people in the audience. On the third night there were 1,034 people in the audience. How many people attended the show in all?

  Ⓐ 2,867 people   Ⓒ 1,977 people

  Ⓑ 2,783 people   Ⓓ 1,840 people

4 The movie theater holds 225 guests. If every seat is sold in the theater, how much money will the theater take in?

  Ⓕ $1,012.50   Ⓗ $10,125.00

  Ⓖ $9,990.00   Ⓙ $1,120.50

5 John and Susanna want to hike the entire Long Trail in Vermont in 3 trips. On the first trip they hiked 87 miles. On the second trip they hiked 105 miles. How many miles do they have left to hike?

  Ⓐ   192 miles

  Ⓑ   18 miles

  Ⓒ   9,135 miles

  Ⓓ   73 miles

Computation

Some tests contain math sections where you must solve a variety of number equations. These questions test your ability to find exact answers to math problems. You will often be allowed to use scrap paper to work out these problems, but the work you show on scrap paper will not count.

Using Operations

Your ability to perform basic mathematical operations (such as addition, subtraction, multiplication, and division) will be tested. Whenever you are solving a math equation, be sure of which operation you must use to solve the problem.

- Even though you will be given answer choices, it's best to work the problem out first using scrap paper. Then you can compare the answer you found to the choices that are given.
- If you have time, double-check your answer to each problem by using the inverse operation. If an equation requires you to add, for example, double-check your answer by substituting your answer choice for the appropriate part of the equation and then subtracting backwards.
- Keep in mind that the same equation may be written differently. Even though these problems look different, they ask you to do the exact same thing. Here are two equations for the same problem:

$$99 - 66 = ?$$

$$\begin{array}{r} 99 \\ -66 \\ \hline ? \end{array}$$

Other Things to Keep in Mind

- When using decimals, make sure your answer choice shows the decimal point in the correct place.
- If your problem contains units (such as 2 centimetres + 50 millimetres = X millimetres), be sure that you find the answer choice with the correct units labeled. Many tests will try to confuse you by substituting one unit for another in an answer choice.
- Finally, if you get to a tough problem, look carefully at the answer choices and use logic to decide which one makes the most sense. Then plug this choice into the equation and see if it works.

Computation Practice

Directions: Mark the letter of the answer to each problem below.

1 5.91 − 2.39 =

(A) 83

(B) 3.52

(C) 3.62

(D) 8.30

2 647 + 692 =

(F) 45

(G) 1239

(H) 1249

(J) 1339

3 $\frac{3}{4} + \frac{3}{4} =$

(A) 0

(B) $\frac{2}{4}$

(C) $1\frac{2}{4}$

(D) 6

4 93 × 6 =

(F) 99

(G) 109

(H) 548

(J) 558

5 $1\frac{1}{5} - \frac{4}{5} =$

(A) 2

(B) 1

(C) $\frac{2}{5}$

(D) $\frac{1}{5}$

6 67 × 5 =

(F) 350

(G) 335

(H) 62

(J) 13

7 962 − 128 =

(A) 834

(B) 844

(C) 846

(D) 1008

8 $12.64 − $5.08 =

(F) $6.56

(G) $7.66

(H) $7.56

(J) $7.76

Concepts

Some tests also test your understanding of important math concepts you will have learned about in school. The following is a list of concepts that you may be tested on:

Number Concepts

- recognizing the standard and metric units of measure used for weighing and finding length and distance.
- recognizing place value (the ones, tens, hundreds, and thousands places; the tenths and hundredths places).
- telling time to the nearest quarter-hour.
- using a calendar.
- reading a thermometer.
- rounding up and down to the nearest ten or hundred.
- recognizing the bills and coins we use for money.

Geometry

- identify flat shapes such as triangles, circles, squares, rectangles, and more.
- identify solid shapes such as prisms, spheres, cubes, cylinders, and cones.
- find the perimetre of flat shapes.
- find the line of symmetry in a flat shape.
- tell about the number of angles and sides of flat shapes.

Other Things to Keep in Mind

- If you come to a difficult problem, think of what you do know about the topic and eliminate answer choices that don't make sense.
- Also keep in mind that you may be given a problem that can't be solved because not enough information is provided. In that case, "not enough information" or "none of the above" will be an answer choice. Carefully consider each of the other answer choices before you decide that a problem is not solvable.

Concept Practice

Directions: Find the answer to each problem below.

1 **What time does this clock show?**

Ⓐ   9:45

Ⓑ   10:15

Ⓒ   10:45

Ⓓ   11:00

2 **What place does the 7 hold in this number? 3070.5**

Ⓕ   tenths place

Ⓖ   ones place

Ⓗ   tens place

Ⓙ   hundreds place

3 **Round the number 46 up to the nearest ten:**

Ⓐ   40

Ⓑ   45

Ⓒ   50

Ⓓ   100

4 **Find the perimeter of a square with one side of 7½ feet.**

Ⓕ   15

Ⓖ   28

Ⓗ   30

Ⓙ   not enough information

5 **Which of these letters is not symmetrical?**

Ⓐ   H

Ⓑ   O

Ⓒ   Z

Ⓓ   X

6 **How many minutes are there in one day?**

Ⓕ   24

Ⓖ   60

Ⓗ   720

Ⓙ   1440

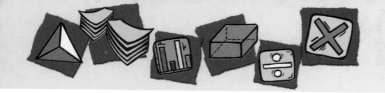

Math: Applications

You will often be asked to apply what you know about math to a new type of problem or set of information. Even if you aren't exactly sure how to solve a problem of this type, you can usually draw on what you already know to make the most logical choice.

When preparing for tests, you may want to practise some of the following:

• how to use a number line.

• putting numbers in order from least to greatest and using greater than/less than symbols.

• recognizing basic number patterns and object patterns and extending them.

• choosing the best operation to solve a problem and writing an equation to solve the problem.

• reading bar graphs, tally charts, or pictographs.

• reading pie charts.

• reading simple line graphs.

• reading and making Venn diagrams.

Other Things to Keep in Mind

• When answering application questions, be sure to read each problem carefully. You may want to use scrap paper to work out some problems.

• Again, if you come to a problem you aren't sure how to solve or a word/idea you don't recognize, try to eliminate answer choices by using what you do know. Then go back and check your answer choice in the context of the problem.

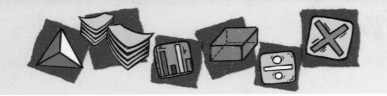

Application Practice

Directions: Find the answer to each problem below.

1 What is the next number in this pattern? 2, 4, 8, 16, 32, _____

ⓐ 36   ⓒ 64

ⓑ 60   ⓓ 128

2 How many more students voted for chocolate ice cream than strawberry?

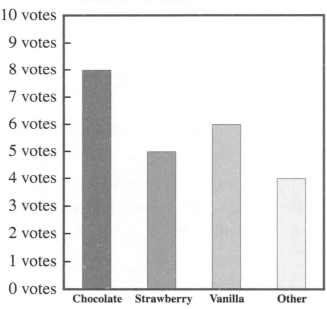

Students' Favourite Ice Cream Flavors

ⓕ 3   ⓗ 13

ⓖ 8   ⓙ not enough information

3 How many students named vanilla as their second choice?

ⓐ 2   ⓒ 8

ⓑ 6   ⓓ not enough information

4 Choose the correct symbol to go in the empty box: $\frac{2}{3}$ ☐ $\frac{3}{2}$

ⓕ <   ⓗ =

ⓖ >   ⓙ not enough information

5 Five friends decide to buy a bag of lollipops and share the lollipops equally. What operation must they use to figure out how many lollipops each will get?

ⓐ addition   ⓒ division

ⓑ multiplication ⓓ subtraction

6 Which letter is missing from this pattern? A, B, A, _____, A, B, A, C

ⓕ A   ⓗ C

ⓖ B   ⓙ not enough information

Mathematics Skills

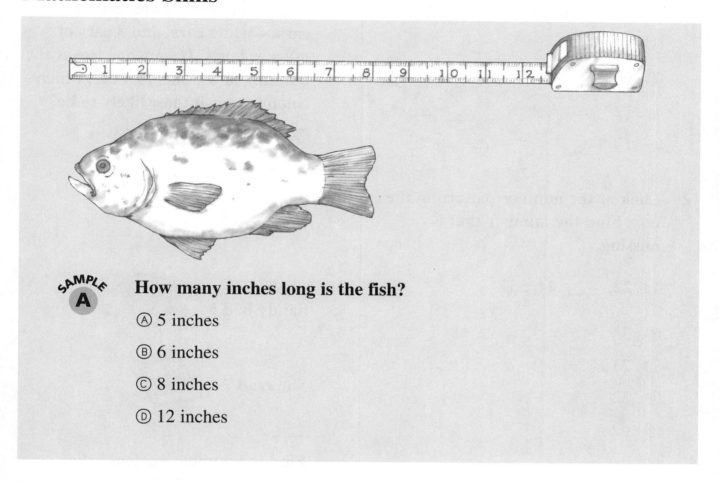

SAMPLE A **How many inches long is the fish?**

Ⓐ 5 inches

Ⓑ 6 inches

Ⓒ 8 inches

Ⓓ 12 inches

Read the problem carefully. Look for key words, numbers, and figures. Look carefully at all the answer choices.

If you use scratch paper, transfer the numbers correctly. Work neatly and carefully so you don't make a careless mistake.

GO

Name _____

1 What is the best estimate of the number of beans on the plate?

Ⓐ 30

Ⓑ 20

Ⓒ 12

Ⓓ 10

2 Look at the number pattern in the box. Find the number that is missing.

11, 22, ____, 44, 55

Ⓕ 33

Ⓖ 23

Ⓗ 32

Ⓙ 42

3 Look at the clock. How long will it take the minute hand to reach the 6?

Ⓐ 3 minutes

Ⓑ 5 minutes

Ⓒ 12 minutes

Ⓓ 15 minutes

4 Marlow noticed that the parking lot at the store had 11 red cars, 6 blue cars, 4 white cars, and 3 cars of other colours. If someone leaves the building and walks to a car, which colour car is it most likely to be?

Ⓕ red

Ⓖ blue

Ⓗ white

Ⓙ another colour

5 Sandy had 5 .

She read 2 .

Find the number sentence that tells how many books Sandy has left to read.

Ⓐ 5 + 2 = 7

Ⓑ 5 − 2 = 3

Ⓒ 2 + 3 = 5

Ⓓ 2 − 1 = 1

GO

Name _____

6 Look at the pattern of fruit. Which of these is the missing piece of fruit?

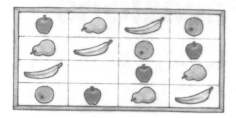

   Ⓕ orange   Ⓗ pear

   Ⓖ banana   Ⓙ apple

7 Mr. Lowell paid $0.59 for a bag of chips and $0.39 for a bottle of juice. How much money did he spend all together?

   Ⓐ $0.79

   Ⓑ $0.88

   Ⓒ $0.89

   Ⓓ $0.98

8 Look at the number sentences. Find the number that goes in the boxes to make both number sentences true.

$$6 + \Box = 7$$
$$7 - \Box = 6$$

   Ⓕ 1

   Ⓖ 0

   Ⓗ 13

   Ⓙ 7

9 Look at the picture. What number tells how many blocks are in the picture?

   Ⓐ 100

   Ⓑ 115

   Ⓒ 110

   Ⓓ 15

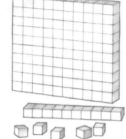

Directions: For numbers 10 and 11, estimate the answer to each problem. You do not have to find an exact answer.

10 Which two things together would cost about $30.00?

   Ⓕ hat and shirt

   Ⓖ belt and socks

   Ⓗ shirt and socks

   Ⓙ hat and belt

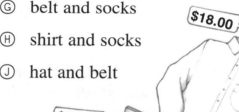

11 Use estimation to find which of these is closest to 1000.

   Ⓐ 591 + 573   Ⓒ 392 + 589

   Ⓑ 499 + 409   Ⓓ 913 + 183

GO

Our Summer Vacations

Directions: The third grade students at Millbrook School made a graph about where they wanted to go on vacation. Study the graph, then do numbers 12–14.

Third Grade Vacations

| | River | Mountains | Lake | Beach |

12 Which of these is another way to show how many students went to the beach?

Ⓕ |||| |||| |

Ⓖ |||| |

Ⓗ |||| ||||

Ⓙ |||| |||| ||/|

13 How many students went to a lake for vacation?

Ⓐ 11   Ⓒ 8

Ⓑ 7   Ⓓ 5

14 Two of the students changed their minds and decided to go to a lake instead of the beach. How many students then wanted to go to a lake?

Ⓕ 7   Ⓗ 5

Ⓖ 8   Ⓙ 9

GO

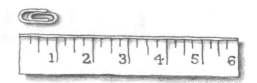

Name _____

15 Look at the paper clip and the pencils. Which pencil is about three inches longer than the paper clip?

Ⓐ

Ⓑ

Ⓒ

Ⓓ

---

16 Bonnie folded a piece of paper in half and then folded it in half again. The picture shows how she folded her paper. What will the piece of paper look like when Bonnie unfolds it?

Ⓕ

Ⓖ

Ⓗ

Ⓙ

---

17 Find the answer that shows 35 peanuts.

Ⓐ

Ⓑ

Ⓒ

Ⓓ

STOP

Name _____

MAIN STREET FAIR

SAMPLE A

Last week, two hundred fifty-three people attended the Main Street Fair. Which of these numbers is two hundred fifty-three?

Ⓐ 235   Ⓑ 20053   Ⓒ 253   Ⓓ 2053

Directions: Study the schedule for the Main Street Fair. Use it to do numbers 1 and 2.

Main Street Fair

8:00 – 10:00
Student-Teacher Softball Game
10:15 – 12:00
Arts and Crafts Sale
12:30 – 2:00
Cookout in the Park
2:30 – 4:00
Pet Show

1   Mrs. Barnes arrived 15 minutes early for the softball game. What time did she get there?

Ⓐ   8:15   Ⓒ   7:15

Ⓑ   8:45   Ⓓ   7:45

2   Exactly 60 people brought their pets to the show. Half the people brought dogs and 20 people brought cats. How many people brought other kinds of pets?

Ⓕ   30   Ⓗ   20

Ⓖ   10   Ⓙ   40

GO

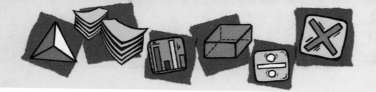

3 Pepper's little brother made this castle with toy blocks. Which shape did he use just once?

Ⓐ circle

Ⓑ triangle

Ⓒ rectangle

Ⓓ square

4 The chart below shows the number of cars parked in a lot. Which of these is the same number as is shown on the chart?

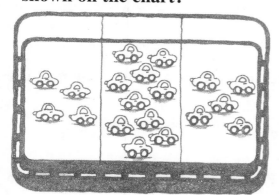

Ⓕ 100 + 40 + 5

Ⓖ 1 + 4 + 5

Ⓗ 400 + 100 + 5

Ⓙ 4 + 10 + 5

5 Paul and Vesta used a computer to solve a problem. Which of these is the same as the number on the computer screen?

Ⓐ three thousand one hundred eight

Ⓑ thirty one thousand eight

Ⓒ three hundred eight

Ⓓ three thousand eighteen

6 Sarah just read that her town has the highest population in the county. Where should she mark on the chart below to show her town's population?

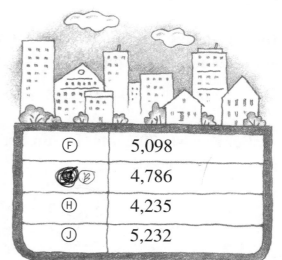

Ⓕ	5,098
Ⓖ	4,786
Ⓗ	4,235
Ⓙ	5,232

GO

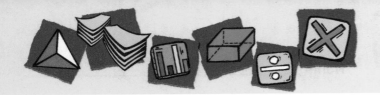

Name _____

Going to the Bank

The Dime Bank
Opens: 9:00
Closes: 4:00

7 **What do the numbers on the sign tell you?**

Ⓐ how much money is in the bank

Ⓑ how many people work in the bank

Ⓒ what time the bank opens and closes

Ⓓ the bank's address

8 **Jawan's sister has four coins. One is a nickel and one is a dime. Which of these amounts might she have?**

Ⓕ 15 cents Ⓖ 20 cents Ⓗ 24 cents Ⓘ 30 cents

9 **A sticker costs 20 cents. Jawan has 12 cents. How much more money does he need to buy the sticker?**

Ⓐ 8¢

Ⓑ 10¢

Ⓒ 12¢

Ⓓ 32¢

 STOP

Mathematics Final Test
BUILDING OUR CLUBHOUSE

SAMPLE A Which of these is most likely measured in metres?

Ⓐ the distance around a room

Ⓑ the weight of a large box

Ⓒ the distance to the moon

Ⓓ the amount of water in a pool

1 Jennie had three bent nails in her pocket. Then she put five straight nails in her pocket. Which answer shows what she had in her pocket?

Ⓐ   Ⓑ   Ⓒ   Ⓓ

2 Ricky carried 4 boxes of tiles into the kitchen. Each box held 12 tiles. What would you do to find out how many tiles he carried into the kitchen altogether?

add   subtract   divide   multiply

Ⓕ   Ⓖ   Ⓗ   Ⓙ

3 Angela wants to measure a piece of wood. Which of these should she use?

Ⓐ   Ⓑ   Ⓒ   Ⓓ

GO

4 Mr. and Mrs. Akers are going to build a deck. It will take 2 weeks to finish. They plan to start on April 24. What date will they finish?

APRIL

S	M	T	W	T	F	S
				1	2	3
4	5	6	7	8	9	

Ⓕ April 10

Ⓖ May 1

Ⓗ April 26

Ⓙ May 8

5 Pam made this pattern of 4 rows of floor tiles. How many grey tiles will she need all together if she adds 1 more row to make 5 rows of tiles?

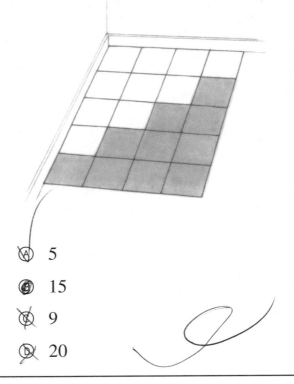

Ⓐ 5

Ⓑ 15

Ⓒ 9

Ⓓ 20

6 Which pattern of letters could be folded in half on a line of symmetry?

AMOMA	BAGGB	VERDT	UNPOS
Ⓕ	Ⓖ	Ⓗ	Ⓙ

GO

7 The children in the Adams family were stuck inside on a rainy day. They decided to make their own games. They each made a spinner for their game. When Jennie spun her spinner, the colour it landed on was grey. Which spinner was probably Jennie's?

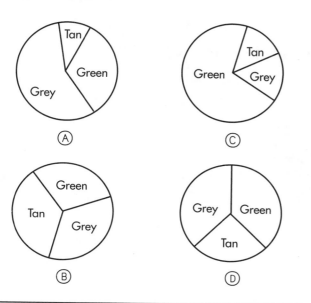

8 This map shows Janelle's yard. She came in through the gate and walked east for 3 metres. Then she went north for 2 metres. What was she closest to?

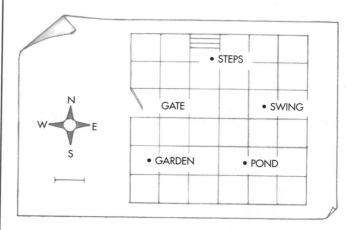

Ⓕ to the swing

Ⓖ to the pond

Ⓗ to the steps

Ⓙ to the garden

9 Rick is carving a pattern in a piece of wood. Which shapes are missing from the pattern?

GO

10 **Which of these is not the same shape and size as the others?**

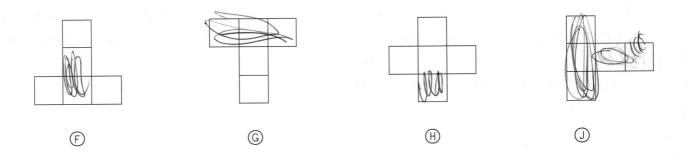

Ⓕ   Ⓖ   Ⓗ   Ⓙ

11 **Look at the group of socks. What fraction of the socks is black?**

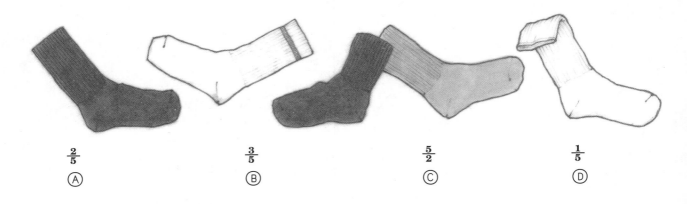

$\frac{2}{5}$ $\frac{3}{5}$ $\frac{5}{2}$ $\frac{1}{5}$

Ⓐ   Ⓑ   Ⓒ   Ⓓ

12 **Look at the graph below and the report Willie made about the coins in his change jar. How many dimes did Willie have in the change jar?**

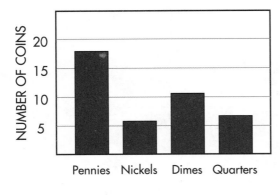

Willie's Report

I had more pennies than any other coin. There were the fewest nickels. I had more dimes than quarters.

7   **11**   **18**   **6**

Ⓕ   Ⓖ   Ⓗ   Ⓙ   **STOP**

Directions: Choose the answer that correctly solves each problem.

13 Which number has a 7 in the ten-thousands place and a 3 in the hundreds place?

Ⓐ 178,234   Ⓒ 498,301

Ⓑ 476,302   Ⓓ 753,092

14 What is the perimeter of the polygon?

Ⓕ 38 centimetres

Ⓗ 26 centimetres

Ⓖ 28 centimetres

Ⓙ not enough information

7 cm   6 cm   5 cm   9 cm   11 cm

15 Which decimal is greater than 1.32 but less than 1.41?

Ⓐ 1.42   Ⓒ 1.31

Ⓑ 1.36   Ⓓ 1.30

16 Which decimal is equal to $\frac{1}{4}$?

Ⓕ 0.25   Ⓗ 0.75

Ⓖ 0.025   Ⓙ .033

17 What could be the next number in the pattern? 3, 7, 15, 31, 63, …

Ⓐ 127   Ⓒ 96

Ⓑ 106   Ⓓ 79

18 Which animal is between 15 and 40 metres long?

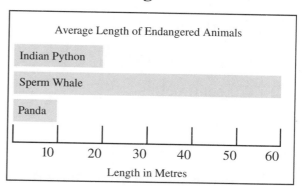

Average Length of Endangered Animals

Indian Python

Sperm Whale

Panda

10   20   30   40   50   60

Length in Metres

Ⓕ Panda   Ⓗ Indian Python

Ⓖ Sperm Whale   Ⓙ Not here

19 What other equation belongs in the same fact family as 17 × 8 = 136?

Ⓐ 8 × 136 = 1,088

Ⓑ 136 ÷ 2 = 68

Ⓒ 8 × 17 = 136

Ⓓ 17 + 8 = 25

20 Which figure shows parallel lines?

Ⓕ S   Ⓗ +

Ⓖ ═   Ⓙ ✳

GO

Name _____

21 A tsunami is a wave created by underwater earthquakes. Tsunamis can reach heights of 37 metres. How many centimetres tall is that?

Ⓐ 37,000 centimetres

Ⓑ 3,700 centimetres

Ⓒ 370 centimetres

Ⓓ 3.70 centimetres

22 What is the temperature shown on the thermometer?

Ⓕ 74° C

Ⓖ 66° C

Ⓗ 64° C

Ⓙ 54° C

23 How can you write 56,890 in expanded notation?

Ⓐ 5 + 6 + 8 + 9 + 0 =

Ⓑ 50,000 + 6,000 + 800 + 90 =

Ⓒ 56,000 + 8900 =

Ⓓ 0.5 + 0.06 + 0.008 + 0.0009 =

24 Which number is not a multiple of 4?

Ⓕ 86   Ⓗ 40

Ⓖ 68   Ⓙ 32

25 In a pictograph  stands for 5 books. How many books does

stand for?

Ⓐ 5 books   Ⓒ 20 books

Ⓑ 8 books   Ⓓ 40 books

26

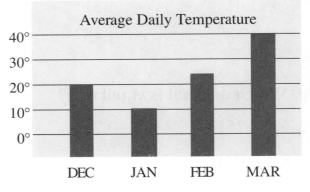

How long is the paperclip?

Ⓕ 3 inches   Ⓗ 3 centimetres

Ⓖ 5 inches   Ⓙ 2 centimetres

27 How much did the average daily temperature change from February to March?

Average Daily Temperature

Ⓐ 25° F   Ⓒ 10° F

Ⓑ 15° F   Ⓓ 5° F

GO

Directions: Choose the answer that correctly solves each problem.

28 8,906 + 3,897 =

- Ⓕ 11,803
- Ⓖ 12,793
- Ⓗ 12,803
- Ⓙ 3,893

29 467.902 − 56.894 =

- Ⓐ 411.192
- Ⓑ 411.008
- Ⓒ 410.192
- Ⓓ 410.008

30 84 × .65 =

- Ⓕ 44.80
- Ⓖ 52.80
- Ⓗ 53.60
- Ⓙ 54.60

31 $\frac{3}{8} + \frac{1}{8}$ =

- Ⓐ 1
- Ⓑ $\frac{5}{8}$
- Ⓒ $\frac{4}{8}$
- Ⓓ $\frac{2}{8}$

32 $\frac{279}{9}$ =

- Ⓕ 3
- Ⓖ 26
- Ⓗ 31
- Ⓙ 42

33 $\frac{1}{3} + \frac{2}{3} + 1\frac{1}{3}$ =

- Ⓐ $3\frac{2}{3}$
- Ⓑ $2\frac{1}{3}$
- Ⓒ 2
- Ⓓ $1\frac{1}{3}$

34 $\frac{1784}{2}$ =

- Ⓕ 876
- Ⓖ 892
- Ⓗ 1,784
- Ⓙ 3,568

35 24.75 + 27.5 + 25.6 =

- Ⓐ 77.85
- Ⓑ 77.4
- Ⓒ 53.10
- Ⓓ 50.35

36 4321 + 2987 =

- Ⓕ 7,308
- Ⓖ 7,208
- Ⓗ 7,108
- Ⓙ 1,334

37 $\frac{15.05}{5}$ =

- Ⓐ 3.01
- Ⓑ 3.1
- Ⓒ 31
- Ⓓ 82

GO

Name _____

Directions: Choose the answer that correctly solves each problem.

38 Michael was at a card convention. At the first booth he bought 8 cards. He bought 6 cards at each of the remaining 9 booths. How many cards did Michael buy altogether?

Ⓕ 54 cards   Ⓗ 57 cards

Ⓖ 62 cards   Ⓙ 72 cards

39 There were 85 boxes shipped to the warehouse. In each box there were 22 cartons. In each carton there were 40 water guns. How many water guns are in all 85 boxes?

Ⓐ 880 water guns

Ⓑ 1,870 water guns

Ⓒ 74,800 water guns

Ⓓ Not enough information

40 Mary measured the length of a room at 8 feet. How many inches long is the room?

Ⓕ 12 inches

Ⓖ 24 inches

Ⓗ 96 inches

Ⓙ None of these

41 Mr. Thomas bought 2 adult tickets and 1 child ticket to the amusement park. How much money did he spend altogether?

Ⓐ $44.85   Ⓒ $29.90

Ⓑ $38.85   Ⓓ $23.90

42 Rita left dance class at 3:30 p.m. She arrived home at 4:17 p.m. How long did it take Rita to get home?

Ⓕ 1 hour, 17 minutes

Ⓖ 47 minutes

Ⓗ 37 minutes

Ⓙ 13 minutes

STOP

Test Practice Answer Key

Page 304
1. A
2. H
3. B

Page 306
1. C
2. F; EXTRA INFORMATION: 36 oranges, 24 bananas
3. A
4. J

Page 308
1. B
2. F
3. C
4. H

Page 310
1. A
2. G
3. B
4. J
5. C

Page 312
1. B
2. F
3. C
4. G
5. D

Page 314
1. D
2. H
3. D
4. G
5. B

Page 316
1. C
2. F
3. B
4. F
5. D

Page 318
1. B
2. J
3. C
4. J
5. C
6. G
7. A
8. H

Page 320
1. C
2. H
3. C
4. H
5. C
6. J

Page 322
1. C
2. F
3. B
4. F
5. C
6. H

Page 323
A. C

Page 324
1. B
2. F
3. D
4. F
5. B

Page 325
6. F
7. D
8. F
9. B
10. F
11. C

Page 326
12. F
13. B
14. J

Test Practice Answer Key

Page 327
15. D
16. J
17. A

Page 328
A. C
1. D
2. G

Page 329
3. B
4. J
5. A
6. J

Page 330
7. C
8. J
9. A

Page 331
A. A
1. C
2. J
3. B

Page 332
4. J
5. A
6. F

Page 333
7. A
8. H
9. D

Page 334
10. H
11. A
12. G

Page 335
13. B
14. F
15. B
16. F
17. A
18. H
19. C
20. G

Page 336
21. B
22. H
23. B
24. F
25. D
26. H
27. B

Page 337
28. H
29. B
30. J
31. C
32. H
33. B
34. G
35. A
36. F
37. A

Page 338
38. G
39. C
40. H
41. B
42. G

Record Your Scores

After you have completed and checked each test, record your scores below.
Do not count your answers for the sample questions.

Practice Test

Number of Questions: 26   Number Correct _____

Final Test

Number of Questions: 42   Number Correct _____

This page was
intentionally left blank.

Tangram Activities

Directions: Use tangrams, or make your own, and follow the directions on each of the tangram activity pages.

A. Cover this shape with one piece.

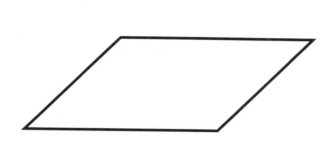

B. Cover this shape with three pieces.

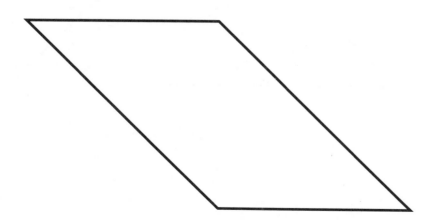

Name _____

Cover each shape a different way.

Match the shapes.

Match the shapes.

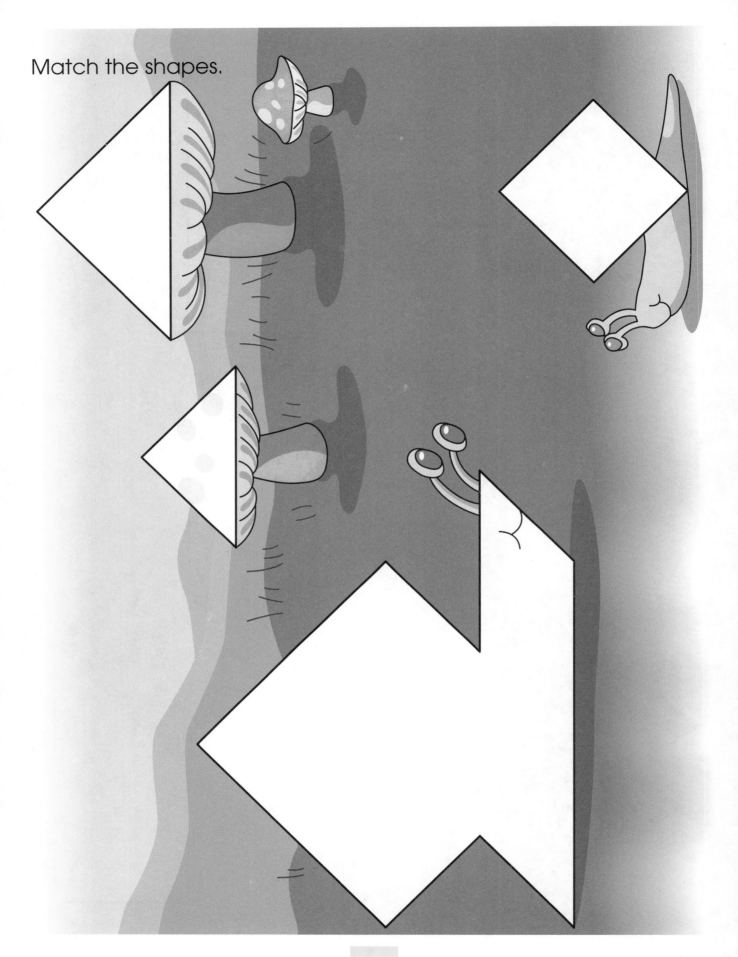

Match the shapes.

Match the shapes.

Match the shapes.

Match the shapes.

Match the shapes.

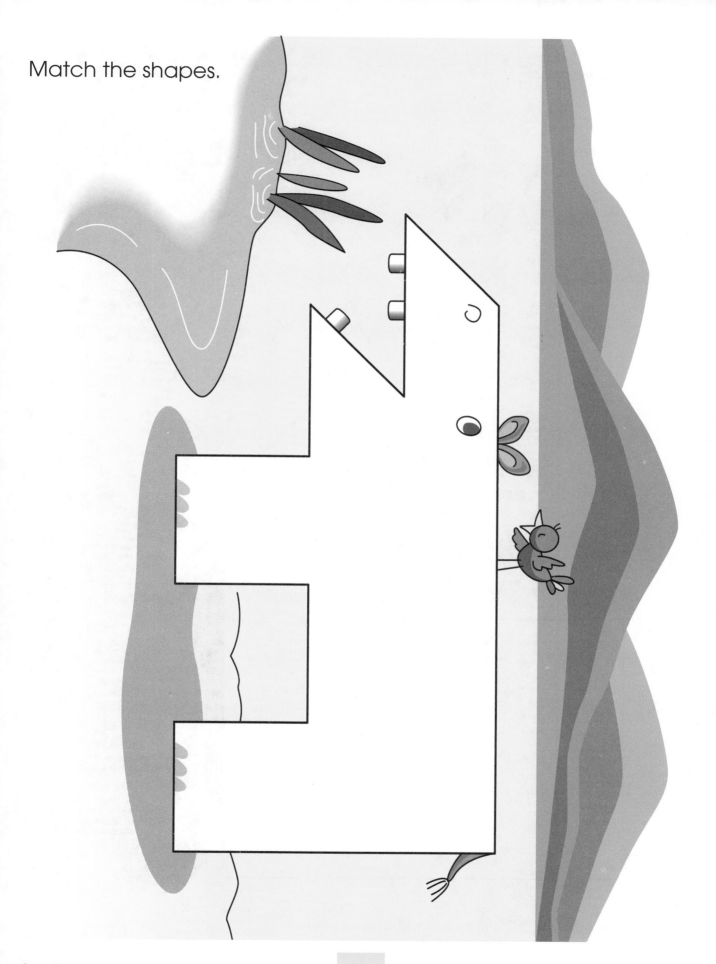

Match the shapes.

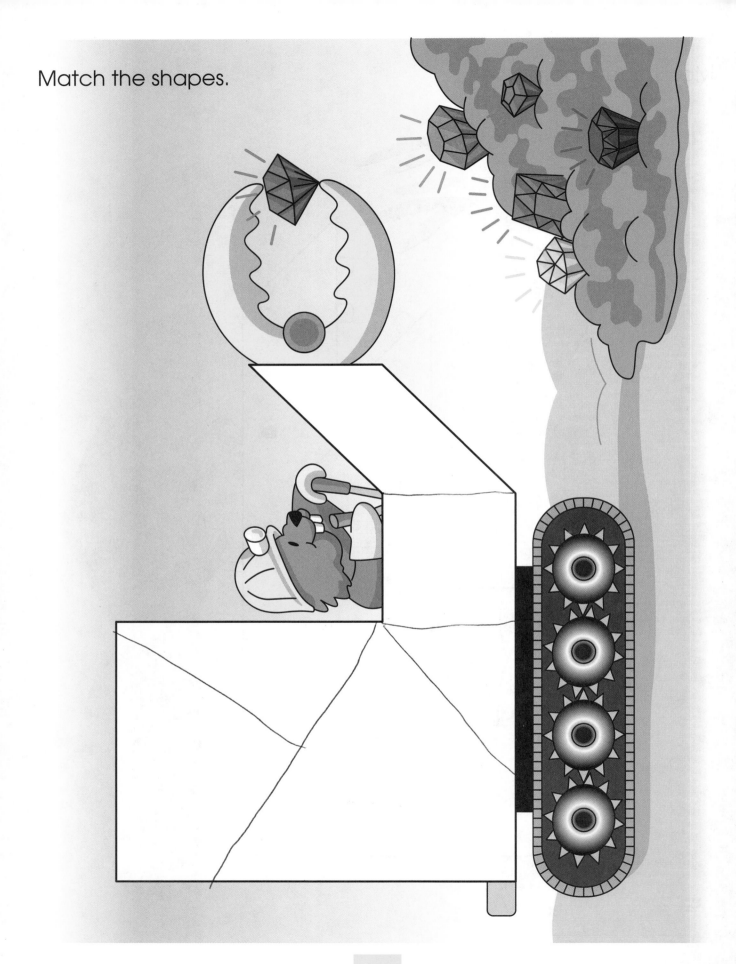